Resources for Ministry in Death and Dying

Resources for Ministry in Death and Dying

Larry A. Platt
Roger G. Branch

BROADMAN PRESS

Nashville, Tennessee

Unless otherwise noted, Scripture quotations are from the King James Version of the Bible. Scripture quotations marked (RSV) are from the Revised Standard Version of the Bible, copyrighted 1946, 1952, © 1971, 1973.

From Eric J. Cassell - "Dying in a Technological Society" in *Death and Dying, Theory, Research and Practice,* Larry A. Bugen (ed.), Wm C. Brown, 1979, pp. 291-298. Reproduced by permission of the Hastings Center.
From Herman Feifel - "Death in Contemporary America" in *New Meanings of Death,* Herman Feifel (ed.) McGraw-Hill, 1974. Reproduced by permission of McGraw-Hill Book Company.
From Judith Stillion and Hannelore Wass - "Children and Death" in *Death, Facing the Facts,* Hannelore Wass (ed.) McGraw-Hill, 1979. Reproduced by permission of Hemisphere Publishing Corporation.
From Miriam Moss and Sidney Moss, "The Impact of Parental Death on Middle Aged Children" in *Omega: Journal of Death and Dying,* Volume 14, Number 1, 1983-1984. Reproduced by permission of the editor, *Omega.*
From Marian Osterweis - "Bereavement and the Elderly" in *Aging,* Number 348, 1985. Reproduced by permission of the editor, *Aging* magazine.
From Jack D. Krasner - "Pastoral Counseling With the Dying Person" in *The Journal of Pastoral Counseling,* Volume 15, Number 2, Fall-Winter, 1980. Reproduced by permission of the editor, *The Journal of Pastoral Counseling.*
From James Giles - "Telling the Truth To The Terminally Ill" in *Journal of Pastoral Counseling,* Volume 15, Number 1, Spring-Summer, 1980. Reproduced by permission of the editor, *The Journal of Pastoral Counseling.*
From Edwin S. Shneidman - "Some Aspects of Psychotherapy with Dying Persons" in *Psychosocial Aspects of Terminal Patient Care,* Charles A. Garfield (ed.) McGraw-Hill, 1980. Reproduced by permission of McGraw-Hill Book Company.
From Regina Flesch, "The Clergy on the Firing Line", Chapter 20 in *Acute Grief and the Funeral,* Vanderline R. Pine et.al. (eds.), Charles C. Thomas, 1976. Courtesy of Charles C. Thomas, Publisher, Springfield, Illinois.
From Paul E. Irion, "The Funeral and the Bereaved", Chapter 4 in *Acute Grief and the Funeral,* Vanderline R. Pine et. al. (eds.), Charles C. Thomas, Publisher, Springfield, Illinois.
From Edgar N. Jackson, "Why You Should Understand Grief: A Minister's Views" in *For Those Bereaved,* Austin H. Kutscher et.al. (eds.), Arno Press, 1980. Reproduced by permission of the author.
From Irene Moriarity - "Sudden Death: Pastoral Presence With the Bereaved" in the *Journal of Pastoral Counseling,* Volume 15, Number 2, Fall-Winter, 1980. Reproduced by permission of the editor, *The Journal of Pastoral Counseling.*
From Erich Lindemann - "Grief and Grief Management: Some Reflections" in *The Journal of Pastoral Care,* Volume 30, Number 3, 1976. Reproduced by permission of the editor, *Journal of Pastoral Care.*
From Raymond G. Carey - "Weathering Widowhood: Problems and Adjustment of the Widowed During the First Year" in *Omega: The Journal of Death and Dying,* Volume 10, Number 2, 1979-80. Reproduced by permission of the author and the editor of *Omega.*
From Larry A. Platt - "Without Warning: The Impact of Sudden Death" in *Thanatos,* Volume 10, Number 4, Winter 1985. Reproduced by Permission of the editor, *Thanatos.*

Library of Congress Cataloging-in-Publication Data

Resources for ministry in death and dying.

Bibliography: p.
1. Church work with the terminally ill.
2. Church work with the bereaved. 3. Death—Religious aspects—Christianity. I. Branch, Roger G., 1934-
II. Platt, Larry A.
BV4460.6.R47 1988 259'.6 87-14298
ISBN 0-8054-6945-1

Gratefully dedicated to the memory of "Doc" Stealey,
Ben Fisher, and Ed McDowell of "The School of the
Prophets"—Southeastern Baptist Theological
Seminary. "There were giants in the earth in those
days."
RGB

To Allison and Tim
Whose short lives have enriched my own
LAP

Contents

Introduction

Although the subject is death, this is a book not so much about endings as beginnings and about the need for individuals to recognize the importance of coming to grips with the beliefs, values, and fears that make us both human and vulnerable. Death is a reality of life; it comes to us all. We must confront our own deaths and the deaths of those we love. Each of us must undertake our search for the meaning of death in our lives amid a society which is constantly changing.

If death is a biological constant in that it visits us all, another constant in the human experience is the process of social change. We are forever altering and modifying the social world in which we live in the hope that we will discover more effective ways of serving God, mankind, and ourselves. Often the incessant tide of social change collides with the barricades we have erected around the reality of death and forever alters the patterns of our lives. As DeSpelder and Strickland (1983) noted, Americans have experienced a profound change in how we die, when we die, and even where we die. These modifications in our lifeways, while neither good nor bad in and of themselves, have produced a more complex form by which Americans interact with death. These fundamental changes have generated a new social milieu in which we respond to death physically, mentally, and spiritually.

Unfortunately many of these social changes have formed new obstacles in our attempts to understand and effectively relate to death. In our search for meaningful ways to confront this new reality of death, we have often engaged in patterns of action that are more destructive and dehumanizing than was true in our past. The forces of change are constant though gradual; they are subtle yet potentially devastating. Clearly we must come to understand the changing character of death in contemporary America if we are to learn how to minister more effectively to the spiritual and social needs of the dying person and the grieving survivors.

Perhaps the most apparent change in America's new world of death has been the alteration in the causes of death. In 1900 the leading causes of death were those which brought about rapid and sudden demise, primarily acute infectious diseases. They included tuberculosis, typhoid, diphtheria, and pneumonia, and they accounted for nearly 40 percent of all the deaths in the United States (DeSpelder and Strickland, 1983). Today, the typical causes of death are cardiovascular diseases and cancer, which often are prolonged in character. Thus there have been fundamental changes in the way people encounter death in today's society. No longer a sudden and relatively short-lived event, death now is frequently a continuing crisis that extends its erosive effects over sufferers and loved ones for lengthy periods of time. Death in America resembles an endurance race in which even the strongest will eventually grow weary from the extended course of pain, anxiety, lack of closure, and financial costs.

These changes in the causes of death have in turn modified the ways we interact with one another regarding death. Today, upon hearing the news that a loved one has cancer or other terminal illness, we as family members brace ourselves not only for the immediate crisis surrounding the onset of the disease but also for the extended process that we and the dying person will endure. We subconsciously save a portion of ourselves out of fear that we will become consumed during this marathon run with extended illness. This leaves less of ourselves to give to the dying person, less of ourselves to give to each other.

As was true of causes of death in contemporary America, the locus of death has also changed. In the early 1900s nearly 80 percent of all people died at home, in their own beds. Now nearly 80 percent experience death in an institutional setting (DeSpelder and Strickland, 1983). No longer is it common for family members to be at the side of the dying individual. Instead, when we become seriously ill, we are removed from the family setting and placed in specialized facilities. Modern hospitals and nursing homes provide the most technologically advanced forms of treatment environments and have as their major function the provision of medical care to keep people alive. They are designed not so much to meet the unique and pressing needs of a single individual but to administer health care to a large number of people with a variety of conditions. Consequently, health-care institutions are bureaucratically organized in order to dispense the prescribed medical services. Since these environments are unfamiliar to both the dying person and the family members, death is propelled from the familiar to the strange. It has been transferred from the home to the institution. As we commute to death by visiting the health-care institution, we must daily confront an environment in which we are the stranger, the outsider, and in which we must obey the rules and governance of those who manage them. In order to receive the benefit of the treatment of an institution, we must accept its rules. People find the dominance of institutions unpleasant; they find the strangeness of the environment intimidating. So death is made more threatening, more imposing, than in the past. These new places of dying have fostered a greater fear of death and of its consequences.

When death occurred in the early 1900s, we were surrounded by family members who lived nearby. We lived in towns that were smaller, and we were woven into large extended families. We lived in family circles where aunts, uncles, cousins, nephews and nieces were all close by. Brothers and sisters were but a moment away. However, in the last half-century

America has become one of the most geographically mobile societies in history. More Americans move every year than any other people in the world in our pursuit of opportunity and achievement.

One major result has been the displacement of the family. Typically, brothers and sisters no longer live in the same village or hamlet, but thousands of miles apart. When death confronts the modern family, the immediate comfort of a caring circle of those we know and love may be unavailable. There is instead the rush and harried chaos of distant relatives trying to assemble for a brief time. This geographical fracturing of the emotional support system has made death a more lonely event, a more isolated event. To be surrounded by strangers who try to serve as surrogates for distant family members amplifies the sense of loss and exposes the frailty of our personal defenses.

Americans value independence; they value success; they value achievement. The ability to move about makes for favorable opportunities for this success and achievement, but it robs us of the strength of family life that has been our bulwark in times of trouble. As we confront our deaths and the deaths of others, we now turn to a family system so fragmented by geographic mobility that it offers little help. It leaves us to die alone—more fearful than we need be, more unprepared than we should be. In earlier times, death in America was not nearly so fearful an enterprise. Death is never easy, but to die surrounded by the loving arms and caring hearts of those who are our family and friends eases the pain, lessens the fear, and gives us strength.

Perhaps the most publicized feature of the changing character of death and dying in modern America has been the development of life-extending medical technologies. With our advances in technology and our increased understanding of scientific principles, we have developed a vast array of medical skills and equipment that can postpone and alter the nature of our deaths. These great strides in methods of medical care have been accompanied by ethical and moral dilemmas, clusttered around the issue of intervention in the process of dying.

Of even greater significance has been the evolution of a set of values and beliefs under which the medical profession has assumed authority over death and dying. Death has increasingly been perceived as a medical issue for which there are medical solutions. Contrary to these trends, death is and always will be a moral and spiritual issue in which humans must come to terms with the realities of their deaths in the spiritual context. Machine technologies that provide a respite from the realities of death offer only a temporary solution to the human problems that surround death. The marriage of medicine and its technologies in American society has created a host of new dilemmas surrounding our own deaths and the deaths of those we love. Medical technologies may offer an extension to life; they may prolong, postpone, or prevent what otherwise would be fatal malfunctions in the human system. However, they also demand that we answer the question of whether we are saving a life or simply prolonging the dying process.

Alvin Toffler in his book *Future Shock* (1970:207) offered this perplexing view of the future and medical technology:

> At a major midwest hospital not long ago a patient appeared at the emergency room in the middle of the night. He was hiccupping violently, sixty times a minute. The patient was an early pacemaker wearer. A fast thinking resident realized what had happened: a pacemaker wire, instead of stimulating the heart, had broken loose and had become lodged in the diaphram. Its jolts of electricity were causing the hiccupping. Acting swiftly, the resident inserted a needle into the patient's chest near the pacemaker, ran a wire out from the needle and grounded it to the hospital plumbing. The hiccupping stopped, giving doctors a chance to operate and reposition the faulty wire. A foretaste of tomorrow's medicine?

As the excerpt from Toffler's book illustrates, we live in a world of life-extending technologies. How we come to deal with those technologies and develop our responses to both the preventions of death and the occurrences of death that result from these technologies is a significant question that must be answered.

These four major changes in the character of death in American society—(1) changing causes of death, (2) displacement of death from the home into a health-care institution, (3) reduced contact among family members, and (4) development of life-extending technologies—have created fundamental alterations in how we experience our own death and the deaths of those around us. The overall effect has been to shift the way Americans view death and relate to one another about death. By and large the process of change has created a contemporary view of death that is more fearful than the past, one that is more impersonal than ever before, and one which leaves us isolated without the human circle of caring that we desperately need.

Thus many writers suggest that what we have witnessed is the loss of "death with dignity" in the United States. Mary Nash (1977) and others concluded that death with dignity means that in the past we maintained a high degree of control, though not absolute, over our own management of pain, our sense of loneliness in the face of death, our ability to maintain independence in relating to the dying process, and our ability to control the environment in which we existed. Nash argued that the institutionalized setting and the impact of medical technologies have reduced the individual patient and family members to subordinate positions in which we control little in our lives and little in our deaths. This loss of control, with its erosion of medical independence and the diminished ability to have close at hand family and friends for comfort and support, has made death a modern-day nightmare in American society.

Today's cancer patients undoubtedly benefit from the latest in medical advances for the care and treatment of their illness. However, the price for that capability has been high. We must give up the comforts of home for the coldness of modern hospitals. We must give up autonomy over our bodies and surrender ourselves to the judgments of others and even machines. We must abandon the circle of friends and relatives who give us emotional strength and replace them with strangers and technicians who administer medical care. No doubt we are medically far better off for these changes. It is highly doubtful, however, that we are in any way better equipped to confront our deaths and the deaths of those we care for than in the past. Indeed, the newly evolved American way of dying has robbed us of any personal dignity we might impose upon death.

Resources for Ministry in Death and Dying seeks to address this crisis. We seek to offer insight into the ministry of death and to suggest how, despite the changing environment, we can restore much of what has been lost in human caring for the dying and the bereaved. We attempt to clarify the nature of modern problems surrounding death and to propose realistic solutions to those problems. Our four primary objectives are (1) that we will help to restore death to its proper place in the life cycle, (2) that it will be seen as a less fearful and threatening aspect of life, (3) that you will come to view death as an opportunity for giving and growing, and (4) that we all will learn again that death is an experience of the greatest spiritual significance. We hope death will come to be seen as it was in the past—as part of life and of living, not the end but the beginning.

References

DeSpelder, Lynn and Albert Strickland. 1983. *The Last Dance: Encountering Death and Dying.*

Nash, Mary. 1977. "Dignity of Person in the Final Phase of Life: An Exploratory Study." In Richard Kalish, ed. *Caring Relationships: The Dying and the Bereaved.* Farmingdale, New York: Baywood Publishing Company, Inc.

Toffler, Alvin. 1970. *Future Shock.* New York: Random House, Inc.

Part I

Death in America

Part 1

1
Death Ministry in Modern America
Roger Branch and Larry A. Platt

Every juncture where mortality confronts ultimacy is a crisis point in human experience which cries out for ministry. At the diagnosis of terminal illness or at death, human creatureliness and finiteness are overwhelmingly obvious. For many people these events become crises of faith for which they are poorly prepared because they have limited spiritual foundations or none at all. Indeed, the experience of death—one's own or that of a loved one—can devastate even spiritual giants temporarily because the anguish of physical and emotional pain penetrates the very center of being.

In imitation of Christ and at His command, those who are called by His name are also called to minister to all others who experience these ultimate events at life's extremities. Christians serve those who so suffer because His grace is at work in us and thrusts us into a mission of love. We must always be keenly aware that those who mourn can be completely comforted only by the presence and power of God, and we must be ready to help them open their lives to Him for healing. For some people these extreme moments of vulnerability are the only times when they will allow God to touch them. Death, dying, and bereavement, therefore, are events or processes which demand ministry in the name of Christian love and offer opportunity to reach people who usually are indifferent to the call of Christ to salvation.

Dick Young, pioneer practitioner, teacher, and author in the field of pastoral counseling, and his long-time associate Al

Meiburg made the point well twenty-six years ago (Young and Meiburg, 1960:161).

> There is no greater crisis than can come to a family than the loss of one of its loved ones through death. Historically man has always called upon whatever religious beliefs he possessed in the face of this mystery. Despite any effect secularism may have had upon the minister's role in our culture today, he remains the chief figure in our society charged with the responsibility of bringing comfort to the bereaved.

Young and Meiburg understood that this challenge was not an easy one. For example, they were prescient in their conclusion that acute grief is a serious problem affecting many victims, as they stated, "It is the belief of the authors that unresolved grief is complicating the emotional lives of far more people than most ministers realize" (1960:160).

However, in the quarter century since Young and Meiburg wrote these prophetic words, the issue of death ministry has become far more complex and challenging than they envisioned. Changes in how, where, and with whom people die have made special ministry to those who are dying both more desperately needed and more difficult to achieve. These and related changes also have made more complicated the task of aiding the bereaved. Moreover, the results of a large body of research done during the past twenty-five years demonstrate that the dynamics of dying and grieving are far more complex and the impact of grief is far more devastating in many cases than previously had been supposed. Thus, death ministry becomes more crucial and more difficult.

The matter of "death with dignity" is a good case in point. To die with dignity is to die in character, with essential personhood intact and as much in control of one's own dying as possible. Modern dying usually places the person under the control of medical personnel who further consign him to batteries of medical gadgetry. Generally designed for saving life, it becomes inappropriate where, in any meaningful sense, life cannot and sometimes should not be saved. It interferes with dying, which is the natural and appropriate end of each human life. As machines have usurped the right to choose death from the dying, they clearly take away death with dignity.

The questions of patients' rights in decision making and of appropriate use of life-prolonging equipment are moral and ethical issues of the ultimate order. Christian moral theology has some answers, but they have been interjected into these debates with great timidity or not at all. Most people seem content to delegate all treatment decisions to physicians, assuming that they will always decide in the best interest of the patient. In fact, typical caution, occasional greed, and a general fear of malpractice suits usually result in decisions to keep the machine plugged and the full range of drug treatments going. From the pulpit and through counseling, ministers can play an important role in helping people regain enough direction of their last days and hours to die with dignity.

Why has death ministry become both more badly needed and more difficult in our society? Many factors contribute to the present state of affairs.

Erosion of Traditional Support Systems

The growing population of the United States is geographically mobile and urbanized. The rural and small-town communities typical of the past provided a strong network of extended kin and friendly neighbors who immediately stepped into crisis experiences with practical assistance and socioemotional support.

Today the family, as a supportive network, is usually confined to spouses and their offspring with little effective linkage to aunts, uncles, and cousins. Thus, the "outer ring" of the family network is weak while members of the nuclear family are often too disturbed by hurt and grief to be of much help to one another. Mobility frequently separates family members by great distances, which make it difficult to help one another over the weeks and months through which grief typically continues. In urban society interpersonal relationships are usually secondary, instrumental, and impersonal and, therefore, useless in helping to deal with personal loss and grief.

However, other social forms can sometimes substitute for the family. The church provides an important focus of belonging, meaning, and interaction. If church members are filled with a sense of calling to minister to one another and others with special needs, they can become worthy substitutes for the kinship network. New Testament concepts of brotherhood (1 Thess. 4:6; Jas. 2:15) and of fellowship, *koinonia* (1 Cor. 1:9) and the command to "bear one another's burdens" (Gal. 6:2, RSV) demonstrate that Christians should be and act as family to fellow believers. Contemporary churches are faced with great opportunity and responsibility in developing active and caring ministries to the dying and bereaved, with close and regular personal contact as their essence. A thoughtful pastor can provide leadership, inspiration, and guidance in developing these systems of service.

Nature and Content of Death Ministry

Little more than a generation ago the minister's responsibility in a death situation was to conduct the funeral. In some cases he had opportunity to visit the victim before death but was not strictly obliged to do so and often could not. If he lived in the community, although in rural churches he often lived miles away, he would visit the home where the body lay in state. But mostly he "preached the funeral," and that was his ministry.

Today people are more vulnerable because of weakened family support systems. We now also know that grief is far more potent and long lasting than we ever suspected. Moreover, dying often takes longer and in its process ravages both the dying person and loving family and friends. Before and after the funeral, a lengthy, multifaceted ministry is required to meet the broad spectrum of human needs generated by the illness and death.

The minister must be counselor and confidante to the terminally ill, sometimes for months or even years. He must understand something of the physical and psychological dynamics of dying slowly. He must know how others, including intimate loved ones, react to this peculiar experience. He must search for ways to help all of them in a situation that has no pat answers or precise guidelines.

The contemporary minister must also know what grief is, its effects, how it works, how to detect it, and how to help. Grief makes people behave in unusual ways, but it is normal, even necessary. Judging when grief has passed beyond the "normal" range and should be defined as "complicated" (Wordon, 1982) is not easy, but the minister needs to be able to do so. While he will try to aid both types of mourners, those suffering from complicated grief require more and different help.

Effective ministry to the dying and bereaved demands careful preparation, emotional strength, and spiritual maturity. The pastoral ministry in general has become far more complex and challenging (Brister, 1964; Oates, 1959; Young and Meiburg, 1960), due in a large part to the same social conditions that have complicated death ministry. Regularly upgraded training, vigorous spiritual discipline, and careful shepherding of one's own physical and emotional health will be required of pastors if they are to mend modern America's brokenness. Now and then, most of us feel the need to escape, as Jeremiah (9:2) did, to "a wayfarers' lodging place" in the desert but we cannot, anymore than he did.

Again Dick Young (1954: 106) said it well over thirty years ago:

> It is a moving experience to stand and see a person die. The average man or woman usually shrinks from any association with the dying. Yet those who are often in the presence of

death learn that it need not be depressing but may be made beautiful by the way in which the dying person and those around him face it. Not only should the pastor consider it an honor to participate in the last moments of an individual's life, but he should also regard it as a sacred opportunity. Attendance at a death is without doubt the most difficult of pastoral ministries, but any shirking of responsibility is bound to leave one with a sense of guilt.

In addition to preparing himself spiritually, intellectually, and emotionally, the pastor can improve the effectiveness of his death ministry by preparing church members. If they know in advance what to expect of the experiences of death, dying, and bereavement, they will be somewhat prepared for the onslaught of pain, fear, general anxiety, depression, and other grief-linked emotions. Understanding the pastor's role in such situations, they will know how to call on him and how to use his services to meet their needs. Moreover, if properly prepared, church members can join the pastor in this vital ministry, which demands all the helping hands and caring hearts that can be found.

Institutional Settings

Not long ago most people died at home, and our research indicates that most people would prefer it to be that way today. However, in reality most people die in hospitals or, in a much smaller number of cases, nursing homes. This almost certainly will be a continuing pattern as far in the future as we can project at this time. Such settings pose major challenges to effective ministry.

The first challenge in that the locus of death occurs in settings in which the pastor is out of control. Death does not occur in the church building or the patient's home, where the pastor ordinarily holds great authority. Instead, the bureaucratically structured management of the hospital that is home to the dying makes and enforces the rules and generates the routine of activity within which he must operate (Rando

1984). This is further overlaid and complicated by the greater, professionally founded authority of the physician.

Finding himself in a position of limited authority and as an outsider in this treatment system, the minister must find ways to adapt. The first step is to learn the system from physical layout to the names of the housekeeping staff. Learning the management system, the structure of the hospital bureaucracy and the specific rules it promulgates, is particularly important for the minister (Sudnow, 1967). He will then know how to follow the rules and how to challenge them on humane and spiritual grounds when necessary. He will do well to forge strong alliances with caring and influential physicians and to establish a positive, professional relationship with the hospital administration. In most cases this will secure for the pastor all of the freedom he needs to carry out his ministry to the dying and bereaved.

New Complex Issues

When is a person dead? How is death to be defined? Once the answer was simple. Lack of pulse or heartbeat and absence of certain neurological responses to stimuli declared a person to be dead. Now the heart-lung machine can keep a body technically alive when the brain has been irreparably damaged. When are the machines to be turned off? This finally reduces to a moral issue to which Christianity should speak, but no clear and consistent answer has yet been advanced. Unfortunately one of our physician friends could have been right when he predicted that the answer will finally come from a government bureaucrat who will decide at what point financial coverage for a procedure will be terminated.

What right has a dying patient to decide when to cease treatment? If "every right" is the answer, does the minister have a duty to help the patient? The medical profession generally has a built-in tendency to try to prolong life. Thus, the pastor trying to help a dying friend seize control over his dying could be in the middle of a struggle with powerful authority figures.

The complexity of death and its definitions surround the dying person and generate social and psychological issues that distress the patient. Ministry demands response. To respond, the pastor must not only be caring but also knowledgeable, capable of translating that knowledge to patient and family, and prepared to help the patient gain information and seek his own best interests as he sees them.

While much has changed about death and dying during the past half century, some things remain the same. For all of its technology, its banishment of mystery, and its secular overtones, modern society has not lost the sacred (Lewis, 1961). Ultimate issues remain and become starkly evident in the experience of death. Therefore, the legitimacy of the presence of the minister with the dying and bereaved is certain. However, it is difficult to be present, challenging the minister's professional capacities, personal strength, capacity for giving, and spiritual resources. In return, the blessings received are profound—the assurance of having been an instrument of our Lord's in comforting those who mourn.

References

Brister, C.W. 1964. *Pastoral Care in the Church.*

Lewis, C. 1961. *A Grief Observed.*

Oates, Wayne E., ed. 1959. *An Introduction to Pastoral Counseling.*

Rando, T. A. 1984. *Grief, Dying, and Death: Clinical Interventions for Caregivers.*

Sudnow, David. 1967. *Passing On: The Social Organization of Dying.* Englewood Cliffs, N. J.: Prentice-Hall, Inc.

Worden, J. W. 1982. *Grief Counseling and Grief Therapy: A Handbook for the Mental Health Practitioner.*

Young, Richard K. 1954. *The Pastor's Hospital Ministry.*

Young, Richard K. and Albert L. Meiburg. 1960. *Spiritual Therapy.*

2
Dying in a Technological Society
Eric J. Cassell

The care of the terminally ill in the United States has changed as the business of dying has shifted from the moral to the technical order. The moral order has been used to describe those bonds between men based on sentiment, morality, or conscience that describe what is right. The technical order rests on the usefulness of things, based in necessity or expediency, and not founded in conceptions of the right. The change of death from a moral to a technical matter has come about for many reasons based in social evolution and technical advance, and the effects on the dying have been profound.

One reason for the change has been the success of modern medicine in combating death. For most, in the United States, premature death is no longer imminent. The death of infants is unusual, the death of children rare, and the death of young adults so improbable that it must be removed from the realistic possibilities of young life. Further, the nature of death has also changed. The degenerative diseases and cancer have become predominant. Lingering sickness in the aged is a less common event because medicine is able to combat the complications of chronic disease that so often in the past kept the sick person from functioning. Accompanying these changes brought about by technical advances, there has been a change in the place where death occurs. Death has moved from the home into institutions—hospitals, medical centers, chronic care facilities and nursing homes.

From the Moral to the Technical

There are other reasons for the shift of death in the United States from the moral to the technical order. One is the widespread acceptance of technical success itself. Because life expectancy has increased, the dying are old now. But, life expectancy is not an individual term, it is a statistical term. For individuals, what has changed is their death expectancy; they do not expect to die. They may use fantasies of early death or fears of death for personal or psychological reasons, but the reality belief is that death need not occur in the foreseeable future, that death is a reversible event. That belief in the reversibility of death, rooted in the common American experience of modern medicine, begins to move death out of the moral order. Death is a technical matter, a failure of technology in rescuing the body from a threat to its functioning and integrity. For the moment, it does not matter that the death of a person cannot be removed from the moral order by the very nature of personhood; what matters is the mythology of the society. The widespread mythology that things essentially moral can be made technical is reinforced by the effect of technology in altering other events besides death; for example, birth, birth defects, or abortion.

The fact that technology can be seen so often as altering fate nurtures an illusion that is basic to the mythology of American society—that fate can be defeated.

From the Family to the Hospital

Another reason why death has moved away from the moral order lies in the changes in family structure that have occurred over the past decades in the United States. The family remains the basic unit of moral and personal life, but with the passing of functionally meaningful extended families have come changes directly related to the care of the dying. The old, both the repository of knowledge about what is right and the major recipients of moral obligation, have left the family group. For many reasons, not the least their desire for continued independence in the years when previously material dependency would have been their lot, the aged frequently live alone. In retirement they may live far from their roots or their children, associating largely with others of their own age. An age-graded way of life has emerged that depends again on technical success and public responsibility (such as old age benefits) to solve problems for the aged that previously would have been the primary concern of the family. There is the belief, reinforced by the advantages of the change in family structure and geographic mobility, that essentially moral problems—obligations to parents, for example—have become part of the technical order amenable to administrative or technical solutions.

On the other hand, in his search for continued independence and comfortable retirement, the old person has allowed his family to separate, allowed the young to achieve their independence. In previous times and in other cultures, the mantle passed to the next generation only with the death of the old. Here it is voluntary. But, a problem is created for the dying patient. The old person who is going to die is already out of the family. To die amidst his family he must return to them—reenter the structure in order to leave it. Reenter it in denial of all the reasons he gave himself and his children for separation, reasons equally important to them in their pursuit of privacy and individual striving and in their inherent denial of aging, death, and fate.

Thus, by reason of technological success and changes in family structure that are rooted in the basic mythology of America, death has moved from the moral order to the technical and from the family to the hospital.

The Context of Dying

It is interesting to examine some of the consequences and corollaries of the shift. In individual terms, moving the place of death from the home to the hospital, from familiar to strange surroundings, means changing the context of dying. The picture of the old person, independent and swinging free—promulgated as much by the old as by others—while part fact, is also a partial fiction dictated by the old person's love for, and nurturance of, the independence of the young. Becoming a burden is the great fear not only for what it may mean personally, but for the threat it poses to the fragile economic and personal structure of today's nuclear family. But part fiction or no, the hallmark of "golden age" is independence. With independence and its mobility, the belief arises that each person is the sole representative of his own beliefs, values, and desires. In health that may seem to be true, but the fact is as fragile as the body. In health a person can struggle for his rights, pronounce his values, and attempt their fulfillment. But the sick, bound to their bodies by their illness, are different. The values and desires dearly held during life give way in terminal illness. Pain and suffering erode meaning and deny dignity. The fiction of independence and the denial of fate give way to reality. In terminal illness, the individual must give over to others and to the context of his dying the defense of his dignity and the statement of his values. But the context of dying and the people at the bedside have changed. The aged no longer die surrounded by their loved ones. An essentially private matter takes place in the public sphere surrounded by symbols of individual sameness, not personal difference. The family and its needs are the intruders. The patient's values, spoken by others, compete with the values of the institution. There is a final, ironic independence as the person dies alone.

Thus, there are personal or value problems created for the individual when death moves from the moral to the technical order. Characteristically, our society seeks solutions to these problems not by reasserting the moral, but by attempting technical solutions for moral imperatives. We are seeing increasing attempts in the United States to find quasi-legal or legal means to reassert the rights of the dying—some technical means to give as much weight to the person who dies as the hospital gives to his body.

Mechanical Events in the Moral Sphere

In the process of the shift of death from the moral to the technical, a basic confusion arises that confounds the usefulness of technical solutions in what are essentially moral problems. The mechanical events involved in a body becoming dead, which occur in the technical sphere, are confused with the process of dying, which occurs in the moral sphere. It is a natural error but one that we do not frequently make in health. That is to say that while we are aware that the mechanical event that is a beating heart is essential to life, we do not confuse ourselves with our heartbeat. As a matter of fact, if someone becomes too conscious of his heartbeat, we consider it a symptom, or neurosis. But in the sick or the dying the confusion is rampant. There are two distinct things happening in the terminally ill, the death of the body and the passing of the person. The death of the body is a physical phenomenon, a series of measurable events that are the province of physicians. The passing of the individual is a nonphysical process, poorly defined, largely unmeasurable and closely connected to the nature of the dying person. It is the process by which he leaves the group and during which we take leave of him. Indeed, in the manner in which many act toward the newly dead body—as though it still contained some part of the person—the passing of the individual, at least for the onlooker, may not end with death. It is obvious that in sudden death a person may pass away who was never dying; or conversely, in the depressed, the person may be dying with no evidence of impending death.

The passing of the individual is also part of the work of physicians; but, of more importance, it is the province of family, friends, and clergymen—indeed the entire group. But in a technical era, the passing of the person, since it is unmeasurable and does not fit the technical schema, is not a legitimate subject for public discourse.

Those feelings within that relate to the dying person are difficult to organize, to deal with, or to speak about. The social rituals that previously enabled those confused meanings and feelings to spend themselves appropriately have diminished or disappeared along with the extended family. In the moral order, time slows down for those around the dying; but in the world of things, of necessity or expediency, time moves on relentlessly, making its case for those around the dying to return to that world. Furthermore, with decreasing practice in moral matters, even when social forms remain, the content becomes increasingly sterile. Men obscure the moral content of the passing of the person by using the facts and artifacts of the death of the body as the vehicle for their interchanges—much as talk about the weather or sports draws the sting on other occasions.

The confusion of the mechanical events of the death of the body with the personal and social nature of the passing of the person confounds attempts to solve the essentially moral problems of the dying—problems of sentiment, conscience, or the knowledge of what is right. Thus, in matters such as when the respirators should be turned off, and by whom—essentially moral questions—the mechanical events loom so large that attention is diverted away from the moral, back to the technical. And this is the corollary problem to that raised earlier: the context of death no longer gives weight to the values of the dying person and forces a resort to legal or administrative protection of his rights.

Depersonalization of Care

The confusion of mechanical events for moral processes creates the further problem of depersonalization of care. And it is seen in the greater attention paid to diseases than to people by doctors and their institutions—a common complaint about physicians and particularly about physicians in their care of the dying. Frequently we explain this depersonalization by saying that it is the physician's psychological defense against the emotional burden imposed by the care of the dying. Though that may be true, it is only part of the truth. We have seen how the whole society has shifted its public focus from moral to technical in many areas of life: doctors are no exception to the trend. The problem cannot solely lie among physicians, or the society would not let them get away with it. Social forces would drive doctors back toward a more holistic view of their patients. Indeed, such a change is beginning to occur in response to the increasingly vocal dissatisfaction with medical care.

Because depersonalization is so much a part of the technical order, not only in medicine, and so antithetical to the values of personhood, let us further examine how depersonalization takes place. Each dying patient is not only a person, but also the container of the process or events by which his body is dying. By definition, since he is dying, these processes or events cannot be controlled by existing technology. Because of the inability of the technology to control such things —and cancer or heart failure are examples—they acquire independent meaning apart from the person containing them. From the viewpoint of caring for the terminally ill, such depersonalization may be justly deplored. But from the viewpoint of medical science, the pursuit of the meaning of the resistant body process, apart from the person containing it, is a legitimate end in itself. That is to say, the heart as an abstraction, as a pump, an electrical system, or what have you is a proper object of technical concern and quite distinct from the fact that human hearts are only found in humans. Further, it is the nature of any system of abstract or formal thought not to be content with mystery but to continue operating on any problem until understanding results. Mystery is a threat to the adequacy of the system of thought itself. Consequently, the disease process must be probed and probed, not only because of its relevance to the care of the sick and dying, but also because lack of a solution poses a threat to the entire logical construct of which the body process is thought to be a part. Thus, the depersonalization and abstraction of body mechanics is both necessary and legitimate within the framework of science, and understanding of the body-as-machine is impeded by consideration of human values.

The problem of depersonalization depends in part on the degree to which the dying person's disease process is understood. For example, in the care of the patient with bacterial pneumonia, easily treated with antibiotics, depersonalization poses little difficulty. The abstractions necessary for understanding microbes, antibiotics, and so forth are so much a part of the physician's thinking that he or she is able to integrate them back into a total concept of man, patients, etc. Withdrawal and depersonalization are not frequent, I think, when experienced doctors and nurses care for the dying, if the cause of death is something acceptably inevitable, such as pneumonia in the very old, or stroke. If it is correct that persons dying of a poorly understood process are more likely to be depersonalized by their physicians, we can better understand why the accusation of depersonalization is most often brought against young physicians. To the inexperienced doctor almost everything about the dying person is unfamiliar or poorly understood, thus requiring the abstraction that leads to depersonalization. Effective integration of the learned technical material with human needs, values, and desires comes only at a later stage of learning.

Temples of the Technical Order

In the United States the modern medical center is the very temple of the technical order, revered both by medicine and the public. As medical science, in its effort toward understanding, has taken the body apart system by system, it has departmentalized the intellectual structure of the hospital. By that I mean not only the well-known division of medicine into specialities, but the further subdivisions that represent specific body functions. The corridors of any American medical center reveal rooms whose doors bear titles such as pulmonary function laboratory, cardiographics laboratory, nuclear medicine, sonography, and so forth. Each of these specialized functions has contributed immeasurably to the diagnostic and therapeutic power of the modern physician, and no doctor who has grown accustomed to their use will feel wholly comfortable in their absence. They are unlike the traditional clinical or research laboratory which, when examining a function of the patient's body, takes the whole patient along; it is not his blood or urine that goes to the laboratory, it is the patient. But it is not the person who holds the interest for the specialized laboratory; instead the interest centers on the person's lungs, or heart, or whatever. A good coronary arteriogram is not necessarily a good patient or even good for the patient, it is merely a technically good example of coronary arteriograms. Patients are usually not aware of or interested in those distinctions, and all too frequently, but in an opposite sense, neither is the physician who performed the test. One can see the hospital, thus compartmentalized, as the concrete expression of the depersonalization resulting from the abstract analytic thought of medical science. Thus, the dying patient in the modern hospital is in an environment ideally suited for the pursuit of knowledge and cure, but representing in its technology and idealized representative—the young doctor— technical values virtually antithetical to the holistic concept of person. This does not imply that the most personal and humane care cannot be and is not given in such hospitals, but rather that those who do give such care must struggle against their technical, depersonalized thinking about the body and against the structure of the hospital that such thought has produced.

No discussion of the care of the terminally ill in the United States can avoid the problem of the nursing home. Whereas the modern hospital represents the positive strivings of medical science and the technical order—the belief that nature, disease, and fate can be conquered—the nursing home represents the tattered edges of that philosophy. Medicine and medical care are seen primarily as the application of medical science to disease: if science fails the body, medicine fails the person. Nursing homes contain the failures and frustrations of medicine as well as the homeless or unwanted sick. They are a place to linger and to die. Walking their halls is deeply depressing because hopelessness is overwhelming. It is the hopelessness one experiences whenever one sees the sick completely overtaken by their sickness, forever apart from the comfort of group. None of the many reasons for their proliferation and crowding explains why they are the hopeless places that they usually are. We know they can be better because of the success of the occasional institution given over to the care of the terminally ill in a positive sense. Such successful nursing homes are often run by religious orders or by others whose belief in their mission is deeply moral. Thus, what we see in the usual American nursing home is by no means inevitable in the way that death is inevitable, but rather a vacuum of care. The promise of science and technology has failed here. The old family solutions to the problems posed by the care of the terminally ill have been altered past utility by social change. No new solution has come forward to fill the void.

We have seen how the care of the terminally ill has changed in the United States. They are older now and die more frequently in institutions. But that bare frame of facts conceals increasing distress within the society over the quality of their dying. When death occurs in the modern hospital, there seems to be more concern for the disease than for the dying person, more concern for life as a succession of heartbeats than life as meaning. When death occurs in nursing homes, it is as if life just dribbled out—custodial care seemingly inconvenienced by individual difference or tenacity for life.

A Balance of the Moral and Technical

We have seen that the problem is larger than widespread insensitivity which might be corrected by new educational programs. Rather, there has been a shift of death from within the moral order to the technical order. The technical, the expedient, the utilitarian that has worked so well in so many material ways seemed to promise easier solutions to the problems previously seen as matters of conscience, sentiment, or obligations between men. But the promise has not been fulfilled; not in the United States nor elsewhere where the technical order spreads its dominance.

Even if it were possible, the solution is not a return of American society to technical innocence. I do not believe that men were inherently more moral in the past when the moral order predominated over the technical. The path seems to lie in the direction of a more systematic understanding of the moral order to restore its balance with the technical. Understanding the body has not made it less wonderful, and the systematic exploration of the moral nature of man will not destroy that nature but rather increase its influence. In the care of the dying, it may give back to the living the meaning of death.

Note

1. Robert Redfield, *The Primitive World and Its Transformations* (Ithaca: Cornell University Press, 1953), pp. 20 *ff.*

3
Death in Contemporary America
Herman Feifel

People have spoken about life and thought about death since the beginning. Still, modern day discussion of death has never quite reached the major-league status of sex, sports, politics, or the weather. Nevertheless, there is no denying that surface consideration of death these days has become lively—almost chic—a surprising outgrowth of a culture portrayed as death-denying. There are a number of reasons for this development. Recent advances in innovative medical technology are altering the character of dying and compelling us to look more steadily at death. Blows from an impersonal technology are alienating us from traditional moorings, and weakening institutional and community supports. The consequences are increased loneliness, anxiety, and self-probing. It is a historic phenomenon that consciousness of death becomes more acute during periods of social disorganization, when individual choice tends to replace automatic conformity to consensual social values. Thus it was in classical society after destruction of the city-state and in the early Renaissance period after the breakdown of fuedalism. Finally, ever since the day when the age of mathematical physics came to a climax at Alamogordo when a black cloud covered the sun and announced, "I am become Death—the shatterer of worlds," there has been a growing pessimism concerning the future of humanity.

Yet, despite these wellsprings of contact, Americans still approach dying and death warily and gingerly. As Woody Allen recently personalized it on his fortieth birthday, "I shall gain immortality not through my work but by not dying." A number of factors contribute to this state of affairs. Foremost among these, I think, is the fact that many of us no longer command, except nominally, conceptual creeds or philosophic-religious views with which to transcend death. People of the Middle Ages had their eschatologies and the sacred time of eternity. And although death portended judgment, it was accompanied by the possibility of atonement and salvation. Death was a door. More recently, with the waning of traditional belief, temporal man lived with the prospect of personal immortality transformed into concern for historical immortality and for the welfare of posterity. Today we are vouchsafed neither. With the advent of the H-bomb, physical science has presently made it possible for us all to share a common epitaph. Not only descendants and social immortality but history as well is being menaced. Time along with space can now be annihilated. Even celebration of the tragic will be beyond our power. Death is becoming a wall.

Further undercutting our capacity to integrate personal death is an impersonal technology which is steadily increasing fragmentation of the family and dismantling rooted neighborhood and kinship groups. Today, the family is essentially nuclear—composed of a husband, wife, and children. No longer do we live in a community abounding with uncles, aunts, siblings, and cousins, and possessing homogeneous values. Consequently, when death intrudes into our lives, previously existing emotional and institutional supports to cushion its impact are absent.

Allied to this development is a spreading deritualization of grief, related to criticism of funerary practices as being overly expansive, irrelevant, and exploitive of the mourner's grief. An aftermath of this orientation is removal of an additional buttress which in the past bolstered many in the face of dying and death.

Another circumstance which has made death more difficult to confront is the gradual expulsion of death from common experience. Death has become a mystery to most of us. It is now a rare phenomenon for the average person to see an untreated dead person. A piece of domestic technology familiar in most nineteenth century households—how to deal with a corpse—has vanished. It is paradoxical that while direct exposure of children and young adults to dying and death is decreasing because of medical advances, dying and death are being given considerable but unrealistic attention in the gothic fantasies of horror films and in derivative TV renditions. These bring to our awareness disaster and battlefield deaths, but they are usually removed from the realm of feeling to that of impersonal statistics, black comedy, and fictive experience. Dying and death are now the province of the "professional," i.e., physician, clergyman, funeral director. Unfortunately, too many of them tend to use their professional knowledge as a buckler against unprotected encounter with death to bind their own anxieties. Accordingly, when the professional is called upon to blunt the edge of grief, to interpret death to family and survivors, he usually is unsuccessful.

Finally, in a society that emphasizes achievement and the future, the prospect of no future at all and loss of identity is an abomination. Death is seen as destroyer of the American vision—the right to life, liberty, and the pursuit of happiness. Hence, death and dying invite our hostility and reputation. I submit that it is this outlook which, in substantial measure, lies behind our general negativity toward old age, herald of death.

In light of these vying and contradictory factors propelling us toward both accepting and denying death, it is understandable why ambivalence toward death is so characteristic of much of modern America's adaptation to death. Or maybe it is, as Avery Weisman has suggested, that we really are not that more accepting of death these days—it's just more difficult to hide from.

Unified and systematic findings are relatively sparse thus far in the thanatological field, but some commanding perceptions are beginning to take hold. What are they?

Developmental Orientations

It is becoming clear that death is for all seasons. It is not the restricted domain of the dying patient, elderly person, combat soldier, or suicidal individual. Children as young as 2 years of age are already contending with the idea of death. We have disabused ourselves of the fancy that sex is a happening that comes to life at puberty, as a kind of full-bodied Minerva emerging from Jupiter's head. In a similar vein, it is fitting that we now recognize the psychological presence of death in ourselves from infancy on. We have come to realize the mental hygienic aspects of being candid about birth (sex). Research studies and clinical experience direct that we do the same for the topic of death. We do not protect children by shielding them from the realities of death. We only hinder their emotional growth. This ban usually mirrors more the adult's and parent's own anxieties and apprehensions about death than the child's actual ability to handle the impact of death. Children are more capable of withstanding the stress brought on by their limited understanding of death than its mystery and implied abandonment. Further, recognition by children of the authenticity of death helps them make better sense of the world. Naturally, such aspects as individual differences, cultural context, method of explanation, and timing have to be considered. In broad perspective, what is truthful and helps sustain the reality-sense of the child will ordinarily prevent a child's adverse reaction to death.

At the other end of the chronological continuum—old age —it is manifest that the older person must joust not only with the possibility of body-image changes, beleaguered hopes, and the shrinkage of his or her social world but with the inescapable certitude of personal mortality. Ironically, we find that though many older persons want to share their feelings and thoughts about dying and death, they are frequently prohibited from doing so by our general reluctance to examine death. A net result is that too many elderly persons turn to regressive and in appropriate patterns of conduct in dealing with their fears, even hopes, about death. The periods of adolescence and middle age likewise share a strong consciousness about death.

What is increasingly apparent is that disregard of the intellectual and emotional predicaments arising from self-consciousness about personal death, present in the mental functioning of the healthy as well as the sick, bars our access to a dominant gyroscope of individual and group behavior. As Kastenbaum has aptly phrased it, "Death is not just destination, it is part of our getting there as well."

Clinical Management

The forward march of medicine has had marked impact on the present character and duration of dying, at least in the more technologically developed countries. Major communicable diseases such as tuberculosis, influenza, and pneumonia are being replaced by more chronic and degenerative types associated with aging, notably heart disease, cancer, and stroke. Additionally, medical headway has lengthened the average time which now elapses between the onset of a fatal illness and death. This is bringing in its wake exacerbated problems of chronic pain, fear, dependency, loss of self-esteem, and progressive dehumanization for many persons.

Medical practice has also altered the locus of dying. No longer do most of us receive death in the privacy and security of our homes. Nowadays, we die in the "big" hospital, convalescent or nursing home, where our lot is often the death of a sickness rather than of a person.

There is expanded recognition of the psychotherapeutic value of open communication with the dying person. Seemingly, the unknown can be feared more, at times, than the most known dreaded reality. Further, clinical experience suggests that, for a goodly number of patients, information received about the seriousness of their situation can galvanize a "will to live" not available to them before. Untapped potentials for responsible and effective behavior as well as less depression and blame of others become evident. Additionally, honest and sensitive talk from physicians, nurses, and family about the gravity of the patient's condition tends to attenuate feelings of guilt and inadequacy not only in the patient but in professional personnel and family as well.

In truth, most dying patients do not expect miracles. What they ask for most of all is confirmation of care and concern. The summons is to help the person recreate a sense of significant being, to be an individual even though dying. The paradox in much of our current treatment is that at the very moment we enhance attention to the patient's physiological needs, we isolate the patient psychologically and socially. When efforts to forestall the dying process fail, professionals usually lose interest and transfer their motivation and resources elsewhere. After all, the saving of life is the paramount goal of the health professional. Therein is where the professional attains his emotional and financial rewards. In a corresponding vein, institutional structures dealing with death and dying seem to be more organized to meet anxieties and requirements of the helping professional than genuine needs of the dying person. A hospital's usual perception of operations and appropriate utilization of personnel classifies dying as a relatively ineffective and inefficient enterprise. The unhappy result is that the dying patient is often left to die emotionally and spiritually alone. We hardly tolerate his farewell.

In this context, I find it perplexing that so many professional colleagues still feel that truth and hope are necessarily mutually exclusive. Obviously, truth can be cold and cruel, but it can also be gentle and merciful. Deceiving disavowal and raw confrontation are not the only options in speaking about death. Indeed, if we were to act in the light of what we know about psychology and responsibility, we would follow a policy of first informing the adult patient about his or her diagnosis and plan for treatment. Then patient and physician would determine what to tell the family. The will, wishes, and integrity of the person should be a sine qua non in any decision making about the dying patient. In current parlance, the dying person needs to recapture his or her "civil rights." We should remember that although the dying do not possess much political or social clout, sooner or later we shall be *they*.

Fortunately, numerous nurses, physicians, the clergy, and other health professionals have not renounced the human, comforting, and emotionally sustaining aspect of their relationship with the dying patient. A superb application of this approach is exemplified by St. Christopher's Hospice in London, under the invigorating directorship of Dr. Cicely Saunders. Here, time is viewed as a matter of depth and quality as well as length. Being in a dying state does not veto respect for the sanctity and meaningfulness of life. The felicitous effect is a dying characterized by minimal physical pain, and a living until death—a *finis coronat opus* (the end crowns the work). The model that is St. Christopher's, hearteningly, is now being replicated in various parts of the United States and Europe. We must appreciate that the essence of dying extends beyond biology. It is a psychosocial as well as biological process, and the attitudes of physician, hospital, family, and friends all influence how the dying person feels and responds.

This leads to another facet of work in the area—the professional's own sensibilities about dying and death. Few undertakings are more emotionally exacting. Pain and death are themes not comfortably encompassed by theory and skill alone. Ministry to the dying is extremely difficult if we ourselves are not quite reconciled to the truth of personal death.

Lastly, the transition in expectations about life and death along with new alternatives available as a result of medical expertness (organ transplantation, hemodialysis) have brought with them awareness that social, economic, and legal, as well as manifestly medical, aspects are inherent in dealing with the dying experience. Communal and ethical relevancies loom large nowadays along with those of medicine and psychology. Adequate concern for the dying requires reassessment of existing social organizations and public policy responsible for health care and delivery.

The Survivors

The ache of death does not end with the death of a person. Its legacy of deprivation, void, sharpened sensitivity to our own transience, even stigma, is transmitted to family and friends—the "significant others." Grief and mourning tend to be too curtailed these days. Accumulated evidence indicates that there is a lot of mental-hygienic wisdom in the Irish wake and Jewish shiva. We are rediscovering that expression of grief is not a sign of weakness or self-indulgence. Rather, it is a normal and necessary reaction to loss or separation from a loved or significant person, and represents a deep human need. Funeral and ritual are important because they underscore the reality of death, bring the support and warmth of fellow human beings when needed, and provide a transitional bridge to the new circumstances brought about by the death of an intimate person.

In this regard, we are more alert to the fact that the positive by-products of mourning are enhanced when we allow room for expressions of anger, guilt, abandonment, even relief at times, along with the more accepted ones of privation, love, and idealization of the dead person, *de mortuis nil nisi bonum.* We are also learning that if we do not lament close upon the death of a loved one, we shall do so later on, only more discordantly. And, indeed, certain demonstrations of adolescent delinquency and significant increases in physical and emotional illness among bereaved persons have already been linked to a negligent mourning. There is the additional implication that avoiding grief is associated with rejecting it in others, a contribution of doubtful value in these days of callousness to human needs.

Two further findings are of importance. One is the phenomenon of anticipatory grief—grief which occurs even before the loss or death takes place. This can characterize the dying person as well as involved family members and professional personnel, and has functional as well as dysfunctional consequences. It is important to keep this dynamic in mind in understanding seemingly varying behaviors reported for family and health-care professionals facing the same death and dying. The second is that normal mourning, in most of us, lasts for at least 1 year after death. Even the more fortunate among us are usually bereft of support after the first month of a death. It is essential that community resources be available to mourners for at least that first year. Newly initiated widow-to-widow programs and similar enterprises are encouraging moves in this direction.

Overall, it is plain that we not truncate the grief and mourning process. The dead must die before we are able to redefine and reintegrate ourselves into life. And the greatest gift we can offer to the bereaved is to be with, not treat, them.

Responses to Death

The anguish of selfhood in contemplating death is not tolerable for most of us without resources, be they transcendental, inspirational, or existential. Major ways of establishing bearings with the idea of death have been religion, art, love, and intelligence. Choice has usually been determined by a confluence of such factors as life experiences, personality, cultural context, age, value-belief system, and level of threat. Unfortunately, knowledge of the specific interactive contributions of these variables is still not available to us in organized fashion. We do, however, possess glimmerings. For example, let us consider religious sentiment. Surprisingly, religious predisposition per se does not appear to be associated significantly with the strength of fear of death. Influence of cultural imprinting with respect to perception of death, at least in the United States, seems to be of a magnitude that subdues major differences in religious conviction.

An emerging datum of some salience is that the attitudes toward death of most persons reflect a kind of coexisting acceptance-avoidance orientation toward fear of death. The governing conscious response to fear of death is one of limited fear; on the fantasy level, one of ambivalence; and on the nonconscious level, one of outright aversion. This patterning appears to serve adaptational requirements, allowing us to maintain communal associations and yet organize our resources to contend with oncoming death. What is clear is that assessment of reaction to personal death must utilize a variety of outcome measures to capture differing levels of awareness. In the face of death, the human mind seemingly operates simultaneously on various levels of reality or finite provinces of meaning, each of which can be somewhat autonomous.

We are now more cognizant of the dissembling garbs with which fear of death can cloak itself. The depressed mood, insomnia, fears of loss, varying psychosomatic and psychological disturbances—all, at times, exhibit affinity to anxieties about death. In this regard, there is the suggestion of a possible tie between violent behavior and a person's ideas concerning death. Some of the violence of our times can be construed as an aggressive reaction to psychological death. An industrial society engenders feelings of impersonality in many of us. We find ourselves small cogs in a big unresponsive machine. Violence then becomes a means of revenging ourselves against a life which permits this alienation. We destroy presumably that which stands in the path of our attaining selfhood, identity. This conceptualization may have explanatory pertinence for presently prevalent intensified expressions of ethnicity—expressions which may serve as channels for conquering feelings of insignificance, i.e., symbolic death.

Violence can also be perceived as an active response to

unmastered dread of death. The ideological attempt is made to transform death from an internal inevitability against which one is helpless to an external threat over which one has some control. Death is then understood as resulting essentially from the hostility of others, and violence is employed to vitiate or kill the person or institution seen as threatening injury or death. Mastery over death is gained symbolically by "killing" or "conquering" death. Additionally, violence supplies individuals with a type of ascendancy, or sense of triumph, in enabling them to decree when and under what conditions they can inflict injury, murder others, or kill themselves. Unhappily, if apathy is a retreat from life—a withdrawal from risk taking—violence is a striking out against death, an assertion of identity that devalues life even as it defies death.

We are no longer in a zealous partnership with God. The quality of sin has changed. When God and State are discerned as halting and enfeebled in punishing violence, and when the grave painfully symbolizes nothingness, the commission of violence and its meaning fall more actively into the bailiwick of self-judgment and criticism, with its potential for legitimizing violence. Herein may lie much of the irrational and absurd, so manifest and marked in the moral temper of our times.

If death were less of a stranger to us, it is conceivable that our compulsive need to extrovert fear of death and kill might be somewhat muted. Indeed, in contrasting manner, appreciation of finiteness can serve not only to enrich self-knowledge but to provide the impulse to propel us forward toward achievement and creativity. It was no less a person than Michelangelo who said, "No thought is born in me that has not 'Death' engraved upon it."

In the chapters that follow, the book's contributors bring to bear their scholarship and thinking to further advance our understanding of how death operates in and influences our lives.

References

Aries, P. *Western attitudes toward death: From the Middle Ages to the present.* Baltimore: Johns Hopkins, 1974.

Brim, O. G., Jr., Freeman, H. E., Levine, S., and N. A. Scotch, (Eds.) *The dying patient.* New York: Russell Sage, 1970.

Feifel, H. (Ed.) *The meaning of death.*. New York: McGraw-Hill, 1959.

Feifel, H. Philosophy reconsidered. *Psychological Reports,* 1964, 15, 415-420.

Feifel, H., and Branscomb, A. B. Who's afraid of death? *Journal of Abnormal Psychology,* 1973, 81, 282-288.

Feifel, H. Religious conviction and fear of death among the healthy and terminally ill. *Journal for the Scientific Study of Religion,* 1974, 13, 353-360.

Fulton, R., and Fulton, J. A psychosocial aspect of terminal care: Anticipatory grief. *OMEGA,* 1971, 2, 91-100.

Glaser, B. G., and Strauss, A. L. *Awareness of dying.* Chicago: Aldine, 1965.

Gorer, G. *Death, grief, and mourning.* New York: Doubleday, 1965.

Jackson, E. N. *Understanding grief, its roots, dynamics and treatment.* Nashville: Abingdon, 1957.

Kastenbaum, R. Death and development through the life span. In H. Feifel (Ed.), *New meanings of death.* New York: McGraw-Hill, 1977.

Kubler-Ross, E. *On death and dying.* New York: Macmillan, 1969.

Morgenthau, H. J. Death in the nuclear age. *Commentary,* 1961, 32, 231-234.

Parkes, C. M. *Bereavement: Studies of grief in adult life.* New York: International Universities Press, 1972.

Weisman, A. D. *On dying and denying: A psychiatric study of terminality.* New York: Behavioral Publications, 1972.

Weisman, A. D. The psychiatrist and the inexorable. In H. Feifel (Ed.), *New meanings of death.* New York: McGraw-Hill, 1977.

Part II

Death and Bereavement Across the Life Cycle

4
Children and Death
Judith Stillion and Hannelore Wass

Introduction

Children and *death*—the two words seem contradictory. Children symbolize life and growth whereas death marks decay, the end of growing and being. Why, then, when the subject is so foreign to the nature of children should we try to educate them about the inevitability of death? In the twentieth century the answer of U.S. culture to this question has been, we should not. Many well-intentioned adults fear that facing the facts of death straightforwardly with children will rob them of their essential innocence and, therefore, of their childhood. Some adults go so far as to believe that children, confronted with the concept of death, will become so terrified that they will not be able to face living in a courageous way. A third reason that adults fail to face the question of death with children relates to the adult's own needs for denial and repression of the inevitability of death. Finally, many adults feel that since death is an unknown it is unrealistic to try to teach anyone to prepare for it.

Historical Perspective

That death and children have not always been so foreign to each other is evident in children's games, prayers, and chants that have been passed on from generation to generation. Peek-a-boo, a game that delights infants, is said to be derived from an old English word meaning "dead or alive" (1). It teaches babies their first lessons in object permanence. One of the first games children learn, ring-around-the-rosie, with its chant, "ashes, ashes, all fall down," grew out of children's reaction to death during the great plague of the Middle Ages (2). Even today children very commonly learn as their first prayer, "now I lay me down to sleep, I pray the Lord my soul to keep. If I should die before I wake, I pray the Lord my soul to take." Public awareness of death anxiety has caused the latter line to be changed by many teaching agents. However, its original form serves as a reminder that in earlier days children were supposed to recognize life as transient and death as a constant possibility at a very young age. A rope-skipping chant familiar to many children contains the lines, "Doctor, Doctor, will I die? Yes, my dear, but do not cry," or a variation of this rhyme, "Doctor, Doctor, will I die? Yes, my child, and so will I." Many other games, including hide-and-seek and many tag games, have been offered as evidence of children's lasting tendency to explore the contradictory nature of life and death (2, 3).

Until this century children were common witnesses to death. Infant mortality was high, and it was a rare firstborn who did not experience the death of a younger sibling. Similarly, life expectancy was significantly shorter. According to Lerner (4), life expectancy in 1900 in the United States was 47.3 years. Children often attended the funerals of their parents as well as of siblings before they reached adulthood. In earlier days death occurred most often at home and children were aware of it in all its aspects. They helped care for the sick family member, were often present at the moment of death, and were included in the planning of the funeral and attended it. In short, children lived continuously with the fact of death from infancy through adulthood.

As medicine became more specialized and sophisticated, as infectious diseases and others were conquered, death became more and more remote. The past two generations are the first in known history in which many middle-aged adults have not experienced the death of an immediate family member.

Adults' Death Denial and the Child

Death has come to be viewed as an unwelcome stranger rather than an expected companion, and many adults refuse to discuss it or even think about it. Their denial of death has extended to their children. In a survey by Wass 144 high school seniors were asked, among other questions: "When you were a child how was death handled in your family?" "Death was never talked about," responded 39 percent. An additional 26 percent said that death was talked about only when absolutely necessary, and even then only briefly. The majority of students reported that this death taboo in the family was true for the present time as well. It is safe to say that in the United States parents, as a rule, do not discuss the topic of death with their children. This avoidance of death stems largely from the adults' own discomfort and anxiety concerning dying and death. It is difficult, for example, for the mother of a 4-year-old to provide a calm and well-deliberated answer to the child's totally unexpected question "Mommy, do I have to die?" What mother is not horrified at the prospect of her child's death? Even if she manages a straightforward answer such as "Yes, everybody has to die sometime, but we hope you will not die for a long long time, not for many many years," she is likely to communicate a great deal of anxiety to the questioning child. Such transmission of anxiety from adults to children may be unavoidable, and the best we can strive for is to keep the amount of anxiety at a manageable level. In addition to anxiety, adults frequently feel frustrated and sometimes angry about these death questions, and when these feelings are communicated the child may come to feel guilty as well as anxious.

Avoidance of the topic of death on the part of parents is well intentioned. Most parents have a great need to shield their children from the harsh realities of death. In fact, until recently adults generally believed that children are not concerned about death and that those who are need psychiatric help. The fact, however, as shown in many studies and supported by the authors' experiences is that children are very much concerned. This interest in death is a normal part of human development. The question of life and death is an existential question and an expression of the child's basic curiosity and search for meaning. Children, like other people, seek to understand themselves, their relationship with others, and the world in which they find themselves. Even very young children ask existential questions such as: Where do babies come from? Where was I before I was born? Do I have to die? Who deaded Grandpa? And in their everyday world, children experience death by coming in contact with dead insects, birds, and other animals. With their all-encompassing curiosity, children try to understand the difference between the warmth, motion, and vitality that marks life and the cold, pallor, and silence that marks death. All too often when they broach their questions to adults they are met with not only evasive but often incomplete answers or disapproving silence. In this way a child learns that death is a taboo subject, and a child may well come to believe that death must be a horrifying, terrible thing, too awful even to mention.

Attempting to protect the child from the facts of death is a futile exercise. In addition to their real life experiences with dead animals, children observe death on television news and inordinate amounts of fictional death in movies and television plays. Much of the death portrayed by the media creates a totally unrealistic picture in the mind of child viewers. For example, Wiley Coyote on "Road Runner" is smashed, mashed, blown up, dropped into ravines, shot, stabbed, and run over, and yet he emerges with nothing worse than a frazzled coat and a new determination to catch the Road Runner.

In the human television world, children frequently see a central character on a soap opera die a drawn-out death only to appear on a different soap opera within a week or two. On "cops' and robbers" shows characters die violently every night but are seen on other shows the next day or week. Perhaps even more disturbing, actors such as Freddie Prinze die and their deaths are publicized, but they continue to appear on reruns and syndications for years following their deaths. What impression of the nature of death can a child glean from such exposure? While realistic attempts to deal with death, bereavement, and grief are not widespread in our media, at least one notable exception is that of the Emmy award-winning show produced by Family Communications, in which death and grief were both explored at a level preschool children could understand and to which they could relate (5).

Children's Views of Death

In order to answer children's questions concerning death, an adult must be aware of the child's age, experience, and prior understanding. In general, children's understandings of death seem to follow the cognitive developmental model rather closely. This model, developed by the acclaimed Swiss psychologist Jean Piaget, states that a child's level of reasoning is dependent upon both maturation and learning. Children pass through certain cognitive stages as their mental structures mature and as they interact with the world around them (6). Thus a child of 3 confronted with the death of a parent will not react or understand in the same manner as will a child of 12, even if he or she is given the same explanations and treatment.

Developmental Stages in Understanding Death

Nagy (7), in the now classical study done with Hungarian children between the ages of 3 and 10 years of age, concluded that there are three stages in children's understanding of death and that these three stages are age-related. The *first stage* in understanding death encompasses the age ranges of 3 to 5 years and is similar to what Piaget calls the preoperational stage (6) in that it reflects the egocentric mind of the preschool child. Because children know that they need to eat and breathe, they cannot imagine a human body without those characteristics. Therefore, they describe death either as a kind of sleep or as a gradual or temporary state. While there is a recognition that death differs from life (for example, most young children know that dead people are buried in the ground [8]), there is an incomplete and almost wistful tone to the child's understanding. Nagy (9) illustrates this point by recording a preschool child's remarks:

> Child: It can't move because it's in the coffin.
> Adult: If it weren't in the coffin, could it?
> Child: It can eat and drink. (p. 274)

Similarly, a small child may urge a parent to take a dead puppy to the doctor to make it well.

This stage in the child's cognitive development is also characterized by magical thinking. The lines between fact and fantasy are often blurred, and for small children many things are possible. A small child believes that flowers whisper and that mountains open up if you tell them to, and that princes can turn into frogs and vice versa. Fairy tales support the child's unrealistic concept of death: The beautiful princess sleeps for a hundred years and then a prince awakens her with a kiss (10). While young children are saddened by death, they do not yet grasp the finality and irreversibility of death at this first stage.

The *second stage*, beginning around age 5 or 6 and lasting through age 8, is comparable to the stage of concrete operations in Piagetian theory. Piaget describes this stage as the age of the scientist. During this period, children are consumed with questions concerning the workings of the world around them. They are sorting out impressions, classifying objects, and discovering laws of cause and effect (6). Their understanding of death reflects the growing awareness of the way the world operates. They now recognize that death is final.

Nagy's children frequently personified death as a skeleton or powerful monster, perhaps in an attempt to bring the topic into a more easily understandable cause-effect relationship. Death personified comes to get you, but if you are fast enough or clever enough you may get away. At this stage, children worry about the mutilation of the body brought about by the death monster. This is well illustrated in poems written by children (11). Obviously the 6- to 8-year-old child, while recognizing that death is final, also sees it as capricious. The child has not yet incorporated the ideas that death is inevitable, natural, and universal. A typical conversation with one of Nagy's (9) children reveals this lack of understanding:

> Adult: Do you often think of death?
> Child: I often do. But such things as when I fight with death and hit him on the head and death doesn't die. (p. 273).

Nagy described the *third stage* of death as that of mature understanding. In Piaget's theory this stage reflects the complex integration of the formal operational stage of cognitive development. Nagy's study indicates that this stage may begin as early as 9 years of age. Children who have reached this level of reasoning realize that death is inescapable and universal; "Death is the termination of life. Death is destiny. Then we finish our earthly life. Death is the end of life on earth" (9, p. 273). In addition, children view death as personal. It is no longer something done to people from the outside (except in the case of accident) but rather the result of a natural, internal destruction process that will happen to everyone including themselves. Childers and Wimmer (12) conducted a study of the awareness of two aspects of death, universality and irrevocability, in children from ages 4 to 10. Of the 4-year-olds, 11 percent recognized that death is universal, but by the age of 9, 100 percent recognized death as universal. Of the 10-year-olds, 63 percent as compared to 33 percent of 4-year-olds recognized death as irrevocable.

However, even strict Piagetian theorists do not maintain

that very young children have no concept of death. Being and nonbeing seems to be one of the first differences to which a child attends and tries to understand. Kastenbaum (13) tells the story of a 16-month-old boy who is engrossed in watching a caterpillar moving along a path. When the foot of a passing adult crushes the caterpillar, the child looks to his father and says, "No more." Kastenbaum maintains that the solemnity of the tone and the facial expression of the child are powerful indications that the child comprehends (at least at a preconceptual level) the state of death. Such everyday experiences with death can provide the impetus for an informal death education program within the home.

The Influence of Life Experiences in Understanding Death

Children vary by age in their understanding of death, but their views are also shaped by their life experiences. For example, two 15-year-olds sharing similar backgrounds and IQs can vary greatly in understanding depending upon their religious background and their firsthand dealings with death or lack of them. One 15-year-old might have learned at a young age that talking about death made the adults in his family uncomfortable. By circumstance he may not have confronted death among family or close friends. He may even have trained himself to deny curiosity about the subject. When contrasted with a 15-year-old who has had to cope with the death of a parent, sibling, or friend, there may be as much difference in comprehension of the topic as we would expect to find between the 5- and the 9-year-old of Nagy's study. A replication of Nagy's study (14) showed that children in the United States, in contrast to the Hungarian children of nearly 30 years ago, express concepts of death that could be classified into four categories:

1. Relative ignorance of the meaning of death (ages 0-4).
2. Death as a temporary state. Death is not irreversible

and the dead have feelings and biological functions
(ages 4-7).
3. Death is final and irreversible but the dead have biological functioning (ages 5-10).
4. Death is final. It is the cessation of all biological functioning (ages 6 and beyond).

Other attempts to replicate Nagy's findings in this country
(12, 14-16) have generally found a relationship between age
and breadth of death awareness but have not found the personification of death among 6- to 9-year-olds that Nagy
found. This may lend support to the idea that cultural beliefs
and experiences also shape concepts of death. Nagy's children were all firsthand witnesses of a terrifying, bloody war
in which death could be delivered from the skies unexpectedly. Most of them undoubtedly knew families who had lost
loved ones during the war. Perhaps it was more natural for
those children to try to make the concept of death more
understandable by personifying it. However, their words may
also reflect a personification tendency more prevalent in
Europe than in the United States.

Family and Social Class Influences

The importance of the family in the development of ideas
and feelings about death was also demonstrated in a study by
Wass and Scott (17). They found that children aged 11 to 12
whose fathers were college educated theorize and verbalize
more about death than do children whose fathers only completed high school. Interesting also was the wide variability
found in the sample concerning concepts of death. They
ranged from an "immature" belief that death is a long rest to
a "mature" belief that death is a natural, irreversible, and
universal event. It is important to note that the need to discuss death and dying should be viewed as a sign of normal,
healthy development rather than as an indication of morbid
preoccupation with abnormal material. Older children in particular welcome the chance to discuss their views of death and

dying. The protocols that follow are typical of responses made by 11- and 12-year-olds who were invited to tell what they thought and felt about what happens when one dies.

> Girl age 12: I would like to die of old age. Just go to sleep and never wake up, a nice quiet way to go. I would like to be buried. Then whatever the spirits wanted to do with me they could do.
>
> Boy 11 years: I think if death came slowly I would just fade out. But if it was instant, I would suddenly be gone. I believe that after you die, you have another life and you might come back from anything like a cockroach to a royalty.
>
> Girl 11 years: I think when someone knows they are going to die, they are very scared. I would be. I think after someone dies they just lie there forever and disintegrate. I hope I never die.
>
> Girl 12 years: When you die, you lay there wondering if you will go to Heaven or Hell. I get scared and don't want to die. Whenever I think about it, I get all spooked out. I don't know about you, but I am going to Heaven.
>
> Girl 12 years: When I die, some people will probably come and put me in a coffin with cobwebs in it; and they'll put me in a dark hearse, and the spiders will probably eat me before they get me in the ground. Next they'll put the coffin in a real deep hole and let me rot!
>
> Girl 12 years: I think you would be surrounded by darkness. You would be absolutely without movement. You couldn't talk or see or use any of your senses. You would be that way forever. It's like taking a very long rest.
>
> Boy 12 years: Well, to me death is a natural thing. Everybody has to die sometime. Nobody can live forever. I know that my mother and father will die sometime. I just hope it's not soon. Then, later, I myself will be threatened by this natural thing called death (17).

A 1974 study (18) supported the impact of the environment in children's conceptualization of death. These authors studied 199 children between the ages of 3 and 9. They grouped the children by age according to socioeconomic class. The results showed that lower class children, whose environment is more violent, tend to be more aware of death at younger ages. They concluded that "The lower class children's fantasy content indicates that they are attempting to deal in a realistic, sensible manner with their environment" (p. 19).

In summary, whereas there is ample support for the cognitive-developmental approach to children's concepts of death, it should be remembered that development involves more than maturation; it results from an interaction of biological readiness with environmental factors. Life experiences, intelligence levels, family attitudes and values, self-concepts, and many other as yet unexamined factors all seem to play a part in each child's individual attainment of meaning for death.

Loss, Anxiety, and Death in Children

Children begin to experience loss at a very young age. Birth itself might be regarded as a form of loss as it involves giving up one state of being (the protective womb) to enter another (the world, which requires many adaptations). Weaning represents the loss of the major source of comfort, security, and pleasure in an infant's life. Toilet training also is a milestone away from the comfortable dependency of babyhood. Each loss might be thought of as representing a "small death" to the child and each loss brings with it anxiety. The toddler moves out of the soft security of his mother's lap in an uncertain, vaguely worried way. The 5-year-old worries over the loss of her first tooth until the adult mollifies her by assuring that the "tooth fairy" will pay for the loss. The early teen watches with anxiety as the well-known, compact child body begins to assume new proportions.

The process of growing is intimately tied in with loss; and loss produces anxiety. The very young child, from infancy through preschool, manifests this anxiety over separation. The need for mother is almost equivalent to the need for survival and so to be separated arouses a form of death anxiety in the infant. The child between 5 and 9 years old, who is rapidly gaining a strong self-image, shows mutilation anxiety (fear of destruction of some part of his or her body) but is not yet able to verbalize death anxiety per se. It is the adolescents, with their newly acquired ability to think symbolically, who can torture themselves with the concept of nonbeing.

Even strong adults cannot regard nonbeing with equanimity. As children become more mature in their view of death, it is reasonable to suppose that they also become more anxious. Wahl (19) has suggested that many of his child patients' "anxieties, obsessions and other neurotic symptom formations are genetically related to the fear of death or its symbolic equivalents . . ." (p. 27). Von Hug (20) found support for Wahl's suggestion when he obtained a curvilinear relationship between age and death anxiety in normal children but a linear relationship with neurotic children. However, there is evidence that supports the environmental point of view, namely that a child's death anxiety is also largely influenced by the environment. Wass and Scott (17) found that children with college-educated fathers theorized more about death than those whose fathers only completed high school. And children who theorized showed less death anxiety than those who did not theorize.

Positive self-regard is generally viewed as a sign of mental health. Bluebond-Langner (21) suggested that the self-concept may be an important factor in children's concepts of death. It may relate importantly to children's management of death anxiety. This hypothesis is supported in the Wass and Scott study (17) in which it was found that the self-concepts of 11- and 12-year-olds were inversely related to their death anxieties, that is, the higher their self-concepts the lower their death anxiety.

It seems possible that healthy children can grow toward low death anxiety, especially if they are provided with adult models who have worked through their own attitudes toward death and who encourage children to express their fears rather than repress or deny them. Neurotic children, on the other hand, tend to grow more anxious as their concept of death matures.

Implications for Parents

During the early years, parents can help most by merely being available to children and assuring the child that he or she is loved and will not be abandoned (22). Children need honest answers no matter how unpleasant, offensive, or seemingly morbid their questions may be. Grollman (23) points out that parents should answer their children's questions factually and uncompromisingly and at a level they can understand. To tell fairy tales about death to children is not only misleading but may create serious problems in trust between the parents and the child as the child grows older. One of the problems with parental answers is that they are frequently spiritual answers to children's physical-chemical questions. Children want to know what happens after a person has died, but they are equally curious about the physical aspects of dying, particularly in the middle years. They ask questions such as: Why do people die with their eyes open? Why does the blood turn blue? Do people get buried alive? Could a doctor say a person is dead when he really isn't? How long does it take for the body to disintegrate? If parents do not know the answers to such questions it is all right to admit to ignorance. It would be wise to consult a physician or books. Evasiveness or refusal to answer children's questions may also lead to heightened anxiety (22).

Adolescents may clothe themselves in an illusion of invulnerability in order to deny anxiety brought about by their mature understanding of death (24). Kastenbaum (25) has reported that about 75 percent of the adolescents he studied shut the idea of death out of their minds. They were interested in living fully in the present, seeking their identity in the here and now. Adults working with teenagers may find invitations to discuss death go unanswered. However, meaningful dialogues on grief and life after death are also possible if and when the adolescent seeks them out.

Terminally Ill Children

How they view death. Since children's firsthand knowledge of death is a powerful environmental influence for learning about death, it would follow that the terminally ill child should have a far different conception of death than would a healthy child of the same age and intelligence. At least one researcher, Bluebond-Langner (21), makes a case for the idea that terminally ill children not only become aware that they are dying but also understand death as adults do. She discusses five stages in the process of the acquisition of information that are progressive and lead to concomitant changes in self-concept. These changes are dependent upon significant cumulative events occurring throughout the course of the illness but follow the sequence as outlined below:

Information acquisition	Self-concept changes
Diagnosis	Well
"It" is a serious illness	Seriously ill
Names of drugs and side effects	Seriously ill, but will get better
Purposes of treatment and procedures	Always ill, but will get better
Disease as a series of relapses and remissions minus death	Always ill, and will never get better
Disease as a series of relapses and remissions plus death	Dying

Death anxiety. Other researchers working with terminally ill children have found support for Bluebond-Langner's view (21) that many know of the seriousness of their illness. Waechter (26) reported that anxiety scores of a group of fatally ill children were twice as high as those of other hospitalized children. She suggested that the fatal nature of a child's illness is communicated to the child by the changed way that persons react to him or her after the diagnosis is made. She stated that it is meaningless to argue about whether a child should be told that his or her illness is fatal. Rather, "the questions and concerns which are conscious to the child should be dealt with in such a way that the child does not feel further isolated and alienated from his parents and other meaningful adults" (26, p. 172). Her study reported a significant relationship between children's projective anxiety scores and the degree to which the child has been allowed to discuss his fears and prognosis. She concluded that accepting and permitting dying children to discuss any aspect of their illness may decrease feelings of isolation, alienation, and the sense that the illness is too horrible to discuss completely. Her final plea is that helping professionals not allow the existence of "a curtain of silence around the child's most intense fears" (p. 171).

In another supporting study (27) fatally ill children between the ages of 6 and 10 who were treated as outpatients were compared to a group of chronically but not fatally ill outpatient children. The dying children told stories that revealed significantly more preoccupation with threats to body function and body integrity as well as significantly higher general anxiety than the stories of the less severely ill children.

Most of the studies examining the attitudes of fatally ill children have included storytelling or the use of projective techniques in order to circumvent the child's initial reluctance to discuss death. Vernick and Karon (28) state that "the initiative for talking about death must come from the adult who is in possession of more emotional strength" (p. 395). These authors are representative of many health workers who feel that fatally ill children know more than they feel safe in saying. Yudkin (29) points out that children signal deep anxiety about the possibility of death in many unspoken ways: "Depression out of keeping with the effects of the illness itself; unspoken anger and resentment toward his doctors; resentment toward his parents of a child old enough not to be affected by mere separation in the hospital. These all suggest anxiety about death" (p. 39).

In children under 5 years of age, death awareness often

takes the form of separation anxiety. Natterson and Knudson (30) define death awareness as the "individual's consciousness of the finiteness of his personal existence" (p. 457). Young children, totally dependent on their parents for physical and emotional comfort, often equate separation of parents to physical death. Such separation fear is not dependent upon strong ego and intellectual development. Separation anxiety is most commonly seen in children who have not yet attained language skills but may be the most prevalent fear up to 5 years of age (31). Terminally ill children between the ages of 6 and 10 often display mutilation fear. Children during this period are still working to develop a concept of death but they have well-developed body images. Threats to that image, whether from medical intervention or from the disease itself, cause severe anxiety. The third and final maturational step in death awareness is death anxiety per se. When death is certain, death anxiety must be regarded as a rational fear rather than as a neurotic symptom.

Viewpoints for working with terminally ill children. The medical profession in the past decade has begun to address itself to caring for the psychological health of dying children as well as their physical health. Many health practitioners (32-35) are advocating open honesty in dealing with dying children. Certainly, if it is true that a child may well understand that he is going to die long before he can say it (31), it would seem productive to open lines of communication as fully as possible so as to prevent loneliness, depression, and inward anger in the dying child.

However, the stance of total honesty is not shared by all health professionals. Evans and Edin (34) reflect the more widespread practice of attempting to shield the dying child from death and the fears involved in dying. They believe that this approach is advisable for the following reasons: a) the fear of death is real and cannot be dissipated by discussion; b) suppression and rejection cannot be used as mechanisms for dealing with fear if open discussion is encouraged; and c) children need the support of their parents during terminal illness and parents frequently cannot cope with their children's awareness of imminent death. Evans and Edin appear to favor a less direct method of dealing with children rather than encouraging them to meet the fears head on.

There is a midway position between total honesty and encouraging denial, which is reflected by Green (36). He encourages doctors to remain open to children's questions and to plan for time to talk with their parents. Basically three questions are generally asked by the child between the ages of 6 and 12. The first is: "Am I safe?" The second is: "Will there be a trusted person to keep me from feeling helpless, alone, and to overcome pain?" and the third is: "Will you make me feel alright?" (p. 496). Successfully dealing with these three questions may be enough to allow the child to explore his own potential for growth in the time remaining. Even young children need an atmosphere of psychological safety in which to express themselves. Green relates a story of a 4-year-old who, though sheltered from the prognosis of his terminal illness, nevertheless told the doctor that he was afraid to die. Allowing the child to express that fear is an important part of total care for the dying child as it results in direct comfort to the child and in freeing up of energy that the child can then use to fight the illness or to engage in intensive living in the time remaining.

Care giving and the dying child. In caring for a dying child the natural core conflict of compassion and nurturance for one in pain versus repulsion against impending shock of separation and loss is heightened (37). Somehow death of a child evokes depths of anger, guilt, and frustration that adult deaths do not raise. Perhaps the child's death awakens one of our deepest fears: death before fulfillment (36). Furthermore, patients' failure to get well often leads to feelings of frustration on the part of the health care workers, since one of their primary goals and needs is to restore health. Frustration may lead to feeling angry toward the dying one, which in turns leads to guilt feelings. Since one of the reactions to grief is to become angry at those who invoked the guilt feelings, "a self-sustaining emotional chain reaction" may ensue (37, p. 509). This reaction may be fully conscious, partially conscious, or unconscious to the care giver, but it affects treatment of the dying child, perhaps leading to overprotection and overindulgence or to isolating the child emotionally and caring only for his or her physical needs.

Helping parents. How much more pronounced these feelings must be in the caring parents of the dying child! One father, in a letter to a friend, expressed his anguish in the following way:

> As you are probably interested, Brian is quite bad. We wait each day for him to die. His discomfort and ours is now so great that I believe we now hope each day for him to die. But the human body does not die easily. We're like weeds in a garden. It's ironic, but waiting for a baby to die is quite similar to having a baby: you wait helplessly, you can't do anything to speed it up or slow it down, it's too late to change the course of things, you call home wondering what stage you're in, doctors and hospitals are involved, you wonder what you're going to do with the other kids when it happens, you have to call the grandparents, your friends are anxious, you want it to happen and you don't want it to happen, you're afraid and yet you desire relief from the long wait. So alike and yet so different. (38)

Friedman (39), in discussing care of the terminal child, points out that there is probably no other area in which "anticipatory guidance" is so helpful in promoting rapport between the physician and the patient's parents. Several authors (40, 41) have offered suggestions for working with parents of the dying child. At the base of all suggestions are the dual principles of open honesty and support. A summary of points to be covered with parents after the initial diagnosis is known includes the following:

1. Recognize the depth of shock and despair the parents must be feeling.
2. Explain the basis for the diagnosis and the nature and type of disease.
3. Explain the fatal outcome and type of therapy to be undertaken. Make every attempt to gain parental support both in the physical and emotional care of the child.
4. Assure parents that medical support will always be available in times of need.
5. Try to help parents anticipate problems involved in the initial telling of others and during the child's illness. Go over possible reactions of siblings (e.g., anger, jealousy, fear, guilt).
6. Discuss causes of the problem with emphasis on relieving possible parental guilt.
7. Emphasize any hope possible. If there is hope for remission, dwell on that. If there is not, discuss scientific research going on, if appropriate. If nothing is available, emphasize the support the child will get throughout the illness from the medical staff. While the good physician will discourage excessive optimism (42), parents must be allowed some hope, especially during the early stages of a disease.
8. Discuss anticipatory grief both as an attempt to educate parents about their own feelings in the coming days and to prepare them to recognize stages their child may be passing through.
9. Stress the importance of maintaining continuity in raising the child. It is essential that parents assume the child will live to adulthood and raise him or her consistent with their prior values and ideals. The alternative is that parents in their grief and guilt will indulge the child, who in turn will become confused and often test new limits until parents are forced to discipline him or her. This often leads to greater feelings of guilt both for

the child and the parents. Children need the security of consistency in their parents' behavior.

10. Try to assess family's strengths and weaknesses and encourage building on the strengths. It is important to ask each parent how the other will accept the death, thus encouraging empathy and visualizing problems in advance.

11. Finally, there is evidence that a follow-up talk after the death of the child is often appreciated by the family in order to provide closure for the family and to permit them to express feelings after the death.

Parents are an integral part of total treatment of the dying child. Morrissey (43) showed that high-quality parent participation leads to better adjustment in hospitalized children. Not only can parents be of help to the ward staff throughout their child's illness, but also by doing this they work off some of their own anxiety, guilt, and grief before the child's death (30). In almost all cases of children who survived 4 months or more after the initial hospitalization, the caregiving parents (usually the mother) reacted with calm acceptance and some were even able to express relief at their child's death. There was a triphasic response among mothers whose children survived at least 4 months. In the first phase there was shock and denial often accompanied by anger, excessive weeping, and a tendency toward overprotection. In the second phase there was an acceptance of the situation coupled with the parent's willingness to expend energy in realistic ways that offered hope of saving the child. During this phase the psychological separation of the mother from the child often began. The third phase coincided with the terminal phase of the child's illness. Mothers directed their energy toward other sick children as well as their own. Sublimation was often evident in their desire to give physical and psychological comfort to parents of other terminally ill children. It is noteworthy that in cases where mothers reacted hysterically or clung to hope unrealistically, their child's death usually occurred less than

3 months after the fatal prognosis was given. It would appear that 4 months is the critical period for the working through of anticipatory grief (30).

Children and Grief

There are at least three distinct types of grief reactions that are appropriate to examine in a discussion of children and death. The first is preparatory grief, the emotional reaction of a child becoming aware that he or she is dying. The second is bereavement as a child faces the fact of the death of a loved one. The third is anticipatory grief as the parents of the terminally ill child attempt to cope with the realization that their child is dying.

Preparatory Grief

Preparatory grief seems to be a universal aspect of the dying process if the person has adequate warning of his or her condition. It involves the following emotions: denial ("This cannot be happening to me"); anger ("How can you let this happen to me?"); resentment ("Why me? Why not you?"); fear ("What will dying be like? Will I suffer? Will I be alone? What will happen after I die?"). Sometimes guilt also is a part of preparatory grieving, as in the case of children who feel that this disease is punishment for earlier behavior. The idea of death as punishment as well as the child's assumption of parents' omnipotence is chillingly portrayed in Hailey's *Airport* (44) when the child in the crashing plane is heard to say, "Mummy! Daddy! Do something! I don't want to die . . . Oh, Gentle Jesus, I've been good . . . Please, I don't want to . . ." (p. 142). If care givers can recognize the complexity of these interrelated emotions and encourage the child to verbalize them according to his needs, the child may be able to work through some of them, thus freeing up energy to be spent in more positive ways. Even if the child cannot work through the emotions, he or she will not feel so cut off and alone during the illness. Often, creation of a positive climate for communication with a dying child stems from the way the disease is presented to the child in the beginning. Foley and McCarthy (35) describe a typical physician's explanation to a leukemic child as follows:

> You have a serious blood disease, leukemia. Ten years ago, there was no treatment for leukemia and many people died. Now there are a number of drugs which can be used to treat leukemia. There are several types of leukemia and the type you have is the one for which there are the most drugs.
>
> Treatment to keep the leukemia cells away will last 3 years. You'll miss at least a month of school, the time needed to get the disease in control. The main problem right now is infection. If you stay free of infection you will be out of the hospital in about 5 days, if an infection occurs, you'll be hospitalized for at least 2 weeks. (pp. 1115-1116)

Allowing children to ask questions after such an explanation and making time to talk even when they have no questions creates the setting of mutual trust so necessary for growth during the final period of life.

Death as Loss

Death is above all else loss. The young child (aged 3 to 5) usually has experienced only temporary loss, as when a parent leaves for a short time. These children do not understand permanent loss but they know the discomfort of being without their caretakers. Bowlby's work (45) suggests that since preschool grieving and adult grieving are very similar in their intensity, the longing and mourning that are intrinsic to the grief process may be largely instinctive rather than cognitive. Spitz (46) described a syndrome that he called "hospitalism," in which the young child from infancy through preschool reacts to separation from his mother first with anger, then with a kind of quiet, resigned despair. Some of the children actually refused nutrition, turned their faces to the wall, and died. This was not learned behavior. Rather it was a natural response on the part of the child who had suffered an overwhelming loss.

Dying children suffer not only from physical separation from their home and parents but also from pain and loss of function as the disease progresses. Older children (6 years and beyond) begin to have the cognitive capacity to grieve over the loss of the future. They can understand that their tomorrows are numbered. It is difficult for the child as well as the adult to make sense of such an intrinsically unfair situation. However, many children have a need to discuss these feelings. If, when they first mention them, they are met with embarrassment, disapproval, or emotional outburst, the children learn that this is not a safe area for discussion. They must deny those feelings in themselves and retreat into the loneliness of their own loss without the support of those they love. Preparatory grief is real and it can become debilitating. Many health workers today agree that the final cruelty added to the already unbelievably cruel dying situation is to encourage these children to pretend they are *not* suffering the greatest loss of all. In dying the child loses everything: possessions, friends, parents, personality, and self. It is right to grieve then, if he or she realizes even a bit of this loss. Health workers can facilitate the grieving process not by silence but by being available to listen, empathize, and support the child in attempting to cope with the illness.

The Bereaved Child

Just as dying children profit from being able to communicate their feelings of grief, loss, anger, and bewilderment, so children who have lost a loved one profit from communication. The death of a parent can be particularly tragic for a child (47). Mingled with all the other negative emotions is a feeling of betrayal. It is almost as though the young child feels that if the parent had loved him or her enough, the parent would not have left. Bereavement is accompanied by physical symptoms including feelings of panic, insomnia, lack of appetite, nightmares, and others. Unresolved grief, especially in children, can lead to ongoing somatic illness as well as deep psychological problems. In one study (48) 41 percent of the population of 3216 depressed adult patients had lost a parent through death before age 15. In a later study (49) 27 percent of patients in a highly depressed group reported the loss of a parent before the age of 16 as compared with 12 percent of adults in a nondepressed group. Furthermore, an appreciably larger number of patients in the highly depressed group lost a parent before the age of 4. It appears that the loss of a parent is a traumatic psychological event for a child and that the earlier that loss occurs, the more potentially devastating the effect can be.

Parness (50), in working with preschool children who have sustained the loss of a parent or sibling, points out that "very young children have resiliency and fortitude in the face of some of the painful and unpredictable experiences life has to offer" (p. 7). However, she goes on to say that death and loss must be worked through with children. She points out that teachers and mental health workers can encourage healthy coping in children by beginning work with the assumption of loss as a universal human emotion. The adult must also be willing to share feelings of grief honestly and in a positive way that communicates faith in the children's "resources, resiliency, and power over their future lives—in spite of the unexpected" (50, p. 7).

Parental Anticipatory Mourning

The final type of grief to be considered in this chapter is parental anticipatory mourning. Futterman and Hoffman (51) defined it as "a set of processes that are directly related to the awareness of the impending loss, to its emotional impact and to the adaptive mechanisms whereby emotional attachment to the dying child is relinquished over time" (p. 130). It involves the following steps:

1. *Acknowledgment:* growing awareness of the approach of

the inevitable moment of death accompanied by alternating feelings of hope and despair.

2. *Grieving:* the emotional reaction to loss that starts off as an intense undifferentiated response but gradually mellows in quality and the intensity becomes subdued.

3. *Reconciliation:* one step advanced from mere acceptance, it involves attempting to find meaning for the child's life and death and moving beyond that to a stage where the parents can be grateful for their blessings.

4. *Detachment:* this is the process whereby the parents gradually withdraw their emotional investment from the child.

    One parent has described a very rapid detachment reaction in the following way: "As soon as the doctor told me that B. had neuroblastoma (a fatal form of the infantile cancer) I looked at him in the bed and felt like he was already dead. Later on, hope revived for a while with a change in medication, but as the disease progressed, I protected myself from too much feeling by viewing him as already lost to us" (38).

    This process, so necessary to the mental health of the parents, sometimes can result in the tragic condition referred to as the "living dead" (52). If parents complete the detachment process too soon or if the child has an unexpected late remission, the family may have completed the detachment process and the child may find himself dying alone or receiving an unwelcome greeting from a family that has already resolved his death.

5. The final stage in anticipatory grieving is called *memorialization*. It involves idealizing the child and results in the parents' developing a mental image of the child which will live beyond his death.

Professionals and the Family
of the Dying Child

Professionals working with parents of terminally ill children can do little to lessen the sorrow that is the dominant emotion from the time the diagnosis is made until the child dies. They can, however, help the parents to anticipate and deal effectively with accompanying emotions such as anger, guilt, and anxiety.

Powerful feelings of anger often threaten to overcome parents of fatally ill children. The obvious unfairness of the situation coupled with their impotence to do anything to change it leads to feelings of frustration that can be destructive. The important question for helping professionals must be: How can the parents be helped to express their anger in positive ways? Sometimes, especially in cases of genetically transmitted diseases, one parent will turn his or her anger on the other one, thus adding to the stress of the situation (53). Other family members, including siblings and grandparents, may also have to bear the brunt of displaced parental anger. Other common recipients of anger include God, the doctors, nurses, and other caretakers, and even inanimate objects such as the hospital bed and machines used in treating the child. If parents turn their explosive anger inward, it can result in depression, suicidal urges, and even psychotic breakdown.

Parents need to be helped to find appropriate channels for venting anger. Such channels might include ongoing group or individual therapy, joining an organization to raise funds for medical research, forming parent support groups, and physical activities to discharge tension.

The second major emotion that parents should be helped to anticipate is guilt. Since the child's birth the parents' role has been that of protection and nurturance. When parents are not able to protect their child from a fatal disease, they may feel irrational guilt. In addition, if the parent-child relationship has been strained, the parents may feel guilt for the negative feelings they have had toward the child. As the illness proceeds, guilt may be compounded as the parents experience recurring wishes for the child to die. Guilt is also exacerbated as the parents become aware of hidden feelings of relief that it is not they who have the fatal illness. Folk tales and scattered heroic stories tell of parents who willingly give their lives for their children. However, it is the exceptional person who would willingly choose to exchange places with one who is suffering through a lingering death, even if that person is one's own child. Guilt can be tolerated better if the parent can be encouraged to express these feelings openly. The helping professional can then accept the parents' feelings of guilt and join them in attempting to understand those feelings as natural parts of most intimate relationships.

Commonly, parents of fatally ill children experience a third emotion, anxiety, which arises from at least five sources (53):

1. *Lack of mastery of the protective parental role,* resulting in the need to reorganize self-concept, self-esteem, and feelings of potency. Any major threat to the stable self-concept arouses anxiety.

2. *Inability to cope with the situation effectively,* resulting in feelings of an imminent breakdown. Whenever environmental stress threatens to overwhelm a person, the major emotion is that of anxiety. It is hard to envision a situation more stressful than having to watch your child suffer and die.

3. *Feelings of isolation and loneliness* caused by the parents' new identity as the parent of a doomed child. Parents have said that after finding out the diagnosis they did not want to see friends who had healthy children. They experienced feelings of resentment that the world continued to go on as though nothing had happened while their whole world was collapsing. In short, they felt that theirs was a unique position in the world, which no one else could understand; they were alone.

4. *Separation anxiety* as the parents anticipated the child's

death and its psychological cost. Parents have reported feelings of loss so keen that it felt as though they had lost a limb or some other part of themselves.

5. *Death anxiety* as the realization of their own inevitable death hits home more acutely than ever before because of identification with the child.

Anxiety is best counteracted by action, and much of a parent's anxiety can be constructively channeled into caring for the dying child (54). However, parents need to know that sleeping and eating disturbances often accompany anxiety and that anxiety, like anger, can be displaced, resulting in irrational fears concerning their own health or the health of their other children.

Siblings and the Dying Child

Siblings of a dying child also suffer, often in lonely confusion, as they watch their brother or sister die and their parents grieve. Often parents react to grieving children in an overprotective and secretive manner. Green and Solnit (55) have coined the term "vulnerable child" syndrome to refer to such children. Studies done with adults who lost a sibling in childhood have indicated some support for this syndrome. As early as 1943, Rosenweig and Bray (56) found that patients suffering from schizophrenia had a higher than expected number of siblings who died in childhood. Perhaps the one axiom that will promote the best adjustment in the brothers and sisters of the dying child is quite simply, include them. They need to know some details about the illness if they are old enough; they need to visit the sibling in the hospital and be encouraged to express their thoughts, fears, and guilt feelings just as the parents are. Young children especially need to be reassured that no hostile thought of theirs is responsible for their brother or sister's illness, as magical thinking is still very much a part of their cognitive method of operation.

Summary

Death is a natural event and it is normal for children to want to know about and understand it. Many parents have a need to protect their children from the harsh realities of life, but by doing so they contribute to misconceptions and increased anxieties.

The understanding of what death and dying means develops as the child grows older. The preschool child is believed to understand death as a temporary stage, a long sleep or departure. During the early school years, the child comes to recognize that death is final, but at the same time it is also personified, seen perhaps as a skeleton or a powerful monster who capriciously snatches people and kills them. Usually by the age of 9 the child understands that death is final but also natural and universal. A number of studies have shown that there is extreme variability with respect to the age at which a child reaches a mature understanding of death. These variations are due to cultural and subcultural factors, family background, personal encounters, and very likely a number of other as yet unidentified factors.

Children experience loss at a young age. Loss produces anxiety. As children become more aware of the reality of death, it is reasonable to assume that they become more anxious. Caring and patient adults can help alleviate a good deal of a child's death anxiety.

The terminally ill child usually becomes aware of his or her dying and experiences fears, but researchers find that these fears are often unspoken or couched in symbolic language. In the very young terminal child the fear of separation from parents is the predominant fear. Older children fear mutilation of their bodies.

Caring for the dying child is the most difficult task. The death of a child evokes depths of anger, guilt, frustration, and helplessness that are difficult to cope with. An important aspect of care of the terminal child is for physicians or other care givers to work with parents to help them cope with this impending loss and the feelings these bring about. When parents are an integral part of the total treatment of the dying child, it is found that parents are able to work off some of their own anxiety, guilt, and grief, while at the same time filling a need for closeness on the part of the dying child as well as assisting the staff.

There are at least three different identifiable types of grieving. First, preparatory grief or the emotional reaction of children who become aware of their own dying. Second is bereavement, as a child faces the loss of a loved one, and third is anticipatory grief, or the feeling that parents of the terminally ill child experience as they attempt to cope with the fact of their child's impending death.

References

1. Crase, D. R., & Crase, D. Helping children understand death. *Young Children*, 1976 (November), 21-25.
2. Kastenbaum, R. J. *Death, society and human experience*. St. Louis: Mosby, 1977.
3. Maurer, A. Maturation of concepts of death. *British Journal of Medicine and Psychology*, 1966, *39*, 35-41.
4. Lerner, M. When, why, and where people die. In E. S. Shneidman (Ed.), *Death: Current prospectives*. Palo Alto: Mayfield Publishing, 1976, 138-162.
5. Sharapan, H. Mister Rogers' neighborhood: Dealing with death on a children's television series. *Death education: 1*, 1977, 131-136.
6. Piaget, J. *The origins of intelligence in children*. New York: Harcourt, Brace and World, 1932.
7. Nagy, M. The child's theories concerning death. *The Journal of Genetic Psychology*, 1948, *73*, 3-27.
8. Koocher, G. P. Talking with children about death. *American Journal of Orthopsychiatry*, 1974, *44*, 404-411.
9. Wilcox, S. G., & Sutton, M. *Understanding death and dying: An interdisciplinary approach*. Port Washington, NY: Alfred Publishing, 1977.
10. Wass, H. How children understand death. *Thanatos*, 1976, *1*, 4, 18-22.
11. Arnstein, F. I met death one clumsy day. *English Journal*, 1972, *61*, 6, 853-858.
12. Childers, P., & Wimmer, M. The concept of death in early childhood. *Child Development*, 1971, *42*, (4), 1299-1301.

13. Kastenbaum, R. Childhood: The kingdom where creatures die. *Journal of Clinical Child Psychology*, 1974, *3*, (2), 11-14.

14. Melear, J. D. Children's conceptions of death. *Journal of Genetic Psychology*, 1973, *123*, (2), 359-360.

15. Gartley, W., & Bernasconi, M. The concept of death in children. *The Journal of Genetic Psychology*, 1967, *110*, 71-85.

16. Hansen, Y. Development of the concept of death: Cognitive aspects. *Dissertation Abstracts International*, 1973, *34*, (2-3), 853.

17. Wass, H., & Scott, M. Middle school students' death concepts and concerns. *Middle School Journal*, 1978, *9*, (1), 10-12.

18. Tallmer, M., Formaneck, R., & Tallmer, J. Factors influencing children's concepts of death. *Journal of Clinical Child Psychology*, 1974, *3*, (2), 17-19.

19. Wahl, C. W. The fear of death. In H. Feifel (Ed.), *The meaning of death*. New York: McGraw-Hill, 1959.

20. Von Hug, H. H. The child's concept of death. *Psychoanalytic Quarterly*, 1965, *34*, 499-516.

21. Bluebond-Langner, M. Meanings of death to children. In H. Feifel (Ed.), *New meanings of death*. New York: McGraw-Hill, 1977.

22. Wass, H., & Shaak, J. Helping children understand death through literature. *Childhood Education*, 1976, (November-December), 80-85.

23. Grollman, E. A. (Ed.) *Explaining death to children*. Boston: Beacon Press, 1967.

24. Elkind, D. Egocentrism in adolescence, *Child Development*, 1967, *38*, (4), 1025-1034.

25. Kastenbaum, R. Time and death in adolescence. In H. Feifel (Ed.), *The meaning of death*. New York: McGraw-Hill, 1959.

26. Waechter, E. H. Children's awareness of fatal illness. *American Journal of Nursing*, 1971, *71*, 1168-1172.

27. Spinetta, J. J., & Maloney, L. J. Death anxiety in the outpatient leukemic child. *Pediatrics*, 1975, *56*, (6), 1034-1037.

28. Vernick, J., & Karon, M. Who's afraid of death and leukemia ward? *American Journal of Diseases of Children*, 1965, *109*, 393-397.

29. Yudkin, S. Children and death. *The Lancet*, 1967, 37-41.

30. Natterson, J. M., & Knudson, A. G. Observations concerning fear of death in fatally ill children and their mothers. *Psychosomatic Medicine*, 1960, *23*, (6), 456-465.

31. Spinetta, J. J., Rigler, D., & Karon, M. Personal space as a measure of a dying child's sense of isolation. *Journal of Consulting and Clinical Psychology*, 1974, *42*, (6), 751-756.

32. Singher, L. J. The slowly dying child. *Clinical Pediatrics*, 1974, *13*, (19), 861-867.

33. Karon, M., & Vernick, J. An approach to the emotional support of fatally ill children. *Clinical Pediatrics*, 1968, 7, (5), 274-280.

34. Evans, A. E., & Edin, S. If a child must die. . . . *The New England Journal of Medicine*, 1968, *278*, (3), 138-142.

35. Foley, G. V., & McCarthy, A. M. The child with leukemia in a special hematology clinic. *American Journal of Nursing*, 1976, 76, (7), 1115-1119.

36. Green, M. Care of the dying child. In *Care of the child with cancer*. Proceedings of a conference conducted by the Association for Ambulatory Pediatric Services in

conjunction with the Children's Cancer Study Group A on November 17, 1966. Edited by A. B. Bergman, & C. J. A. Schultle, 1966, 492-497.

37. Rothenburg, M. B. Reactions of those who treat children with cancer. In Cancer. Proceedings of a conference conducted by the Association for Ambulatory Pediatric Services in conjunction with the Children's Cancer Study Group A on November 17, 1966. Edited by A. B. Bergman, & C. J. A. Schultle, 1966.

38. Dorsel, T. Personal communication, 1976.

39. Friedman, S. B. Care of the family of the child with leukemia. Proceedings of a conference conducted by the Association for Ambulatory Pediatric Services in conjunction with the Children's Cancer Study Group A on November 17, 1966. Edited by A. B. Bergman, & C. J. A. Schultle, 1966.

40. Ablin, A. R., Binger, C. M., Stein, R. C., Kushner, J., Zoger, S., & Mikkelson, C. A conference with the family of a leukemic child. *American Journal of Disabled Child*, 1971, *122*, 362-364.

41. Friedman, S. B., Chodoff, P., Mason, J. W., & Hamburg, D. A. Behavioral observations on the parents anticipating the death of a child. *Pediatrics*, 1963, *33*, 610-625.

42. Lascari, A. D., & Stephbens, J. A. The reactions of families to childhood leukemia: An evaluation of a program of emotional management. *Clinical Pediatrics*, 1973, *12*, (4), 210-214.

43. Morrissey, J. R. Children's adaptation to fatal illness. *Social Work*, 1963, *8*, 81-88.

44. Hailey, A. *Airport.* New York: Doubleday, 1968.

45. Bowlby, J. *Attachment and loss. Vol. II: Separation anxiety and anger.* New York: Basic Books, 1960.

46. Spitz, R. A. Hospitalism: An inquiry into the genesis of psychiatric conditions in early childhood. In *The Psychoanalytic Study of the Child, Volume I.* New York: International University Press, 1945.

47. LeShan, E. *Learning to say goodbye: When a parent dies.* New York: Macmillan, 1976.

48. Brown, F. Depression and childhood bereavement. *Journal of Mental Science,* 1961, *107*, 754-777.

49. Beck, A. T., Sethi, B. B., & Tuthill, R. Childhood bereavement and adult depression. *Archives of General Psychiatry*, 1963, *9*, 129-136.

50. Parness, E. Effects of experiences with loss and death among pre-school children. *Children Today*, 1975, *4*, 2-7.

51. Futterman, E. H., & Hoffman, I. Transient school phobia in a leukemic child. *Journal of the American Academy of Child Psychiatry*, 1970, *9*, (3), 477-494.

52. Easson, W. M. *The dying child.* Springfield, Ill.: Thomas, 1970.

53. McCollum, A. T., & Schwartz, H. A. Social work and the mourning parent. *Social Work*, 1972, *17*, (1), 25-36.

54. Martinson, I. M. *Home care for the dying child: Professional and family perspectives.* New York: Appleton-Century-Crofts, 1976.

55. Green, M., & Solnit, A. J. Reactions to the threatened loss of a child. A vulnerable child syndrome. Paediatric management of the dying child. *Paediatrics*, 1964, *37*, 53-66.

56. Rosenweig, S., & Bray, D. Sibling death in anamnesis schizophrenic patients. *Archives of Neurology and Psychiatry*, 1943, *49*, (1), 71-92.

Annotated Bibliography

We must all face death, our own or that of a loved one or both. Preparation for facing death is not only possible but appears to be necessary in light of physical and emotional hazards that can arise from ineffectual handling of death and grief. Since children are aware of death from an early age, parents and helping professionals need only create a climate of tolerance toward the subject and direct children's natural curiosity. In addition, parents' and teachers' books can be excellent sources of information and comfort. The topic of death has concerned humankind from time immemorial, and for this reason death has been written about not only in the context of various theologies, philosophies, and recently the sciences, but also in the general literature, including children's books. There are, of course, the all-time favorites in which the subject of death is imbedded in the main theme but not specifically concentrated upon, such as the following books:

Armstrong, W. *Sounder*. New York: Harper & Row, 1969.
Buck, P. *The big wave*. New York: John Day, 1948.
Cleaver, V. *Where the lilies bloom*. Philadelphia: Lippincott, 1969.
Gipson, F. *Old yeller*. New York: Harper & Row, 1956.
Hunt, I. *Up a road slowly*. Chicago: Follett, 1966.
Lawson, R. *Rabbit hill*. New York: Viking Press, 1944.
O'Dell, S. *Island of the blue dolphins*. Cambridge: Riverside, 1960.
Rawlings, M. *The yearling*. New York: Scribners, 1939.
Salten, F. *Bambi*. New York: Grosset & Dunlap, 1929.
Speare, E. *The bronze bow*. New York: Houghton Mifflin, 1961.
Sperry, A. *Call it courage*. New York: Macmillan, 1940.
White, E. B. *Charlotte's web*. New York: Harper & Row, 1952.

Also, in recent years in particular, a number of gifted authors have chosen death as the main theme of their stories. These books can be informative as well as therapeutic not only for children but for adults as well. Wass and Shaak (22) have compiled a brief selected annotated bibliography of such books by age groups. That bibliography is reproduced below.

Preschool through Age 7

Brown, M. W. *The dead bird.* Glenview, Ill.: Scott, 1965. A group of children find a bird and feel its heart not beating. They have a funeral for it before returning to their play. Life continues.

Buck, P. *The beech tree.* New York: John Day, 1958. The metaphor of a beech tree is used by an elderly man to help explain his impending death.

De Paola, T. *Nana upstairs and nana downstairs.* New York: Putnam's, 1973. Tommy is heartbroken when his bedridden great-grandmother, with whom he has spent many happy hours, dies. He comes to realize that both the Nana that lived upstairs and the Nana that lived downstairs are "upstairs" in Heaven. The hope of life after death brings satisfaction.

Fassler, J. *My grandpa died today.* New York: Behavioral Publications, 1971. A description of Grandpa sleeping away to a peaceful death in his rocking chair is presented. Knowing his Grandpa was not afraid to die, David is able to continue "running and laughing and growing up with only fond memories of Grandpa." Written in simple story-line but with such factual detail that it could be classed as a nonfiction book.

Grollman, E. *Talking about death.* Boston: Beacon, 1970. The finality of death is presented uncompromisingly in simple direct language without softening the blow. Grollman's intent is to protect the child from destructive fantasy and a distorted view of death as well as guilt that often arises when a child is denied information.

Harris, A. *Why did he die?* Minneapolis: Lerner, 1965. A mother's heartfelt effort to speak to her child about death is portrayed. Death is likened to the leaves falling in autumn with new leaves to come in the spring, and to a worn-out motor. Emphasis is on the fact that, no matter what happens, memories of the deceased will never die.

Kantrowitz, M. *When Violet died.* New York: Parents', 1973. A story of the funeral preparations and ceremony for a dead bird, emphasizing the children's reactions, fascination and fun children get out of ceremonies, even funerals. The children are consoled in the continuity of life as shown through their pregnant cat. Life goes on!

Kuskin, K. *The bear who saw the spring.* New York: Harper & Row, 1961. A story of changing seasons and the changes living things go through as they are born, live, and die.

Miles, M. *Annie and the old one.* Boston: Little, Brown, 1971. Annie's Navajo grandmother says she will be ready to die after the new rug is woven. Annie tries to keep the rug from being finished, but her wise grandmother tells her that is wrong, that the "earth from which good things come is where all creatures finally go." Death is a part of life.

Stein, S. B. *About dying.* New York: Walker, 1974. A "shared" and open story about everyday dying, the kind every child meets early in his own life—the death of a pet and a grandparent. Actual photographs accompany the text of death, funeral, and mourning of Snow, a pet bird, and the Grandpa who had given him to the children. The accompanying adult text serves as a resource for handling the questions and discussion arising from the child's natural curiosity. The book explains reality, guiding a child toward the truth even if it is painful, and gives the children the inner strength to deal with things as they are. Preventive mental health!

Tresselt, A. *The dead tree.* New York: Parents', 1972. The life cycle of a tall oak tree is poetically described, showing that in nature nothing is ever wasted or completely dies.

Viorst, J. *The tenth good thing about Barney.* New York: Atheneum, 1971. The rituals of burial and mourning are observed for Barney, a pet cat. The child is led to understand that dying is as usual as living. Death is a part of life. Some readers may question whether young children will be able to comprehend the abstract idea of Barney's future role as fertilizer.

Warburg, S. S. *Growing time.* Boston: Houghton Mifflin, 1969. Jamie learns to accept the reality and meaning of the death of his dog with the help of his sympathetic and understanding family. He finds out that "death is not easy to bear." Something you love never dies; it lives in your heart.

Zolotow, C. *My grandson Lew.* New York: Harper & Row, 1974. The shared remembrances between a mother and a small child of a sadly missed grandfather keep both mother and son from being lonely. Memories keep the deceased alive in your mind.

Ages 8 through 11

Cleaver, V. *Grover.* Philadelphia: Lippincott, 1970. Ten-year-old Grover is forced to handle the changes that the suicide of his ailing mother brought about in his own groping ways, as his father is too grief-stricken to help. He finds out that there is no formula for overcoming grief other than time, friends, and maturity.

Cohen, B. *Thank you, Jackie Robinson.* New York: Lothrop, 1974. The story of the slowly deepening friendship between 12-year-old Sam Greene and the elderly black cook in Mrs. Greene's restaurant. After following their "main man"— Jackie Robinson—Sam is bereft when Davy suffers a fatal heart attack. Because their relationship seems solid, readers too will mourn Davy's death and sympathize with an honestly grieving Sam.

Lee, V. *The magic moth.* New York: Seabury, 1972. A very supportive family bravely copes with 10-year-old Maryanne's illness and death from a heart defect. A moth bursting from its cocoon as Maryanne dies and seed sprouting just after her funeral symbolize that "life never ends—it just changes."

Orgel, D. *Mulberry music.* New York: Harper & Row, 1971. The efforts of a young girl's parents to protect her from the knowledge of her adored grandmother's impending death result in turmoil, both within the girl and around her, when in her rash and rebellious actions the girl searches for her beloved grandmother. Keeping the truth of an impending death from a child can cause misunderstanding and fear.

Smith, D. B. *A taste of blackberries.* New York: Crowell, 1973. Jamie dies of a bee sting.

His best friend is confronted with grief at the loss and comes to terms with a guilty feeling that somehow he might have saved Jamie. After a period of grief, life goes on.

Zim, H., & Bleeker, S. *Life and death.* New York: Morrow, 1970. This is an answer book for questions young people have about death. The physical facts, customs, and attitudes surrounding life and death are discussed. Death is described as a part of living.

Age 12 and Over

Corburn, J. *Anne and the sand dobbies.* New York: Seabury, 1967. Danny's father tries to answer questions about the death of Danny's sister.

Gunther, J. *Death be not proud.* New York: Harper & Row, 1949. The author writes of the courage of his 17-year-old son while facing death. The book is a celebration of life. It is more difficult for his parents than for Johnnie to accept his death.

Hunter, M. *A sound of chariots.* New York: Harper & Row, 1972. Bridie McShane's happy early childhood during World War I in Scotland is interrupted by the death of her beloved father whose favorite child she was. As she matures, her life is marred by her sorrow, leading her to morbid reflections on time and death, which she finally learns to deal with through her desire to write poetry.

Klein, S. *The final mystery.* New York: Doubleday, 1974. The meaning of death is explored and how people of different religions have coped with it. The on-going war against death is discussed.

Rhodin, E. *The good greenwood.* Philadelphia: Westminister, 1971. A tense and moving story of Mike who lost his good friend, Louie. After time and grief pass, Mike came to realize that Louie was really dead and was not going to reappear around the next corner. He came to remember Louie for the clown and dreamer that he was and for the good times they had together. He was not building another Louie as the grownups were, one that was almost perfect.

5
The Impact of Parental Death on Middle-Aged Children

Miriam S. Moss and Sidney Z. Moss

Separations and losses are crucial events over the life cycle and are the focus of much psychosocial literature on individuals and families. One loss that many persons in their mid-years experience is the death of a parent. This paper explores the impact of that loss on adult children in their thirties and forties. It suggests a number of generic themes that may occur.

A search of the literature examining the impact of the loss of a parent reveals that with rare exceptions the focus is on parental loss by the young child, either as initially experienced [1, 2] or as a root of adult psychopathology or suicide [3, 4]. Only a handful of authors have explored the nonpathological impact of parental death in mid-life [5-8]. Why have we failed to examine the one type of death that outnumbers them all: the death of an older person and its impact on the surviving child? What is it about this modal type of death that appears to be so anathema?

Perhaps some of the explanation for ignoring the impact of the loss of a parent comes in our relative disregard of life tasks specific to middle age—a time when a large number of parental deaths occur. Parental loss may seem to pale in importance against the need to work out marital relationships, career goals, parent-adolescent conflicts and reassessment of the self. Further, traditional formulations in psychology have emphasized the individual at the expense of relationships. Only relatively recently—particularly with the increased emphasis

89

on object relations and family therapy—has the meaning of relationships begun to be a primary focus in psychology.

In our culture parental death for an adult child is seen as relatively unimportant in comparison with death of younger persons [9]. Even cross cultural studies of death and dying pay scant attention to the adult child's loss of parent. Findings suggest that an adult losing a parent does not exhibit intense grief and aggression, and rarely necessitates the formal treatment which is normally given to persons in deep mourning [10]. On the other hand, the loss of parents may be so painful that we as researchers and clinicians flee from it to protect ourselves, to escape facing our unresolved guilts and frustrations. The child in each of us may feel abandoned in losing a parent, and we shy away from the topic.

From another perspective, the loss of a parent is quite positive: a relief from the real or potential burdens of caretaking, a welcome severing of destructive family ties, an opportunity to grow unhampered by parental expectations, and a realization of the all too small reward of an inheritance. Yet our cultural proscriptions inhibit open expression of these feelings. Finally, it may be that a personal response to the death of a parent follows no general patterns and is totally idiosyncratic and reflective of the unique relationship of the child and parent over the previous decades, combined with the current life situation of the child, and a wide range of special characteristics which defy generalization.

The older person is sometimes viewed as having outlived the parental role, as being in a "post parental" stage [11, 12]. Concurrently, the middle-aged adult may no longer be seen to need a parent. Does this suggest that the role relationship is severed? While we know something about frequency of interaction and extent of mutual assistance [13], few have examined the *quality* of the relationship between adult children and their parents [14, 15]. If parenting primarily connotes basic nurturance and meeting daily survival needs, then most middle aged persons neither need nor want parenting;

however, if parenting is conceptualized differently as suggested above, there persists a viable and significant bond between adult children and their parents.

The "Adult Child"

The concept of the "adult child" is enigmatic. What does it mean to be a child and an adult simultaneously? Child brings to mind dependency, immaturity, and youth; adult connotes independence, maturity, and age. The dialectic of the adult child concept is appealing. The man or woman who has achieved mastery over life's tasks does not slough off the tie with a parent. The child in each of us persists throughout the years in which we have a parent (and some would suggest beyond). It is generally not a crippling link to the past, but a part of the human condition in which the past and present are melded. None of us is pure child or pure adult. A dialectic of contradictions allows for the interplay of the past and the present, the attachments and separations, the child and the adult [16]. This theme of a dialectic will recur throughout our discussion.

The next section of this paper examines the child-parent relationship, primarily from the vantage point of the adult child. Factors that tend to weaken and to maintain the tie are examined. The assumption is that the bond is a dynamic bio-social one which persists throughout life.

Quality of the Adult Child-Parent Relationship

This paper focuses on normal, middle-aged children, generally married with children of their own. Their parents are generally in the "young old" category, live active independent lives, and are not subject to major impairments or incapacity. Thus, this section deals with the quality of relationship between basically independent adults and children, not with issues of long term primary care of the impaired elderly. For these adult children, their parent tie is the longest of life's relationships—the prototype of attachment.

For three or four decades the image of the parent has been internalized. The infinite number of transactions throughout life—from infancy on—indelibly imprint the images of each on the other. Shared memories, rituals, and the emotional life in the family weave the past into the present. Unfortunately, there is little research that focuses on this area, and the ideas presented here are exploratory. First we examine factors that strengthen the tie.

The genetic tie underlies the parent-child bond. The link of flesh and blood is underscored in middle age when a look in the mirror most easily brings to mind a resemblance to the parent. A core of bio-socially based care eliciting behavior [17] is a vital aspect of the parent-child attachment. Each finds a need for and is satisfied in the bond. Each identifies with a pervasive sense of family that further cements the parent-child tie. A sense of family solidarity strengthens the bond. Values and beliefs are quite often congruent between generations [18], and this tends to provide continuity. Who else in the lives of adult children has offered the possibility of unconditional love? The marital bond, though more intense for most adults, has proved in recent decades to be quite fragile. It is not unusual for recently divorced persons to exhibit strong ties with their parents and to seek and receive considerable parental support—emotional, instrumental, and financial. Few would suggest that the severance of parental bonds has or will approach the soaring divorce rate.

We know little of the qualitative aspects of the tie, yet they play a crucial role in maintaining the relationship. Affection, caring and warm companionship persist in some situations. Yet, we do not know how pervasive these feelings are. The parent continues to be a model for the child and a parent's coping with transitions (child leaving home, retirement, diminished physical strength) provides continuing anticipatory socialization. More thought should be given to the dynamics of reciprocal socialization where each provides a model and a source of influence for the other [18].

The expectations of the partners in the relationship are significant to the bond—each trying to do the right thing for each other. Repeatedly we hear of older parents seeking to maintain independence from their children, with the pervasive fear of being a burden. On the other hand, the adult children, responding to internal as well as social pressures, seek to fulfill filial obligations in spite of conflicting responsibilities. Ideally this allows for progression toward filial maturity [19] when the child can be dependable in assuming some responsibilities for the parent, and the parent has the capacity to be appropriately dependent [20].

Central to the parent-child bond is trustworthiness built out of parental accountability and filial loyalty [21]. There is a deep sense of mutual committment and responsibility. Most adult children keep in touch with their parents, many live nearby and maintain persistent threads of mutual assistance. The way in which the bonds of duty are meshed with genuine caring in the relationship is yet to be ascertained. No matter how dependent the parent becomes on the child, however, there is no role reversal. In only the most superficial way can one equate an older person's inability to take care of some routine task (previously handled unassisted and with little thought) with the incapacity of a young child. Whereas the child is learning to become independent, the older person is losing some autonomy and dreads the inability to regain it.

In spite of the persistence of the bond with the parents, there is a range of factors that tend to weaken the attachment. The parent-child tie is permeated with conflicting elements and the overall quality is a synthesis of contradictions. The separation and individuation process of a child is a recurrent theme intensified in adolescence. There is a stigma for a young adult who is "too" tied to the parent and living at home. Thus by middle age, normal developmental processes have tended to weaken the bond. Old conflicts indigenous to the relationship may persist with issues of control and blaming often recurring. New conflicts are then superimposed upon the old, where the adult child must balance personal needs and those of the family of procreation as well as the responsibilities to another set of parents—the in-laws.

There is some indication that the parents view their adult children as more important in their lives than the children see them [22]. Each may be involved with the other, but most do not live in the same household, and although "intimacy at a distance" may well occur, the fact that the adult child lives with and responds to demands of a spouse and children may place the older parent on the periphery of the demands of everyday living.

There are real pulls that tend to separate parents from children. Parents have lives and interests of their own—they have friends and pleasures that are largely independent of their adult children. They may often be quite pleased that they can assume some distance from the middle-aged generation—struggling as it does to keep marriages together, to meet spiraling costs for expanding needs, to respond to women's issues and adolescent rebellion as well as strong themes of self-fulfillment. One of the major factors that serves to create stress in the adult child-parent relationship is the lack of clarity in the role expectations of each *vis a vis* the other. This is an anomic situation with guidelines generally missing to prescribe and proscribe patterns of interaction. Though the basic tie persists, the details of how it is to be acted out are vague, and each family may feel it must forge its own pattern.

Since the state now provides some basic care (e.g., social security and medicare) the child is released from some responsibility. Hess and Waring [14] suggest that the parental bond may be seen as primarily a voluntary one and that the model which most closely approximates it is that of friendship and homophily, stressing mutuality of respect, interests, and affect. Does this adequately explain findings that most of the care for older people is supplied by the family, not the formal service delivery network or friends [23]? We suggest crucial elements such as biosocial family underpinnings, life long patterns of interaction, and deep family loyalties should not be relegated to secondary status. Further, it is not clear whether increasing responsibility taken by the public sector tends to weaken the family tie (diluting the child's responsibility) or strengthen it (by reducing the fear of economic burden and supporting an affective base of the relationship) [13]. As the parent ages, the child is increasingly aware of small, often incremental deficits in the ability of the parent to equal or exceed past performance. These signs of decline are painful to the child who may wish to forestall the aging of parents in order to hold on to his or her own youth.

Another major factor in weakening the bond is anticipatory orphanhood, which flows throughout the child's life. From earliest childhood, there is the fear that the loved parent will leave or die. Weisman suggests that anticipatory grief begins as soon "as love is implanted." [24, p. 15] Thus, living and loss are intimately intertwined. When a child becomes aware of death of others there is a natural tendency to imagine the death of a parent. How often does a young child say, "Mommy, when you die" or "Daddy, if you die." The fear of orphanhood comes early. Parents live now, but parents will die. Each of us comes to anticipate the death of parents, yet this death has a place in "some legendary time." [25]

As children become middle-aged, they experience the death of parents of their peers. Each such loss has an impact and is a socialization to the death of their own parent. They learn that parents do not have to be very old or to be sick for a long period of time to die. They are braced for death if it should occur. The adult child recurrently considers and rehearses the potential death of a parent. There is less taboo in anticipating one's parent's death than the death of a spouse or a child. The cognitive and affective process of anticipatory orphanhood may occur over decades, thus preparing the adult child for the fact of parental death.

There is an interplay between the factors that serve to

strengthen the child-parent bond and those that tend to loosen it. The elasticity of the bond enables it to transcend a life time. Troll says of child-parent relationships: "They seem to override geographic and socioeconomic mobility as well as developmental changes in a way no other relationships seem to do." [26, p. 84]

Limitations of this Discussion

Before discussing some generic aspects of the impact of the death of a parent on an adult child, we must stress that there are a number of factors in the situation that this paper does not consider, and each may be very important. These include the following:

- whether the death is of the first parent or the second parent;
- the quality and circumstances of the relationship over the life cycle;
- the degree, intensity and quality of the interaction between parent and child toward the end of the parent's life;
- the circumstancees and timing of the last illness and death of the parent;
- social supports and the life situation of the surviving child;
- objective factors such as the gender of the parent and of the child, whether or not they lived in the same household, and the financial resources of each;
- the cultural, ethnic and religious characteristics of the family;
- the broader family and intergenerational implications of the loss; and finally
- the personality of the parent and the child.

Impact of the Loss:
Severing and Maintaining the Bond

The last formal task of an adult child toward his or her parents is to cope with the death of the parent. The shock at the death generally initiates a brief period of numbing and denial, often followed by some degree of protest. Few young-old parents are seen by their children as having lived long enough; even fewer are felt to die in the right way and at the right time. Yet, the loss is no surprise. The years of anticipatory orphanhood and anticipatory grief have laid a foundation for acceptance. This may decrease the ambiguity of what death means and increase the resources available to the child in coping with the loss. Yet even a profound sense of preparedness may not be equal to the reality of death.

Though the loss may be deeply felt by the child, society does not accept or support profound or extended mourning in this situation. This may leave the adult child in the position of outwardly denying the impact of the loss, while inwardly he or she may be grieving. The bond has been severed, and as part of the grief for a parent there may be an attempt to recapture the essence of the relationship, to dwell on past events and feelings in a life review. The parent who died is recalled in part as the parent of early childhood. Recollections are tinged with grief over unfulfilled wishes and entitlements. While mourning the loss of parents, one also mourns the loss of the family of origin in which they played a central part. The child in us receives the ultimate blow, our parent is dead, and only the image remains.

To the extent that feelings of anticipatory orphanhood had begun prior to the parent's death, there may have been an opportunity to work out some of the life review directly with the parents. But how many adult children can handle this— with the potential threats to self and the imagined threats to parents and to the relationship? Whatever the unfinished business with the parents, after their death the issue is unusually poignant because it cannot be worked out directly. Ambivalence persists and with it the gnawing questions of earlier childhood: Did they really understand me and love me for myself? Did they love a sibling more? What were the secrets I was never privy to?

Feelings of guilt and blame may also arise. There is usually no strong guilt in being a survivor, since it is right for a child to outlive a parent. As de Beauvoir writes, it is a guilt of "carelessness, omission, and abstention," one of "a thousand piercing regrets." [25, p. 108] Blame recurs for a life time when love was not always received in right measure or under the right conditions. Superimposed upon this may be an opportunity for the child to step back and with empathy see the relationship from the parent's perspective and allow for forgiveness instead of blame.

After the death most children continue much the same as they did when the parent was alive, keeping some values and attitudes of their parents and rejecting others. If continuity of life style is evidence of mastery of transition, then most people handle death of a parent quite well. There is, however, a spectrum of reactions ranging from the need to exorcize the ghost of the parent to identifying so strongly with the legacy of the parent that the child strives to complete the parent's tasks in lieu of his own goals. This may include taking on responsibility for another family member, carrying on a family business, or taking over as head of the clan.

Some have written of the "former" parent [27, 28] suggesting that after a parent's death the bond is gone. This paper argues that the tie persists, not only on an unconscious level, but viably in the here and now. This was strikingly demonstrated when Troll asked adults in their sixties and seventies to describe a man and a woman. The modal response for each was a parent [12]. Parents continue to be significant people after their death. Professionals working with very old people often hear emotion-laden references to parents who died three or four decades ago. In the symbolic remnants of the tie are images of parental supports, protection, or challenge, no matter how constricting or enabling they may have been in the past. The tie is not severed, and the image or presence of the parent continues both in the habitual patterns of daily life which previously involved the parent as well as in subsequent life transitions. Thus, a basic contradiction inherent in the loss is that of separateness and connectedness. The parent has died, the interaction has ceased, and yet the bond continues.

Impact of the Loss:
Finitude and Personal Growth

The second perspective from which we view the impact of the loss of a parent focuses on the surviving child as he or she faces both finitude and the challenge of personal growth. The death of a parent is a signal that life is transient and that one's personal time is not forever. It brings the child face to face with death. Note the following strikingly parallel accounts of a mother's death:

> . . . the hour in which I lost my immortality . . . in which I tried on my shroud for the first time . . . came to me when my mother died. I accepted death for both of us [29, p. 114].
>
> The only comfort I have . . . is that it will happen to me too. Otherwise it would be too unfair. Yes, we [sisters] were taking part in the dress rehearsal for our own burial [25, p. 115]

The loss of a parent represents the removal of a buffer against death. As long as the parent was alive the child could feel protected, since the parent by the rational order of things was expected to die first. Without this buffer, there is a strong reminder that the child is now the older generation and cannot easily deny his or her own mortality. A major task of mid-life is to cope with finitude, which is the acceptance of the fact that there is more time behind one than ahead and that death is coming closer. Kastenbaum suggests the possibility of defining the onset of middle age as the time when finitude is accepted [6]. Jacques has written sensitively of the pathology of persons who have been unable to meet this crisis [30].

Not only does the loss of a parent force the child to face death, but also to confront its polar opposite: life and personal growth. Successful coping with a parent's death involves neither reifying the past nor leaving it behind but assimilating it as one's psychological inheritance. The positive aspects of the parental tie can be owned and can enable the child in turn to be a better parent and family member to those remaining in his or her life. A conflict-ridden relationship can be terminated and release the child's energy for use in more satisfying directions. Burdensome injunctions of the parent may be challenged and placed in realistic perspective, thus freeing the person to generate a new core of expectations.

Death of parents may usher in a sense of needing to reorganize the self as a way to deal with the profound impact of the loss. What is desired is a feeling of autonomy that flows from a deep sense of one's identity. This can come out of the willingness to face life as it is or was, not as one would have liked or wanted it to be. This tough-mindedness seems essential particularly when evaluating one's relationship with parents. Personal growth does not demand a rejection of parental legacies but rather a selective integration of them into one's own value system [31].

As the bond is loosened, the child can reevaluate the dynamics of the tie and its personal meaning and come to a better understanding of who he was and who he is in the process of becoming. This calls for a shift in identity, in finding one's true roots, and in being less an extension of parents. Some may find the strength to discover and modify the legacies of their parents and value their own difference and creativity. Thus, loss of a parent may potentially free the person to trust more in the self and to risk new behaviors [32].

The need for attachment is strong. After the parent dies the child may look for other parental figures, not only as a substitute or a replacement, but as a way of retaining a hold on the intergenerational tie and as a surrogate buffer against death. Middle age may well be a time of cathectic flexibility. Reaching out for new relationships does not mean disloyalty to the parent. What we are suggesting, then, is that by the loss of parents, the life force of the child who faces his own death can potentially be synthesized into a stronger sense of identity, a renewed commitment to love and to relate to others, and a deeper cognitive grasp of the world.

In summary, this paper has examined the impact of the loss of a parent on a middle-aged child. A life long process of anticipatory orphanhood has been suggested as preparing for, and possibly reducing, the impact of the death. Reaction to the loss involves two dialectic themes which need to be dealt with by the surviving child: first, the breaking and the persistence of the bond, and second, the finitude and personal growth. It is hoped that the ideas presented can be an impetus to further exploration of parental loss in adulthood.

References

1. J. Bowlby, *Attachment and Loss*, Volume 3, Basic Books, New York, 1980.

2. E. Furman, *A Child's Parent Dies*, Yale University Press, New Haven, 1974.

3. J. Birtchnell, Depression in Relation to Early and Recent Parent Death, *British Journal of Psychiatry, 116*, pp. 299-306, 1970.

4. J. Bunch, The Influence of Parental Death Anniversaries upon Suicide Dates, *British Journal of Psychiatry, 118*, pp. 621-626, 1971.

5. H. Anderson, The Death of a Parent: Its Impact on Middle-Aged Sons and Daughters, *Pastoral Psychology, 28*, pp. 151-167, 1980.

6. R. Kastenbaum, Death and Development Through the Life Span, in *New Meanings of Death*, H. Feifel (ed.), McGraw-Hill, New York, 1977.

7. D. P. Malinak, M. F. Hoyt, and V. Patterson, Adult's Reactions to the Death of a Parent: A Preliminary Study, *American Journal of Psychiatry, 136*, pp. 1152-1156, 1979.

8. M. Schlentz, A Study of Grief: The Affect of Death of Parents on Middle Aged Adults, *Archives of the Foundation of Thanatology, 7*, p. 157, 1978.

9. C. M. Sanders, A Comparison of Adult Bereavement in the Death of a Spouse, Child and Parent, *Omega, 10*, pp. 303-322, 1979-80.

10. P. C. Rosenblatt, R. P. Walsh and D. A. Jackson, *Grief and Mourning in Cross Cultural Perspective*, HRAF Press, New Haven, 1976.

11. R. S. Cavan, *The American Family*, Thomas Y. Crowell, New York, 1963.

12. L. Troll, S. J. Miller, and R. C. Atchley, *Families in Later Life*, Wadsworth, Belmont, California, 1979.

13. M. Sussman, The Family Life of Old People, in *Handbook of Aging and the Social Sciences*, R. Binstock and E. Shanas (eds.), Van Nostrand Reinhold, New York, 1976.

14. B. B. Hess and J. M. Waring, Parent and Child in Later Life: Rethinking the

Relationship, in *Child Influences on Marital and Family Interaction*, R. M. Lerner and G. B. Spanier (eds.), Academic Press, New York, 1978.

15. J. A. Peterson, The Relationship of Middle-Aged Children and Their Parents, in *Aging Parents*, P. K. Ragan (ed.), University of South California Press, Los Angeles, 1979.

16. K. Riegel, Dialectic Operations, *Human Development, 16*, pp. 346-370, 1973.

17. S. Henderson, Care-Eliciting Behavior in Man, *Journal of Nervous and Mental Disease, 159*, pp. 172-181, 1974.

18. V. L. Bengston and L. Troll, Youth and Their Parents: Feedback and Intergenerational Influence in Socialization, in *Child Influences on Marital and Family Interaction: A Life Span Perspective*, R. Lerner and G. B. Spanier (eds.), Academic Press, New York, 1978.

19. M. Blenkner, Social Work and Family Relationships in Later Life with Some Thoughts on Filial Maturity, in *Social Structure and the Family: Generational Relations*, E. Shanas and G. Streib (eds.), Prentice-Hall, Englewood Cliffs, New Jersey, 1965.

20. E. Brody, Aging Parents and Aging Children, in *Aging Parents*, P. K. Ragan (ed.), University of Southern California Press, Los Angeles, 1979.

21. I. Boszormenyi-Nagy and B. Krasner, Trust-Based Therapy: A Contextual Approach, *American Journal of Psychiatry, 137*, pp. 767-775, 1980.

22. S. Weishaus, Aging is a Family Affair, in *Aging Parents*, P. K. Ragan (ed.), University of Southern California, Press, Los Angeles, 1979.

23. U. S. Comptroller General, *Well Being of Older People in Cleveland, Ohio*, U. S. General Accounting Office, Washington, D.C., 1977.

24. A. D. Weisman, Is Mourning Necessary?, in *Anticipatory Grief*, B. Schoenberg (ed.), Columbia University Press, New York, 1974.

25. S. deBeauvoir, *A Very Easy Death*, Warner, New York, 1973.

26. L. E. Troll, Intergenerational Relations in Later Life: A Family System Approach, in *Transitions of Aging*, N. Datan and N. Lohmann (eds.), Academic Press, New York, 1980.

27. M. Taggart, Salvete et valete: On Saying Goodbye to a Deceased Former Parent, *Journal of Marital and Family Therapy, 6*, pp. 117-120, 1980.

28. D. S. Williamson, New Life at the Graveyard: A Method of Therapy for Individuation from a Dead Former Parent, *Journal of Marriage and Family Counseling, 4*, pp. 93-101, 1978.

29. B. Hecht, *A Child of the Century*, Simon and Schuster, New York, 1954.

30. E. Jacques, Death and the Mid-Life Crisis, *International Journal of Psychoanalysis, 46*, pp. 502-514, 1965.

31. D. J. Levinson, *The Season of a Man's Life*, Alfred Knopf, New York, 1978.

32. L. Pincus, *Death in the Family*, Pantheon, New York, 1974.

6
Bereavement and the Elderly
Marian Osterweis

For the elderly, bereavement is very much a part of life. Although people of all ages may experience the death of someone they love, for old people losses occur much more frequently. Now that many people live into their 80's and 90's, it is no longer unusual to outlive one's children in addition to one's peers. For the institutionalized elderly in hospitals or long-term care facilities death is all around. Although the people who die may not have been particularly close friends, their deaths do not go unnoticed. At the very least, they are constant reminders of one's own mortality.

The Bereavement Process

Whether because of some of the popular literature or because of implicit or explicit cultural attitudes, people tend to think that grieving should be over within a year and that there are set stages one should go through. People who have experienced bereavement will often tell you that this is not so, and numerous studies confirm that the normal grieving process may be long and uneven (Osterweis, Solomon, and Green, 1984). Although the acute phase usually lasts only several months, it may take a couple of years for people to resume their normal level of activities and enjoy life again. And in some ways, people never fully get over their feelings of loss.

There are many reactions to loss, including emotional and physiological changes as well as changes in social relations.

And the experience of loss differs from person to person. In addition to sadness, a host of other emotions are common during bereavement, including some that may be surprising. Often survivors feel angry—angry for having been left alone, angry at the deceased for dying. Feeling angry at the deceased can heighten feelings of guilt, which is another common emotion following bereavement. People feel remorse about things they did or didn't say, or they wonder whether the death could have been avoided if only they had done something different. Many people experience rapid emotional changes, and even hallucinations about the deceased are not uncommon in recently bereaved people.

The bereaved typically report physical problems ranging from difficulty sleeping and eating to respiratory troubles and even pains and other symptoms that mimic those the deceased person had experienced. Potentially damaging health behaviors, such as increased drinking and smoking, are common.

Usually these emotional and physical complaints taper off after a while and have no lasting consequences. However, some bereaved people are at increased risk for illness and even death. Bereavement can exacerbate existing illness and appears to have a role in precipitating new illness. Widowed men up to age 75 are about 1½ times more likely to die than married men of the same age (Helsing and Szklo, 1981). Most bereaved people appear depressed for a few months; after one year, an estimated 10 to 20 percent of the widowed population is still sufficiently symptomatic to be considered clinically depressed (Clayton and Darvish, 1979). Given that there are 800,000 new widows and widowers annually, this means that 80,000-160,000 will suffer true depression each year.

Although it is difficult to predict with certainty who will do well and who will experience lasting difficulty following bereavement, there are several factors that appear to have a significant influence on recovery. Social support has repeatedly been shown to be a reliable predictor of adjustment following a death. People who have no support or feel they have no one to talk to are likely to do poorly. People who are already in ill health, physically or emotionally, are more vulnerable to negative health consequences. This is especially true of people who were depressed to begin with. Concomitant life changes and crises can make the grieving process more difficult. Especially among the elderly, the death of a spouse is likely to result in substantially reduced income and may necessitate significant changes in life style, including moving to a new home, changes which themselves are stressful. The elderly are also more likely to experience several deaths within a short period of time.

Finally, the course of bereavement is likely to be influenced by who died and how. It is generally acknowledged that violent and unexpected death, especially suicide, leaves survivors more vulnerable. And, of course, the nature and meaning of the particular relationship that is lost will affect the bereavement process (for detailed discussions of risk factors, see Raphael, 1983; Osterweis, Solomon, and Green, 1984).

Types of Losses

Most of the research and clinical literature on bereavement has focused on the loss of a husband or wife. Very little has been written about the loss of siblings or children in the adult years and even less attention has been focused on the loss of one's friends. Just as each relationship has its own quality and importance, so too, does each death have its own meaning.

Loss of Spouse

The death of one's spouse is a loss in many different ways because marriage has so many different aspects to it. It is the loss of companionship, a sexual partner, co-manager of the household, and partner in decision-making, and for many, it is the loss of one's best friend. The surviving spouse is left alone—alone to make decisions and to perform all household tasks, some of which may be quite unfamiliar. If a couple has lived alone, when one spouse dies the other is often left without anything to structure daily life—there is no one to prepare a meal for and no reason, other than one that is entirely self-imposed, to adhere to any particular routine. In short, the death of a spouse is not only an emotional loss, it is a social loss often requiring major changes in life style and role performance (Parkes and Weiss, 1983).

Today's elderly may be poorly equipped to deal with many of the daily tasks of living that they must take on when a spouse dies. Older men and women were socialized to think in terms of a much sharper division of labor than is the case with many young couples. Elderly widows may know nothing about financial management and suddenly be faced with the seemingly overwhelming task of figuring out how to budget wisely and to decide whether other life changes are necessary or appropriate. Should they move out of the family home and into an apartment if the house is paid off and the apartment will require a substantial monthly outlay of funds? What should be done with the life insurance money? These kinds of questions are difficult enough to answer under the best of circumstances, but when one is not used to thinking about them and one is grieving, they are even more difficult to contemplate.

Elderly widowers are likely to be left with a different, but equally unfamiliar, set of tasks and questions. Many have never done routine household chores such as cooking, laundry, and cleaning. They were the wife's domain. For the widower, these tasks can assume major importance and may affect health. Many elderly men suffer from chronic diseases such as hypertension, heart disease, and diabetes and require special diets and regular medication. Yet, in many families it is the wife who has become knowledgeable about what foods are appropriate and how they should be cooked, and what medicines should be taken when. Inattention to these details can lead to exacerbated illness and sometimes death.

For both men and women, the loss of a spouse alters social status. As a single person, the widowed may be less comfortable or less welcome in couples' activities. Previous friendship networks may be less available in an important time of need for social support than they were when no special need existed. Because the loss of a spouse alters social status and necessitates learning new roles and tasks, many people refer to bereavement not as a crisis, but as a "transition" (Silverman, 1982). Among the frail elderly, the death of a spouse often results in institutionalization if the survivor cannot manage alone, a traumatic move that is frequently associated with further decline.

In addition to the impact of all of the above on the course of the bereavement process, two types of marital relationships —those involving intense ambivalence and/or excessive dependence—make it harder to separate from the deceased and are likely to lead to difficulties in grieving. Although virtually all relationships are characterized by some mixture of positive and negative feelings (e.g., affection and hostility), high ambivalence appears to complicate grieving. Similarly although most marital relationships involve some dependence on one another, when a person has been overly dependent on his or her spouse (often because they did not complete the separation-individuation process in childhood), bereavement reactions may include exaggerated fear, anger, and distress, which result in particular difficulty in coping (Parkes and Weiss, 1983).

Death of a Sibling

Although there is virtually no literature on the special meaning of sibling death in older life, one can extrapolate from some of the literature on loss of siblings in childhood and from discussions of the nature of sibling relationships to gain some understanding of the special meaning of that kind of loss. Brothers and sisters may be emotionally close or distant. They may live near one another and see each frequently or live far apart and rarely get together. Regardless of emotional closeness or level of involvement in everyday activities, when a sibling dies, it is a powerful reminder of one's own mortality. If the sibling dies of an inheritable disease, it heightens feelings of vulnerability.

The death of one sibling often results in a realignment of responsibilities among the surviving children. For example, if the deceased was the one who took responsibility for bringing the family together for special occasions, for looking after an ill family member, or for giving advice about various matters, the survivors will now have to redistribute those tasks (intentionally or unintentionally). Ambivalent feelings are very common among siblings. As mentioned above, such feelings can complicate the grieving process.

Death of a Child

Although a substantial literature exists on parents' reactions to the death of an infant or young child, only one real study has focused on the death of an adult child (Levav, 1982). While some observers claim that the death of a young child is the most stressful, based on his clinical experience, Gorer (1965) believes that "the most distressing and long-lasting of all griefs . . . is that for the loss of a grown child."

Until this century, death in infancy and childhood were fairly common, and it was the rare person who lived much beyond 60. Now we expect to live to old age and we certainly expect that our children will outlive us. This expectation of dying before our children do makes the death of a child especially painful—it is untimely and because it seems unfair for a younger person to die, bereaved parents may have heightened feelings of anger. Although it is common for bereaved people to feel some guilt about the death, however unfounded, and to wonder what might have been done to forestall or avoid death, guilt among bereaved parents is even more common. These feelings of anger and guilt have the potential for complicating the bereavement process.

In addition to the emotional impact, an adult child's death may leave the elderly without a caretaker. As with the death of a spouse, other major life-style changes may be necessary.

Assisting the Bereaved

There are three basic approaches to helping the bereaved: mutual support, psychotherapy, and medication. These methods can be used alone or in conjunction with one another.

Mutual support and psychotherapy may be used in a variety of ways. They may be designed for individuals or families, for bereaved people in general or for special groups of bereaved people (such as relatives of suicide victims, parents who have lost children, widows, etc.). These interventions may also be designed to help prior to or after the death. Both approaches offer the opportunity for the bereaved to express feelings in a safe and supportive (nonjudgmental) environment.

Mutual Support

This approach to assisting the bereaved is premised on the belief that "the person best qualified to understand and help with the problems of the bereaved person is another bereaved person" (Parkes, 1980). Typically, mutual support groups provide information about the bereavement process, offer practical assistance, and, by example, reassure the newly bereaved that things will get better. Mutual support efforts may be directed by lay people, alone, as alternatives to the health care system, or in conjunction with health care professionals.

Most mutual support groups are modeled after the Widow-to-Widow program developed by Phyllis Silverman in Boston beginning in the mid-1960s (Silverman, 1970; Silverman and Cooperband, 1975). Trained widow helpers used an outreach approach to identify new widows. The goal of the program was to assist widows with the life transition by providing information and teaching them the skills they needed to learn to adapt to their altered circumstances. A one-to-one approach was used initially, followed by group interaction. This basic model has been adapted for programs in this country, Canada, and abroad. It has been used extensively for widows, rarely for widowers (for whom few services exist generally), and increasingly for parents of dying or deceased children and other special groups of bereaved people.

One of the most interesting recent adaptations of the mutual support approach exists in hospice programs. Hospices care for terminally ill patients and their families. Because the family is the unit of care, prebereavement support is offered in addition to help after the death. Hospices have a unique opportunity to observe and assist with family functioning, an opportunity that is lacking in the traditional health care system. Most hospice bereavement programs are directed, and heavily dominated by lay people who have themselves been bereaved, although health professionals, especially nurses, are also involved. Like other mutual support approaches, hospices vary greatly in the extent of the services offered. Prebereavement support includes emotional support and validation of feelings, information and education, and practical assistance to the family that is often caring for the dying patient at home. "The entire ethos of hospice care is also likely to lend support through its implicit acceptance of death and willingness to discuss and plan for it" (Osterweis, Solomon, and Green, 1984).

Following bereavement, about 70% of hospices offer support for about one year. The support is often modest—a periodic phone call, social gatherings, or occasional visits. When the patient enters the hospice program, most hospices assign a grief worker to the family to assist during the prebereavement and postbereavement periods. Some hospices, most notably the Boulder County Hospice in Colorado, assign a new person to work with the family after the death, believing that one of the most urgent needs for the newly bereaved is to "tell his story" repeatedly and without fear of correction or contradiction. This need is best served by a person with no previous involvement with the case (Lattanzi, 1982).

Psychotherapy

For people who experience pathological or distorted grief reactions or who feel overwhelmed by their grief, professional mental health intervention may be warranted. A number of different kinds of psychotherapy exist, using a variety of health professionals. Whether psychodynamic, behavioral, cognitive, or systems-oriented, psychotherapy may focus on individuals, families, or groups of similarly bereaved people, and therapy may be brief and time-limited or open ended and long-term.

The most common approach to assisting individuals is probably the psychodynamic orientation that assumes that abnormal reactions derive from preexisting personality factors in the bereaved individual, special life circumstances, or aspects of the relationship with the deceased. Unresolved previous losses, defective defensive and coping strategies, preexisting emotional instability, and ambivalence and dependence are some of the things that may be worked on. The goal is to work through grief by clarifying neurotic conflicts and troubling emotions.

In contrast to this approach, behaviorists tend to focus more on specific behaviors than on internal dynamics, and cognitive therapists focus on restructuring the loss by reliving it in the imagination. Also, numerous interpersonal approaches work with the family group or with an individual patient but with the focus on psychosocial aspects of the problem. Family systems therapists, for example, emphasize the impact of loss on the family system and work on communication issues, clarification of altered roles, and individual patterns of behavior that strain the system.

Impact of Interventions

There have been very few studies of the impact of any of the many types of psychosocial interventions in terms of their ability to reduce the stress of bereavement or mitigate long term negative effects. Furthermore, there is no evidence that all people need or want formal interventions. For the bereaved whose informal social support network is lacking, mutual support may fill this void. Numerous anecdotal reports attest to the helpfulness of various mutual support programs in providing support, reassurance, and information, and there is some suggestion that such interventions may help some people move faster through the bereavement process (Vachon, et al., 1980).

A few evaluations of short-term psychotherapy have been conducted. These suggest that such therapy can be useful in terms of enhancing self-concepts, resolving old conflicts, and ameliorating depressive symptoms (see for example, Raphael, 1977; Horowitz et al., 1984; Klerman, et al., 1984). As the Institute of Medicine report concluded:

"For people who experience normal reactions and who are not seen as being at particularly high risk for adverse consequences of bereavement, the support of family and friends, perhaps augmented by some type of mutual support interventions, will generally be sufficient. However, for people who define themselves or who are seen by others in the community as continuing to be overwhelmed by their grief (or unable to grieve), psychotherapeutic interventions may be warranted. In addition, certain categories of people may be at such high risk following bereavement that they should perhaps be evaluated by mental health professionals and followed for some period of time, with psychotherapeutic interventions as indicated. These groups include . . . people with a history of psychiatric disorders (especially depression), and people related or close to someone who committed suicide. (Osterweis, Solomon, and Green, 1984)."

Drug Therapy

Three groups of drugs—anti-anxiety medications (sedatives, minor tranquilizers), sleeping pills (hypnotics), and antidepressants—are commonly prescribed for bereaved people. The bereaved frequently report using sedatives and/or sleeping pills to reduce anxiety and aid sleep. Tricyclic antidepressants, which are effective in relieving symptoms of clinical depression, have also occasionally been used to control symptoms of grief, such as sadness and feelings of hopelessness.

There have been no clinical studies of the effects of any of these drugs for bereaved people. Even if they were shown to be effective in reducing or alleviating the symptoms of grief, there would be substantial controversy about the use of medications for a condition, which though painful, is normal.

In fact, some people worry that drugs can interfere with grief work and will ultimately lead to complications. Even those who support the use of psychopharmacologic drugs to relieve symptoms during the intense period of grief caution that "the final resolution of loss is better accomplished by psychiatric help than by the use of drugs. Although drugs may be helpful in treating the bereaved, their use is adjunctive, symptomatic, and limited in time" (Hollister, 1972).

Furthermore, all three classes of drugs carry potential risks —they can be lethal in large doses or in combination with alcohol, and some entail risk of drug dependence. Because elderly patients metabolize drugs more slowly than young people (National Institutes of Health, 1983; Solomon, et al., 1979) certain anti-anxiety medications and sleeping pills (long-acting benzodiazepenes) may cause problems in coordination, alertness, and mood that develop gradually and are difficult to diagnose; this adds new hazards to an older person's period of grieving.

Conclusions

For most people, bereavement triggers a long and painful process in which one's emotional, social, and physiological functioning may be substantially altered for more than a year. Everyone needs information and support to help them get through this stressful time. The elderly, for whom losses are increasingly frequent, may have special problems following bereavement because of previous ill health, lack of social support, and lack of resources (financial and skills) needed to accomplish a smooth transition. Most of the research on bereavement has focused on conjugal loss, with little attention paid to other losses (siblings, children, and friends) that are especially common among the elderly. Although there are many programs designed to assist bereaved women, there are few for bereaved men despite epidemiologic evidence suggesting that men are at higher risk than women for negative outcomes. For reasons that are not entirely clear, programs designed for widowers are often underutilized.

References

Clayton, P. and Darvish, J. "Course of Depressive Symptoms Following the Stress of Bereavement." In *Stress and Mental Disorder* (J.E. Barrett, ed.) New York: Raven Press, 1979.

Gorer, G. *Death, Grief and Mourning.* New York: Doubleday, 1965.

Helsing, G., and Szklo, M. "Mortality After Bereavement," *American Journal of Epidemiology.* 114:41-52, 1981.

Hollister, L. "Psychotherapeutic Drugs in the Dying and Bereaved," *Journal of Thanatology* 2:623-629, 1972.

Horowitz, M., Marmar, C., et al. "Brief Psychotherapy of Bereavement Reactions: The Relationship of Process to Outcome," *Archives of General Psychiatry* (in press).

Lattanzi, M. "Hospice Bereavement Services: Creating Networks of Support," *Family and Community Health* 5(3):54-63, 1982.

Levav, I. "Mortality and Psychopathology Following the Death of an Adult Child: An Epidemiological Review," *Israel Journal of Psychiatry and Related Sciences* 19:23-38, 1982.

Klerman, G., Weissman, M., et al. *Interpersonal Psychotherapy of Depression.* New York: Basic Books, 1984.

National Institutes of Health Concensus Development Conference Panel. Conference on Drugs and Insomnia, November 15-17, 1983. *Conference Summary,* Vol. 4, No. 10, Bethesda, MD: NIH Office of Medical Applications Research, 1983. Also as "Consensus Development Conference," *Journal of the American Medical Association* 251(18): 2410-2414, 1984.

Osterweis, M., Solomon, F., and Green, M. *Bereavement: Reactions, Consequences and Care: A Report of the Institute of Medicine.*, Washington, D.C.: National Academy Press, 1984.

Parkes, C. "Bereavement Counseling: Does it Work?" *British Medical Journal* 281: 3-6, 1980.

Parkes, C., and Weiss, R. *Recovery from Bereavement.* New York, Basic Books, 1983.

Raphael, B. "Preventive Intervention with the Recently Bereaved," *Archives of General Psychiatry* 34: 1450-1454, 1977.

Raphael, B. *The Anatomy of Bereavement.* New York: Basic Books, 1983. Silverman, P. "The Widow as Caregiver in a Program of Preventive Intervention with Other Widows," *Mental Hygiene* 54:540-547, 1970.

Silverman, P. "Transitions and Models of Intervention," *Annals of the Academy of Political and Social Science* 464:174-187, 1982.

Silverman, P., and Cooperband, A. "On Widowhood: Mutual Help and the Elderly Widow," *Journal of Geriatric Psychiatry* 8:9-27, 1975.

Solomon, F., White, C., Parron, D., and Medelson, W. "Sleeping Pills, Insomina, and Medical Practice," *New England Journal of Medicine* 300:803-808, 1979.

Vachon, M. Sheldon, A., et al. "A Controlled Study of Self-Help Intervention for Widows," *American Journal of Psychiatry* 137-1380-1384, 1980.

Part III

Dealing with the Dying Patient

7
Pastoral Counseling with the Dying Person
Jack D. Krasner

From ashes to ashes - from dust to dust - oh, that we really knew the mystique of death. Henri Nouwen, in his book *Creative Ministry,* states that

> Neither medicine, nor psychology, neither psychiatry nor social work can ever respond to the final question of why man comes to life, slowly learns to stand on his own feet, attach himself to someone else, gives life to others and allows them to continue what he started but will not see fulfilled. A man who has not been able to give meaning to his own life cycle and accept it in its terminable reality cannot die as a man.

Death has been conceptualized from many different points of view. Biologically, death occurs with the cessation of physiological functioning. The heart stops beating, the electrical impulses of the brain stop pulsating and all other life sustaining organs cease functioning. Philosophical and theological positions have been offered ranging from the notion that the soul leaves the individual's body, permitting a reunification with God. The question, and perhaps the answer, as to the meaningfulness of death will depend upon the respective individual's life experiences and emotional needs. The purpose of this presentation is to offer some guidelines in the counseling of the dying person.

The experience of the author has demonstrated that effective counseling with the dying person requires emotional support, understanding and relating to the respective person where he or she is at the moment. There are a variety of professionals who might serve as mental health agents in working with the dying person, e.g., psychologist, psychiatrist, social worker, physician, nurse and cleric. However, the professional of choice for the most effective outcome is the trained pastoral counselor. "Pastoral counselor" has been defined by Fabrikant, Barron and Krasner in their book, *To Enjoy Is to Live,* as

> members of the clergy, professed brothers and sisters, or selected laypeople. Some pastoral counselors receive advance training in psychotherapeutic theory and technique. Their orientation includes a religious moral value system and a goal of enhancing the individual's ability to experience his innate "lovability." One should bear in mind that being a clergyman or a professed member of a religious community does not automatically make one a pastoral counselor. A guide which may be used as a general criterion for pastoral counseling is the general philosophy of the Graduate Division of Pastoral Counseling, Iona College, New Rochelle, New York. In addition to required specialty training encompassing didactic courses and supervised experience, this philosophy includes:
>
> 1. Men and women have psychological needs to fulfill and emotional conflicts to resolve before they can freely develop and value their innate spiritual being.
>
> 2. The pastoral counselor has a moral value system recognizing the inherent worthiness and lovability of the human individual.

A person must remember that whether one is a psychologist, physician, social worker, or pastoral counselor, the training and education received in any of these areas is not sufficient to enable a person to work as a psychotherapist. The individual should receive specialized and intensive training in the area of psychotherapy no matter what his profession is and what areas he will work in as a psychotherapist. A look at the background and preliminary training of each of these subspecialties will provide a clear picture of what goes into the selection, education, and training of each psychotherapist.

More often than any other professional, the Pastoral Counselor (PC) brings several required attributes into the counseling relationship. Through religious training and experiences the PC usually has established a philosophy of death as well as life. In so doing, he has acknowledged and accepted the existence of a Higher Force. He is able to accept and evaluate the physically dying person's reactions to experiences of fear rather than as a threat to his own belief when God becomes the target of anger or condemnation. His relationship with the patient is that of a "covenant" rather than a "contract." A contract may be dissolved or broken by either or both parties. The well trained PC rarely rejects even when met by rejection. He is the only mental health professional who seeks no personal reward such as fame or fortune, or who does not need a reason for dropping in on the patient. The primary concern of the PC is to aid the dying person with the work of living rather than with mere physical survival.

A major hindrance in any psychotherapeutic endeavor is countertransference. Countertransference is an emotional reaction on the part of the psychotherapist which is determined by his/her needs rather than by the patient's needs. Thus, the mental health helping agent of choice would be the person who in addition to an understanding of human psychodynamics and other psychological processes has developed an acceptable philosophy of life, death, and God. Generally, health service providers persist in their efforts towards maintaining physical survival as their primary effort. For example, physicians are trained to keep their patients alive. Physical death is considered a failure of the profession and, at times, even a sign of personal inadequacy. Most persons, including the health service providers, share differences in the recognition and acceptance of death because of the anxiety related to the unknown. The notion that one is afraid of the "unknown" *per se* is misleading. An unknown makes for non-existence and one does not concern oneself with what does not exist within his/her realm of being. We all become frightened when threatened by a danger with which we are unable to cope or control effectively. The "unknown" in physical death is related to the ambiguousness of the future. The individual fantasizes the worst possible outcome and reacts to the threat of this anticipated hopeless, overwhelming danger. The dying person's denial is a means of avoiding the need to face this anxiety provoking state of the future. Institutions and the professionals representing those situations are supposed to have the appropriate answers. When one has an answer that is definitive, then one is relieved of the need to project what is often the most negative outcome. A small number are frightened that they will no longer be able to maintain conscious involvement or control over activities which are going on about them. As one patient described the feeling, "the big sleep will take over." Other persons experiencing intense feelings of guilt anticipate punitive actions emanating from God.

Psychotherapeutic counseling with the dying person might best be focused on the goals desired. The writer proposes that the goal of choice be the acceptance of the inevitability of the individual's existing options. Utilization of the Kübler-Ross phases of the dying process allows for the establishment of a counseling format in the clinical procedure.

In her work with dying persons, Kübler-Ross has also noted and delineated typical psychological reaction patterns within the process of dying. These phases include 1) denial, 2) anger, 3) bargaining, 4) depression, 5) resignation versus acceptance. Some further elaboration and clarification may be helpful. The underlying basis of the initial sequential phases is the dying person's attempts to counter the painful effects of depression which emanate from the feelings of loss and helplessness. As previously indicated the "denial" serves to avoid the inevitable loss of ultimate control. Acknowledgment exposes the dying person to the threat of loss and anger toward the accountable party. The "bargaining" becomes an admission that some Higher Force sits in judgment and is accountable for one's fate. To attack or thwart the person's attempts to protect himself results in counter efforts to reinforce the defense mechanisms. Therefore, the intensity of threat might best be reduced by focusing on areas related to the underlying depression. This initial goal may be attained by the therapeutic agent's availability to and unconditional acceptance of the dying person's worth for *who* and *what* he is.

Denial is perhaps the most frequent occurrence with the dying person. An obvious manifestation is the individual who experiences "something wrong" but refuses to seek an evaluation because his or her suspicions may be validated. Although consultation, that is seeking a second evaluative opinion may be desirable, some people continue shopping for a diagnosis and prognosis which would contradict what they are unable to accept. This denial is related to the individual's degree of ego strength which in turn, determines the means of coping with the threat to survival. Two examples illustrate this phenomenon: Following surgical procedure for the removal of a malignant lymphoma, the patient's physician described the results of the surgical procedure and further treatment. During the consultation, the patient was informed that two non-operative malignant nodes would be treated with radiation and chemotherapy. The patient accepted the postoperative treatment procedure but never heard that he continued to have a malignant condition. The rationale for the continued treatment was accepted as a measure to prevent recurrence. Two months later when the intensity of the experienced threat to the patient diminished, conversation arose during which the malignancy was mentioned. It was only then that the patient heard, that is, was able to accept, the continued existence of a malignant condition. An oncologist has observed that physician patients with cancer also have demonstrated other manifestations of the denial process. For example, the physician patient would be shown x-ray plates but would be unable to see the evident spread of cancer cells in the body.

The recognition of a fatal affliction tends to provoke anger. This reaction is more readily understandable as we consider the traumatic blow to one's continued infantile concept of personal immortality. Many provocative ideas accompany the notion of death. The individual's aspirations are to be terminated. The future, wherein all the deeds, accomplishments and fulfillments are going to take place, no longer exist. The intense pain emanating from the anxiety provoking frustration would, in itself, typically result in anger. In addition, the question most usually arises, "Why me?" That is, "What did I do? Why am I being deprived of life?" or other similar questions. Considering the notion of punishment inherently raises the question of a Higher Being or Force who or which has judged, evaluated, and condemned the individual. One may only speculate why the individual has contracted this terminal affliction. The illness may be a result of genetic factors, environmental influences such as pollution, self-abuse or a combination of these and other factors. A description of the process or natural history of an affliction is more readily produced than the "whys" which often remain a mystery.

The reaction of anger by the dying person may remain static or be transitory, depending upon the effectiveness of the manner and mechanisms used to cope with this reaction. The major difficulty of working through this phase is that the target varies and is often inconsistent with reality. The dying person's uncertainty of the justification for condemning the target of his anger or the threat of additional negative consequences tends to provoke guilt, alienation and withdrawal. The target may be parents because of hereditary or constitutional factors, spouse, siblings, other family members or friends because of insufficient or inadequate caring; children experienced as a "drain" rather than a fulfillment of expectations; or God as a Supreme Being who screens and determines the specific fate of each respective individual.

Anger may also be a means of temporizing the degree of anxiety provoked by anticipated loss of love objects. An individual more readily accepts loss or separation of a disliked rather than a desired object or person.

Dr. Elizabeth Kübler-Ross includes the phase of "bargaining" which most often arises during the process of dying. This pattern may be identified with the mechanism of magical thinking. When the individual experiences feelings of helplessness, accountability of the future is ascribed to others. The child makes promises if the parent will only gratify the request. The student will become an exemplary scholar if the instructor will give a passing grade. The alcoholic will give up drinking if only his DT's would disappear. The dying person will become devoutly religious if God will let him live. There are occasions when these death-bed promises are fulfilled. The likelihood, however, is that the promises last in proportion to the pain experience of the individual.

Psychodynamic exploration reveals that depression may result from one or more of several factors: These factors may include internalization of anger which cannot be expressed to outside targets, feelings of helplessness or experienced loss of cathected objects. The dying person is confronted with one or more of these experiences. Although other persons may influence the dying person, no one as yet has been able to control death *per se*. An excellent example is the Karen Ann Quinlan situation in New Jersey. In 1976, Miss Quinlan was in a comatose state and was on life sustaining mechanisms with the expectation that the removal of these would result in death. Theological, philosophical and legal discussions and actions occurred about maintaining Miss Quinlan's physical life although she remained in this comatose, vegetable-like state. Legal action brought by the family finally resulted in the removal of the life sustaining mechanisms. Over a year later Miss Quinland, although continuing in a comatose state, maintains physical life. The prognosticated imminent death has as yet not occurred.

An individual's attitude as well as medical interventions may help to sustain physical life. However, the lack of definitive determinations results in a feeling of personal inadequacy and helplessness. Feelings of increased limitation or deterioration of internal organic functioning also intensifies the feeling of loss of integrity. Internalized anger provoked by guilt often occurs as the dying individual experiences failure to meet the expectations of others. This phenomenon often occurs when family members, friends and others, because of dependency and other needs, insist that the person "cannot die and leave me." Here again, the feeling of inadequacy is intensified by one's helplessness in gratifying others wishes and demands.

The individual's depression may persist resulting in marking time, waiting for physical death to occur; developing into a state of total helplessness resulting in suicidal efforts; or, when adequate coping mechanisms are utilized, developing a state of acceptance of physical finality and pursuing options which may bring satisfaction and fulfillment. Kübler-Ross, in speaking of resignation as opposed to acceptance of dying very likely is referring to what is referred to above as "marking time" as differentiated from acceptance by utilization of existing, although limited, options. The writer questions whether these two aspects are mutually exclusive. Personal experiences with the dying person reveal a sequential combination of both resignation and acceptance. Initially, there is resignation by the individual that death will occur sooner or later - more likely sooner than later. The individual becomes resigned to the fact that the future has become more limited in various areas such as fulfillment of former aspirations, of occupational, social, inter-personal and other endeavors. Once having resigned him/herself to these restrictions and having weathered the blow to the fantasy of immortality, the individual is able to accept death as a transitional phase.

Physical life may then be utilized more effectively by taking advantage of those options which are available to the individual.

The Rev. Carl Nighswonger at Billings Memorial Hospital in Chicago pioneered work supporting pastoral counseling as the professional discipline of choice. This effort has been a precursor in many hospitals and clinics to the formation of therapeutic group procedures with the terminally ill and relatives of the dying. *The New York Times Magazine* (November 14, 1971) reports that Nighswonger emphasizes that the function of the "Chaplain" is to interpret and clarify in order for the family to better understand and accept their own behavior.

> If we can help people see that in bereavement it's not wrong to love the person who has just died and at the same time to be furious because he left them, and that they need not feel guilty because of this ambivalence, then we've helped them.

Using a therapeutic group approach, Nighswonger gives clinical attention to the Kübler-Ross psychological phases of dying. He also fosters emotional reaction from and interaction among the patients. Helping dying persons cope effectively with emotional conflicts and barriers enables them to accept that, "To die with dignity is to die with a sense of awareness that life is coming to an end, but it's an end that in itself is a fulfillment."

Interviews with the family members are directed towards ". . . synchronizing their own preparatory grief with the dying relative." Encouragement of natural emotional responses such as uncontrolled weeping, anger, silent grieving or simply a heart-to-heart talk reduces the distancing often experienced between patient and relative.

Life may be defined as a biological process of staying alive. The essential force or instinctual drive of every living organism is to perpetuate this process of "survival." A rather simple illustration of the magnitude of this force is the observation of how a thin blade of grass can surface itself through solid concrete.

Within the human organism, the basic drive for survival is manifested in the many infantile and early primary processes which are directed toward staying alive. As the individual matures, the threat to physical survival diminishes and the individual hopefully directs himself towards *enjoying* living. The author, with colleagues, has defined the concept of "to enjoy" as the recognition of opportunities and utilization of one's own attributes to experience satisfaction and fulfillment.

Psychological counseling with the dying person presents severe difficulties. The hardships are related both to the afflicted person's usual primary drive for survival of physical life as well as the helping agent's difficulty in his/her conflict regarding the meaningfulness of the life-death continuum. With rare exceptions, the severely and especially the terminally ill person experiences specific emotional reations. Dr. E.M. Pattison, in the 1969 Spring/Summer issue of *Voices* describes death as a "crisis event" which may be understood in clinical terms of crisis intervention therapy. The major difficulty for the clinican is *how* to tell the patient rather than to tell or not to tell. The helping agent is unable to deal with the ultimate problem of death but can assist the individual in more effectively dealing with the various aspects involved in the process of dying. Pattison speaks of "part-aspects of the experience of dying" in terms of "fears:" the fear of the unknown; the fear of loneliness; fear of loss of family and friends; fear of loss of body; fear of loss of self-control; fear of loss of identity; and fear of regression.

> The importance of dying as a crisis is that the crisis is experienced as an overwhelming insuperable feeling of personal inadequacy in dealing with the dying process. There is bewilderment, confusion, indefinable anxiety, and unspecified fear. The person is faced with a total problem that he does not have

resources to deal with, and the ensuing anxiety makes it impossible to deal with any of the part-aspects. Here lies our opportunity to intervene for although we cannot deal with the ultimate problem of death, we can help the person to deal with the various parts of the process of dying. By focusing on these part-problems, the dying person can cope with himself and with his dying in some measure to resolve the crisis in a rewarding fashion that enhances his self-esteem, dignity, and integrity. The dying person can take pride then in having faced his crisis of dying with hope and courage and come away having dealt successfully with the crisis. One might call this healthy dying!

The question, "How do you tell someone he or she is dying?" might best be approached by understanding one's philosophy of death. Is death a cessation of a living organism resulting in total non-existence, fini? Or, is death a transitional stage moving the individual from one phase of existence to another? One may argue either extreme or select an intermediate position. For purposes of present discussion, the author accepts the second philosophical position for two basic reasons: 1) Although a traditional-theological position, this point of view fits in with the logical processes of nature. 2) This philosophy has greater value in helping the dying person to accept his own death as well as to enjoy existing options available. The propensity for life is extreme within nature. The ready reproduction of living organisms ranging from the most primitive one-cell organism to complex humans is ever present. Natural science has continued to show experimental evidence that energy forces never disappear but merely change from one form to another. Thus, we may postulate that human life on earth is an energy force initiated by the collaborative effort of egg and sperm. Death may then be viewed as a continuum of existence where the energy force is transferred into another medium. The particular theological process may vary from religion to religion, but the effects appear to be essentially the same. That is, the soul of the individual during life on earth emanates from a higher divine force and death allows the transition or a return of the soul into another energy force or return to the divine power. Some religions, for example, Christianity, advocate that with death there is the opportunity for reunification of the individual with God. In the Judiac religion, the Psalms refer to the concept that during life on earth, man's soul is provided by God and with death, the soul returns to God.

The eventuality of death is ever present although the specific awareness may be absent. The conceptualization of death is usually provoked when an individual experiences a direct threat. That is, severe illness or direct confrontation of having a terminal affliction. There is a very old American saying that "Death and taxes are inevitable." These ideas may be legitimately questioned. Traditionally, we anticipate that everyone will die at one time or another. As long as one person remains alive, the inevitability of death remains an hypothesis. This precept may also be applied to *terminal illness*. Terminal illness is a prognosis based upon statistical probabilities of the past as well as present ignorance as to a cure for the existing affliction. The absolute event of death, however, is an uncertainty. This incident may occur in a day, in a month, in a year, a decade or even later. In counseling the person with a terminal illness, the helping agent may focus on when the person is going to die or what is the person going to do with his remaining time on earth.

During recent years, verification has been sought as to the perpetuation of man's existence after death. Experiences have been recounted where individual's have described having been medically diagnosed as dead and then having recovered. Although the criteria for the termination have varied, usually death has been considered as a termination of vital signs. The validity of the criteria may be questionable, but apparently some expert made the decision. A number of investigators are making determined efforts to verify the possibility of what we may refer to as an *after life*. The materials presented are illustrated by the work of Dr. Raymond Moody, Jr., in his publication *Life After Life*. Dr. Moody describes life as interminable. He proposes that life never ends. The individual transcends from one phase into another and that life on earth is merely one of these phases. He surmises, from the data collected, the notion of immortality of the soul. An important factor is the similarity of experiences reported by those interviewed by Moody. Generally, these individuals report that following their supposed death, they tend to hover over the bed or wherever the body is lying and they observe the action which is taking place. The experience is as if they are watching a scenario in which they are appearing. Also, some people have reported a transcending experience through a funnel-like tunnel. The experience includes an intensification of both visual and kinesthetic sensation.

Some individuals have reported having met and conversed with people who had previously died. One person described meeting with a previously unknown sibling who had died prior to her own birth. The actual existence of the sibling was later verified by the parents who were still alive. These and other similar experiences leave open the question of whether or not these people were actually dead. One may hypothesize that vital psychological signs had temporarily ceased. The individual experienced previously unconscious fantasies, the vital signs spontaneously reappeared and the total process was interpreted as a life/death and then return to life condition. There may be some validity to the statement that these people actually were dead and had transcended from *life* as is commonly conceived to an *after life* and then returned to a live condition. If there is reality to the latter process, the question arises why these individuals returned to their life on earth. When asked, some of those who reported the experience said they returned because there was something pulling them back. There was some unfinished business which they had to complete. A child, spouse or some other force provoked the feeling that their life or their goals on earth were not complete. For example, the dead person experienced the feeling of disappointing a family member. This force apparently was strong enough, resulting in returning to the former life status in order to complete the unfinished phase. Considering the evidence reported, one may question the reality of one dying and then returning to the same life conditions experienced prior to death. Was the individual dead or not dead? Was the experience a fantasy or reality? Exploration of the various factors involved may cause conjecture of many possibilities about what is happening during these reported experiences. One may offer evidence which would be contrary or would contradict the validity of these reports. On the other hand, one may equally offer arguments to substantiate or justify the reality of the process. Regardless of what position one chooses, the reported experiences are thought provoking and accept the notion of immortality of the soul. In this hypothesis, life may be considered to be on a continuum with death rather than that physical death automatically results in a cessation of life and consequent nothingness.

Counseling the dying person is initiated by the development of a therapeutic relationship between patient and counselor. For reasons previously described, the person more likely to foster such a relationship would be an effectively trained pastoral counselor. This position is reinforced by the reported psychological and emotional experiences of the dying person which have been condensed in the Kübler-Ross sequential phases of the dying process. Fabrikant, Barron and Krasner also indicate that an important element in psychological assistance is

> to help the individual recognize and admit this developmental stage, whether it is brought about by aging, internal disease, or externally caused injury. The psychotherapist may then provide the dying person with an opportunity to vent his anger and rage. Inability to express the rage and anger outwardly may result in more intense feelings of rejection and isolation. During this phase the dying patient is often extremely

provocative in his condemnation of society, significant people in his life, and even God. The importance of being accepted and being acceptable to someone during this period of time cannot be overemphasized. Reports from the Nazi concentration camps and from American prisoners of war in the Japanese hands during World War II have indicate that when a prisoner experienced a feeling of alienation, that is, had no one to whom he felt personally significant, he became apathetic and quickly died. These reports further emphasize that a sharing relationship is more effective than a sense of personal adequacy in coping with anxiety. Thus, the psychotherapist should maintain his own relationship with the patient. At the same time he should encourage effective relationships between the dying patient and other significant persons in his life.

Sharing feelings and assisting the dying patient through the phases of the death process lessen his/her fears and encourages the development of his/her ability to anticipate death with dignity. Interpersonal reactions and sharing are involvements in living. Fulfillment in living is the best preparation for physical dying.

Knowledge and understanding that one is afflicted with a terminal illness is not restricted to the adult. Special consideration must be given to the child in that the parents are more in control of the range of the activities than in the case of the adult. Research has shown that even children below the age of ten experience some awareness of their condition. E. Wachter did a comparative study of four groups of children, ages 6-10 reported in the June 1971 issue of *American Journal of Nursing.* Group 1 included children with leukemia, cystic fibrosis, tumors, and cancer. Group II included children with chronic disease with good prognosis. Group III included children having brief illnesses and Group IV included relatively healthy elementary school children. The results showed that children with fatal illnesses experienced twice as much anxiety as other hospitalized children. These children related stories that reflected fears and threats to body integrity and preoccupation with death. Fantasy stories manifested separation, loneliness and death more frequently than those of the other children. Of the sixteen fatally ill children in the study, only two were told of their prognosis. However, there was a general awareness by these children of the seriousness of their affliction that suggests correct interpretation of behavior and attitude of those around them. These children often endowed characters in their stories with their own symptoms as well as frequently depicting death in their drawings.

Wachter found that being open and frank with the fatally ill child conveys acceptance and allows discussion of the affliction as a topic of conversation. In so doing, the parents may aid in reducing feelings of alienation, rejection and isolation. Wachter held interviews with the parents. She noted that these interviews were used by parents to alleviate their own anxieties. She also found that the religious devoutedness of the parents influenced the quality of the concern and the manner in which they coped with their fears. However, this did not affect the degree of anxiety expressed by the children. This openness allows the fatally ill child, as well as adult, the opportunity to express his/her love and feelings for relations, friends and other significant persons.

The primary task in any psychotherapeutic process is the establishment of the therapeutic relationship. This is especially so when working with the physically dying person. Better understanding by the PC may be attained by listening and hearing the revelation of the *new* world which has been forced upon the patient. In working through the early phases of the dying process, the patient may engage in what R.M. Butler terms "the life review." Although Butler describes this process in his work with the elder person, the writer has found the same occurs with the physically dying person. The patient reminisces and thus recalls past experiences. These responses are often accompanied by "resurgence of unresolved conflicts" which reveal existing influences of early developmental problems. The PC may utilize the spontaneous and sometimes uncontrolled reminisces to aid the patient in overcoming feelings of failure, guilt, remorse and depression. The vocational, interpersonal, recreational and other limitations incurred by the affliction may then appropriately be discussed on a reality basis. Resignation to possible limitations and acceptance of existing limited options are then in order. In addition to the role of direct change agent, the PC may be a liaison between patient, significant persons, family and involved professionals. As already stated, the encouragement of open communication is absolutely essential. There are also important *household* matters such as updating of will, family and other business matters which should be put in order.

The confrontation of anticipated physically dying with child or adults, offers two positive aspects for the survivor's future. First, there is the opportunity for a preliminary grieving period. Although the physical death of a love object is traumatic to the survivor, the pre-death grief period tends to diminish the intensity and ill effects of the trauma. Second, the survivor has the opportunity to access his/her own influence on the fatally ill affliction of the dying person. This process may diminish feelings of guilt and subsequent self-directed retribution.

The advances of medical science, research and education generally have resulted in physicians who are highly skilled professionals with the ability to evaluate and diagnose many illnesses effectively. The major difficulty, however, is in the treatment procedure of the special affliction rather than in the evaluation and diagnosis. Surgery may be the most beneficial treatment for a particular affliction. Surgery, however, may not always be the treatment of choice. This procedure may be recommended because the particular physician has no other course of treatment available. The physician's opinions are based upon his own experiences and those of others with which he has become acquainted through personal discussion and reading the literature. At times, the physician may exhibit the attitude that he possesses godlike powers. However, he is neither omniscient nor omnipotent. Regardless of the particular faith that an individual may place in any one professional, it may be advantageous to seek out further consultation when the diagnosis offered has a prognostic outcome of death or when surgery is offered as the only treatment. Any professional who is competent would welcome a consultation by another expert. The consultation offers two advantages: The other professional will confirm the diagnosis and treatment plan or may find and offer additional information which had previously been unobtained. The PC has no vested interest in a particular treatment plan. The PC is therefore able to offer himself as a sounding board for the patient to evaluate all of the proposed alternative procedures and their probable outcome.

Acceptance by the terminally ill person of him/herself is extremely important. The person must accept his/her capacity for thinking, feeling and reasoning. The patient should be encouraged to take advantage of his/her ability to think and reason and to make effective judgments in the course of his/her life. The profession's training and expertise should never negate the patient's intellectual or emotional abilities. The patient should never abdicate his own powers of reasoning and evaluation because any professional speaks from a position of authority. The acknowledgement resignation, and acceptance of approaching death provides a crisis situation in the terms of Erikson's formulation (Erik Erikson). The individual is confronted with alternative life directions. The individual, as already described, may react by marking time or may use this event as a creative force for him/herself as well as the survivors. Ideally, this creative force will stimulate the person to develop a form of life separate from but coexisting with the old life style. The *new lifes,* can borrow many activities of the "old"; add some of the desires that previously had been put off for future times; and, finally, compress all of these into an allowable time-span. This development may circumvent the feelings of deterioration, loss, and lack of fulfillment for the patient. The family and other significant persons also have an opportunity to participate in positive action rather than passive handwringing, declarations of support.

As the treatment progresses, the dying person is able to work through the initial phases of denial, anger, bargaining and depression. The patient is then able to resign himself to the imposed limitations of his terminal affliction. The definitive moment of physical death is known only after the fact. Physical survival may continue for an hour, day, year, decade or more. The answer rather than question is what the individual does during the unknown time left.

Assisting the patient spiritually as well as psychologically, the PC's concern is directed towards the emotional health of the dying person rather than toward a bedside conversion. This, in turn, allows the patient to recognize and evaluate existing options which remain. These options include former activities, aspirations which have been put off as well as potentials previously not considered. Examples of these are the people who always wanted to travel but were waiting until . . . ; the person who always wanted to write a book but never had the time. The options, as emphasized must be evaluated and chosen in relation to their viability. The man with a coronary is no candidate for the 4 minute mile. The woman who is tone deaf is unlikely to develop into a concert pianist.

All options do not have the same chance of successful outcome. The PC is in a position to aid the patient to establish priorities. The patient may then select options which will enhance experiences, fulfillment and satisfaction. Thus, the patient is in a better position to evaluate his philosophy of life and death, to make peace with himself in terms of both his fulfillments and never to be completed dreams and aspirations and to allow for full spiritual development.

8
Helping the Dying Patient:
Guidance for Hospital Ministry
Roger Branch and Larry A. Platt

Few challenges equal those involved in ministering to patients who are dying slowly in hospitals. They severely tax ministers' theological, spiritual, social, and psychological resources.

For the patient, the experience of death itself is stressful. When that experience is drawn out over a period of days, weeks, or even months, the sufferer's courage, patience, and fortitude under the shadow of death become exhausted. Moreover, dying usually involves pain, weakness, and physical deterioration. The body fails and refuses to comply with the patient's expectations and commands. Indeed Kalish's (1985: 107) studies of fear of death emphasize that one of the elements of dying that people fear most is physical pain. While people do not anticipate emotional pain as they do physical suffering, when it does invade they often find it more devastating. The intense and unanticipated character of this emotional pain overwhelms the senses and taxes basic coping skills. In sum, personhood endures massive assault.

Characteristics of the hospital setting may also magnify the nonphysical agonies of dying. Because hospitals are formal organizations, social relationships are impersonal and depersonalizing to the patient (Sudnow, 1967). Modern medicine is organized around complex technology aimed at precision in diagnosing, monitoring, and treating physical disorders. It is a machine technology requiring that the patient be attached to a potentially vast array of equipment. These attachments

138

become bonds, and patients often feel as if they are mere extensions of machines or at least prisoners of them (Smith, 1986). In spite of humanitarian goals, the modern hospital exists as a paradox—an alien environment which tends to dehumanize even as it attempts to heal.

The hospital is foreign territory, an unfamiliar place where the patient never really feels at home (Glazer and Strauss, 1965). Everyday things from the toilet to toothpaste are out of place. Rooms and units designated by strange jargon or just initials, such as E.R., O.R., Oncology Center, or Palliative Care, dominate the patient's experience; he often doesn't know what they are or where they are. Family and familiar friends are visitors, given a limited welcome at best. This place belongs to someone else; small wonder that the desire to "go home" is so strong among patients. Place is part of self; an alien place threatens personhood.

Hospital-bound dying patients, along with family and friends, are especially vulnerable and in need of caring assistance. No single category of helping person is more appropriate to meet these needs than pastors and hospital chaplains. This challenging ministry demands character, insight, preparation, and capacity for self-giving; call it *agape*.

As Figure 1 indicates, hospital ministry to dying patients places the pastor or chaplain in a central position, linking the patient, hospital and health-care professionals, and family and friends in a network of service and communication. It serves to organize our examination of effective ministry within that network.

The Minister's Personal Orientation

Effective ministry to a dying person and his or her loved ones is for many people a profoundly difficult duty. The starting point is to analyze yourself. It begins with coming to grips with death itself—personally, spiritually, and theologically. Ignorance and fear cripple the minister's capacity to serve.

FIGURE 1

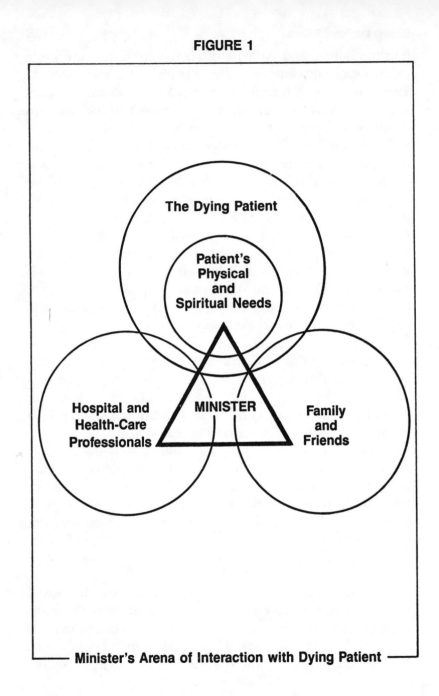

Minister's Arena of Interaction with Dying Patient

Analyze Your Assumptions and Expectations
Regarding the Dying Person

What do you expect to do to or for this individual? Specific attitudes, feelings, and actions flow from fundamental expectations. What is your basic goal with regard to dying patients —to save souls, to perform expected pastoral duties, to minister to the whole person in accordance with changing needs over time? The last is most needed; patience, strength, insight, and love are required. Patience is needed to let the dying person struggle with pain and mortality while the minister waits to be invited to contribute and share. Strength is required to help another wage a losing battle with death. Insight is necessary to see the patient's changing needs, feelings, and thoughts. And love! Only love can make the other three possible. Our first and final goal must be simply to love the dying person. Moment by moment we will try to do what that person needs most to have done, following the model of Christ. Through our caring presence with the dying we are priviledged to become instruments of His grace (Davidson, 1975).

In the quiet moments when we give all that is in us to reach out to the dying patient, a special ministry emerges that is like no other. The process of dying and death offers an opportunity for true Christian caring by which we forge a very personal bond among God, ourselves, and the dying patient. This gift born of dedicated service allows us to experience the glory of God's grace as He embraces both the living and the dying. It is as close as many of us will ever come during our time on earth to touching the face of God.

Assumptions also must be examined. A widespread false assumption is that the dying person does not know that death is inevitable or, if it is known, does not want to talk about it (Weisman, 1972). While such assumptions are rarely true, they affect the way we define our helping roles and react to the terminally ill patient. One who is trying to cope with a fatal illness and with the knowledge of impending death has special needs. Playing games of mutual deception about knowledge of death wastes precious time and energy. Despite its wasteful character, this drama of "mutual pretense" has been noted as a frequent context of interaction that must be confronted (Glazer and Strauss, 1965: 64-80). Since some of the special needs entail talking about death and its consequences, avoidance dooms effective ministry. When the patient is ready to discuss the subject, don't run away.

Be Honest with Yourself About Your Feelings Concerning the Dying Patient

Ministers are human, and they are products of the same culture which impels others to avoid dealing with death. Many find it difficult to accept the approaching death of a church member and friend. Talking to someone about his own impending death is even harder. Such conversation defies a near taboo in this society and requires a high level of mutual trust, vulnerability, and honesty.

Not everyone can handle death ministry. This should be understood. It is no cause for shame. Traumatic personal experience and lack of adequate preparation are but two of many reasons for such a limitation. Not every minister is an apt administrator or spell-binding pulpiteer, either. For a few, counseling and comforting the dying is a great and rewarding calling; others find it an unpleasant task. If you are among the latter, simply admit it to yourself. Not liking to do this thing is not a crime, so it is pointless to carry a burden of guilt (Lewis, 1961). Personal growth, training, and experience can help to make this service less painful and more rewarding. It is only required that you work at it in a disciplined, committed manner.

If for you this is an essential role, come to terms with it. Accept the pain and the inability to do everything every patient needs to have done. Being shaken by death is perfectly normal. Berdyaev (1960) was right in calling death the last great enemy of man. The minister who tries to be a superman is courting self-destruction. To know and admit your fear and limitations in the face of death is to know the truth "and the truth will make you free" (John 8:32, RSV).

Even those who can work effectively with *most* terminally ill people may find difficulty in dealing with *some* patients in the same condition. How you feel about *that* particular dying patient or *that* particular type of illness can be critically important. Close relationships or relationships that are strained, superficial, or reserved can interfere with counseling. Personal experience with such "dreaded diseases" as cancer or Alzheimer's disease can so sear the psyche that working with others who have the malady brings back anguished memories.

The point is that the minister must examine the situation carefully. Feelings of reluctance and limitation are normal. However, the question of why the reluctance exists and how deep it runs must be answered in order to understand oneself and know how to minister to this person in the midst of life's deepest need.

Interacting with the Patient to Meet Physical and Spiritual Needs

The focus of the arena of interaction depicted in Figure 1 is that which goes on between the minister and the dying patient. The latter is at one of life's most extreme points, frequently a spiritual and emotional as well as physical crisis time. Ministers who serve dying patients will find the following guidelines useful.

Put Yourself in the Patient's Place

The need is for profound empathy, not sympathy, in serving the dying person. "Getting inside" the other person involves understanding her or his total pain. The condition is terminal and predictably the physical pain is often intense. The fear and anxiety of facing one's own death also create a special kind of anguish, although some discover a way to conquer it and find security.

One aspect of this total pain is the loss of autonomy or dominance over oneself. Inside a hospital and under the control of medical professionals and staff members, the patient gives up major slices of the self. While the loss of control over one's own body usually meets with some resistance, pressures to "be a good patient" by conforming totally to rules and directions may lead to the "learned helplessness" (Salingman, 1975) syndrome.

In the name of treatment and the efficient management of hospital activities, medical and organization personnel return patients to a childlike condition of dependency. Patients learn to be helpless again because they are praised for being cooperative or because they don't know what else to do in this unfamiliar setting. Although men tend to struggle more against this loss of being "in charge," both men and women generally surrender to learned helplessness. This development is often associated with marked degeneration of physical and emotional well-being. It represents withdrawal from living because the self has been impoverished.

Part of the loss of personhood during this terminal state in a medical facility results from the enduring character of the condition. Being controlled by machines and coolly detached medical personnel in even the most intimate aspects of physical functioning is fundamentally dehumanizing, even over a short period of time. For most patients this is but a temporary humiliation. However, dying takes a long time for many people due to the nature of most of today's terminal illnesses and of the life-prolonging techniques of modern medical science. This unremitting erosion of personhood is crushing and often leads to the "social death" of the person well before the onset of "physical" death (Sudnow, 1967).

Dying patients endure many sorts of pain. This might include religious doubts, feelings of being betrayed or abandoned by God, and questions about life after death. You must imagine yourself in that person's place. Be sensitive to interactional cues—direct statements, aside remarks, oblique references, and physical gestures—that help to define patient attitudes (Kübler-Ross, 1969). Remember that attitudes change, in some cases quickly, in response to changing conditions, feelings, and needs.

Respond to the Changing Needs of the Dying Patient

Following an early work by Elizabeth Kübler-Ross (1969), a number of people have written and spoken of "stages of dying" in describing patterns of change among dying patients. In fact people do not all follow an invariant path of progressive stages in their feelings and behavior, and counselors who wait for this to happen are naive (Fitchett, 1980). The real goal of the stages concept was to draw attention to the fact that patients do change. Different needs and issues become paramount. Anticipating this change, helping persons can more effectively respond to the needs as they arise (Kalish, 1985: 132-136).

Understand that the dying person will not be the same every day. Be prepared for changes beyond the predictable physical ones. When the patient is different, he must be treated differently. For example, sudden displays of resentment and anger are not unusual, even among people of strong faith and even temperament. While the minister is losing one friend and church member, the dying person is losing everyone. Responses to this crushing knowledge include anger, resentment, and depression. In a sense, any or all of these are appropriate for such an overwhelming experience (Turnbull, 1986).

What is the best way for the minister to respond? In some cases perhaps a reassurance of eternal salvation works best. In other cases a different approach might be most helpful. Try asking, "What bothers you most?" This allows the patient to vocalize pent-up frustrations and fears, and talking it out may be highly therapeutic. Asking, "What could we do to make things better?" often leads to practical actions that fill heart-felt needs of the patient.

In response to such a question, one man stated emphatically that he wanted to see a son and his family who lived in another section of the country. He indicated that he knew that he was dying and understood that his son could afford to come only one time. "I don't want him to wait until the funeral to come because I will not get to see him or his wife and children. I wish he would come to me now and not be concerned about the funeral." The son came, and the father's depression lifted.

Remember the Value of Humor and Laughter

Just as there is no single patient condition but a stream of changing needs, so also there is no single approach to helping. Humor is a normal part of human life. It has important uses under the circumstances of terminal illness.

We need humor to help deal with the obviously strong emotional burden of self and others. Thus, it becomes a tool for evoking positive mood changes, lifting depression, and diffusing anxiety.

With some people, humor works well in communicating profound truth. It can be valuable in producing insight. Injected with unusual twists, humor lets us think the unthinkable. Then it will later become possible to speak further about the unspeakable.

Don't Expect Instant Resolution of Problems

Part of the American mind-set expects problems to be solved, and quickly. Troubled people cannot be pressed into timetables. Usually time is needed just to develop the sort of mutual trust necessary for a dying person to share the thoughts and feelings generated by the terminal condition. Only then can the counselor begin to help.

Moreover, the patient does not follow a neat and satisfying pattern of progressive adaptation. Regression to previous emotional and spiritual conditions should be expected. Counselors should also accept that the final resolution of certain problems for the dying person may not be possible.

It Is Not Necessary for the Patient to Die in a "Therapeutic State of Grace"

Counselors tend to develop goals for terminal patients. Insight, acceptance, and tranquility are defined as necessary accomplishments in order for a person to die properly. They often forget that these people are not going to get well. Except for the benefits of the moment, having a positive attitude may have little value for a person who cannot use it as a step toward a happier future.

A dying person does not have to die in such a way that others will approve and declare it appropriate. There is no right way to do it, no set of stages which must be followed to a "therapeutic state of grace" (Shneideman, 1978).

The appropriate ministry is to bring comfort, caring, acceptance, and assistance in every way possible. Resist the temptation to establish an agenda for psychological progress or positive adaptation. Remember that dying is a very negative experience for most people. Unrealistic expectations lead to frustrations and feelings of failure.

"Success" may be to help the patient cope as much as possible with pain, anxiety, loss, and fear. If at the end he still cries out in fear or anger, you have not failed. Never forget the wideness of God's mercy—the patient has not failed either.

Be a Good Listener

Death is an assault on what is all too often our oversimplified conceptions of life. Under such stress, the prevailing tendency is for helping persons to talk too much. Allowing patients to talk is a cardinal rule if their state of physical health permits. Pay attention. Active listening (Trotzer, 1977) is a powerful therapeutic strategy. There may be messages at more than one level of communication. What needs or meanings, conscious or unconscious, are being sent to you?

Express your willingness to enter the world of the dying patient. Your genuine desire to share in the experience of the dying person is often enough even if the invitation from the dying patient is not forthcoming.

Be willing to sit in silence. Feel good about a relationship in which a patient is comfortable with the passage of long periods of time with neither person speaking. More than one thoughtful visitor has been surprised at the end of a virtually silent visit by hearing the patient say, "Thank-you so much for coming; you've been such a comfort to me." One pastor's wife with a special touch in hospital ministry will sometimes say, "You look like you could use a little rest. If you don't feel like talking, I'll just sit here with you and read a bit. I'll be right here if you need me for anything."

This sort of silence is not empty. It communicates caring, concern, and real presence. It is far better than superficial conversation. Glib phrases fill the air; a caring presence fills a room.

Be Aware of the Patient's Energy Level

What you attempt to do on a given day should depend upon the patient's condition, both in terms of needs and capacities. The latter are defined to a great degree by level of physical energy. Low energy accompanied by considerable pain might signal a brief, quiet visit or none at all. Judging energy level requires careful observation, sensitivity to communication cues, and an honest relationship which encourages the patient to say how he feels.

Be There

The patient must be able to depend on you. Maintain a regular schedule as far as possible. Leave information about where you can be located in an emergency. The terrible task of dying is the patient's full-time job. Your faithfulness as a helping person in that task is crucial. As a terminally ill nurse wrote in an open letter to Elizabeth Kübler-Ross (1975: 26), "We may ask for whys and wherefores, but we don't really expect answers. Don't run away—wait—all I want to know is that there will be someone to hold my hand when I need it. I am afraid."

The Hospital Setting: Working with Health-Care Professionals

Effective hospital ministry requires familiarity with the hospital environment: its arrangements, facilities, terminology, basic routines, and procedures. Most of all, it demands a good working relationship with physicians, nurses, and other staff members. The minister must devote time and attention to learning these details and ask some carefully chosen questions to become familiar with the hospital and its workings. Fortunately hospitals are similar in many ways, and lessons learned in one tend to carry over to others. Each hospital also differs from others in various ways, so learning the peculiarity of each is necessary.

A positive working relationship with health-care professionals and the hospital administration is critically important and sometimes difficult to establish. Bluntly stated, some of them have little respect for or confidence in ministers. Many sorts of people bear the title of minister. Unfortunately their knowledge, professionalism, and skills vary radically. Sometimes their influence is disruptive and threatening to the well-being of patients. Don't be surprised if you have to win the confidence of physicians and hospital personnel. Remember also that some health-care professionals are profoundly aware of their status and authority and are often reluctant to share the information which is basic to their power (Mauksch, 1975).

The best way to develop effective working relationships is to state your goals simply and straightforwardly. You might arrange a five-minute spot to introduce yourself during a hospital staff meeting or work through a process of meeting personnel on a one-by-one basis. The hospital administrator should know who you are. Don't be a snob; lower status personnel, such as housekeeping staff, should never be ignored. Most of all, let your professionalism, training, common sense, tact, and courtesy be obvious. The minister does not have an inherent right to know about a patient's physical condition or to have extraordinary access to the patient. However, those who are in charge of the patient's welfare may decide that such knowledge and access might help the patient. It is up to the minister to demonstrate his value and trustworthiness.

Beyond this fundamental step of establishing an accepted role in the hospital, four dimensions of that role would be explored.

Learn About the Patient's Condition Before Visiting

A good starting place for a hospital room visit is the appropriate nursing station. If possible, it is a good idea to ask about the patient's present condition and any recent changes. This information could affect one's visit, even postpone it. For example, if the patient has just completed some painful or exhausting tests and received medication to relieve the discomfort, visitation should be delayed to encourage rest and recovery from the ordeal.

A similar issue is medication. You might want to ask if the patient is receiving any medication or undergoing any procedures of which you should be aware. First, you should not do anything that might interfere with any sort of medical treatment. Second, the effects of such treatment could impact what you are able to do in the way of counseling at that time.

Become Familiar with the Hospital

Know the overall facility—its physical arrangements, what goes on where. Unfamiliarity breeds anxiety. Therefore, to feel comfortable you need to know your way around. This knowledge also may be valuable in explaining the hospital to patients, easing some of their anxieties about the unfamiliar place.

While it is not necessary to become an expert in medical care, one should understand the treatment gadgetry encountered in hospital rooms. "What does this piece of technology do and how does it work?" If you can answer this question, you will be unlikely to interfere with its performance. In a room full of such equipment, you must be aware of where you sit or stand. For example, sitting on the patient's bed is usually not a good idea. While it may seem a natural response, it is sometimes painful to the patient and contrary to operating policy in some hospitals.

Be Prepared to Serve as a Link Between Patient and Health Care Professionals

Sometimes the minister is called upon to serve as liaison person between patient and health-care personnel. Reluctant or uninformed patients may feel intimidated, unsure of themselves, and awed by either high-status, knowledgeable health professionals or by huge, complex, mysterious hospitals. Thus, they fail to report problems, communicate adequately, ask questions, or demand service (Hinton, 1972). In attempting to meet the total needs of patients, ministers can intercede as a channel of communication and help interpret their needs to appropriate caregivers. Avoid interference in patient-physician relations and overpresumptuousness in speaking for a patient, but don't remain silent in cases that cry out for assistance.

In fact, health-care specialists sometimes ask trusted ministers for help. Knowing their church members well, ministers may be able to communicate with them better than anyone in the hospital. They also can provide useful information about patients whom they know well, information that might be difficult to secure anywhere else. Do not be reluctant to consult with the health-care staff concerning things you need to know about the patient or possible ways you might help them in serving the patient.

Be There

The minister must provide a dependable presence. Getting to be known and trusted by medical and administrative personnel requires time. You must be observed in action. Intercessory or liaison activities can happen only if the minister is available, if not instantly then at least within a reasonably short time.

Interacting with Family and Friends

Dying is a traumatic experience for the victim's entire social network. Oftentimes a meaningful ministry to the dying person requires the establishment of effective communication and interaction with the broad circle of family and friends who are linked to the terminally ill patient. The opportunities for Christian service are manifold and encompass the needs of both the living and the dying.

Serve the Family as Well as the Patient

Like the patient, family members face uncertainty, fear, loss of roles and part of the self, emotional agony, and a type of defeat. The net result is sometimes a crisis of faith. The special need for spiritual help and guidance is so obvious as to require no further comment.

Consider the Special Needs of Children

A widespread assumption seems to be that diminished size means diminished feelings or that children don't understand what is happening and, therefore, aren't very disturbed by it all. They are not too young to know. Even when they fail to understand, they are aware that something is seriously wrong and are made anxious by the fact that no one tells them anything. If any people fail to have a chance to talk or to become adequately informed, it will be the children.

Many hospitals have rules that bar children under age twelve to fourteen. Thus, children frequently see hospital settings as awful places that swallow up a parent, a grandparent, or a sibling (Wass and Corr, 1984). The minister should offer to the children special words of explanation and reassurance and remind adult family members about the children's needs. In the case of a dying patient, the minister can often arrange a relaxation of rules to allow a visit for the children. Make the most of such occasions, encourage as much expression of love and concern as possible. The value of these experiences is beyond measure for patients and children alike.

Do Not Neglect the Needs of the Dying Person's Friends

When the patient's condition becomes critical, friends are often shut out. They may be just as loving, caring, and emotionally pained as the family but barred from their sick friend's presence. If the patient is in an intensive care unit, as is often the case near the end of a terminal illness, friends are denied access by many hospitals. Quite simply, the critical character of the dying patient's physical condition may not allow everyone to visit who shares a deep concern for the patient. The minister can serve these friends by helping to keep them informed, carrying messages for them, and counseling them in terms of their spiritual and emotional needs.

Act as a Liaison Between the Medical Staff and Family and Friends

If the minister can achieve something of an insider position in the treatment system, he can perform valuable services. Just as some patients find it difficult to deal with the health-care professions who attempt to serve them, their loved ones may have similar difficulties. When this is the case, the minister can serve as a communication link among all involved. "Doctor, what can I tell Bob's friends about his condition when they ask about him at prayer meeting tonight?" Such a tactfully phrased question usually brings reliable information.

Conveying this information is a valuable service to family and friends.

Be a Facilitator in Secular as Well as Sacred Matters

Doing some ordinary things needed by patients and their families constitutes genuine service and often undergirds the more obviously religious aspects of ministry. Pour a glass of water; write a letter; help make arrangements for drawing up a will. Prayer and insightful counseling are not the only valid expressions of ministry. In the "inasmuch" passage of Matthew's Gospel (25:32-46), Jesus defined ordinary acts of mercy to people in need as service to Him.

Prepare to Make the Transition to
Meeting the Needs of Family and Friends
Following the Death of the Patient

As death approaches, the role of the minister takes on additional dimensions in working with family and friends. The minister can help them prepare for and move into the transition from dying to death. If death is treated as real and certain, they will experience anticipatory grief (Lindemann, 1944). It is as real and painful as that which occurs after death and requires the same caring ministry. Some writers contend that anticipatory grief, if managed well, reduces the intensiveness of after-death grief in many cases (Fulton and Fulton, 1970).

The minister can sometimes assist the patient and family in tying up loose ends even before death occurs. It is not unusual for people to want to deal with funeral arrangements, place of burial, the issue of avoidance of "heroic measures" to maintain life in a terminal situation, and other important matters when an atmosphere of open, honest communication exists. Helping the dying patient and the family and friends resolve any unfinished business can be a significant service.

Finally, in collaboration with the physician, the minister can help to assemble family and friends at the approach of death.

Helping the survivors reach distant loved ones and assisting in notifying the many close friends and associates is of invaluable aid and will be remembered as an act of compassion and concern.

Be There

Be dependably available for family and friends during the dying of a loved one, as well as for the patient and those who provide medical care. This crisis time lays bare many needs, some of which require the comfort and guidance of a minister. Although the physical death may have been anticipated, people often do not confront the true reality of loss until the official pronouncement of death. When death finally comes, it triggers severe emotional stress. The deep pain fostered by the realization that the deceased is permanently lost to them now rushes in, and the comfort of the minister is never more needed or appreciated.

References

Berdyaev, Nokalai. 1960. *The Nature and Destiny of Man.* London: Geoffrey Bles, Publishing.

Davidson, Glen. 1975. *Living with Dying.* Minneapolis: Augsburg Publishing House.

Fitchett, G. 1980. "Its Time to Bury the Stage Theory of Death and Dying." *Oncology Nurse Exchange* 2(3):1-5.

Fulton, R. and J. Fulton. 1977. "A Psychosocial Aspect of Terminal Care: Anticipatory Grief."

Glaser, Barney and Anselm Strauss. 1965. *Awareness of Dying,* Chicago: Aldine Publishing Company.

Hinton, John. 1972. *Dying.* Middlesex, Eng.: Penguin Books.

Kalish, Richard. 1985. *Death, Grief and Caring Relationships,* 2nd Ed. Monterey, Calif.: Brooks/Cole Publishing Company.

Kübler-Ross, E. 1969. *On Death and Dying.*

Lewis, C. 1961. *A Grief Observed.*

Lindemann, E. 1944. "Symptomology and Management of Acute Grief." *American Journal of Psychiatry.* 101:141-148.

Mauksch, Hans. 1975. "The Organizational Context of Dying." In Elizabeth Kübler-

Ross, ed. *Death, The Final Stage of Growth.* Englewood Cliffs, N.J.: Prentice-Hall, Inc.

Shneidman, Edwin. 1978. "Some Aspects of Psychotherapy with Dying Persons." In Charles Garfield ed. *Psychosocial Care of the Dying Patient,* New York: McGraw-Hill Book Company.

Seligman, M. 1975. *Helplessness: On Depression, Development and Death.* San Francisco: W. H. Fresman.

Smith, W. J. 1985. *Dying in the Human Life Cycle.*

Sudnow, David. 1967. *Passing On: The Social Organization of Dying.* Englewood Cliffs, N.J.: Prentice-Hall, Inc.

Trotzer, James. 1977. *The Counselor and the Group: Integrating Theory and Practice.* Monterey, Calif.: Brooks/Cole Publishing Company.

Turnbull, R. ed. 1986. *Terminal Care.*

Wass, Hannelore and Charles Corr, eds. 1984. *Helping Children Cope With Death: Guidelines and Resources.* New York: McGraw-Hill Book Company.

Weisman, A. D. 1972. *On Death and Denying: A Psychiatric Study of Terminality.*

9
Telling the Truth
to the Terminally Ill Patient
James E. Giles

The diagnosis of terminal illness occurs in a medical context. It follows, then, that the initial decision whether or how much to tell the patient depends on how well he "can take" being told that he is terminally ill. He tends to create the boundaries within which others—clergy, therapists, counselors, nurses, and even family—must operate. That is, few would tell a person that he is terminally ill when the physician has deemed it inappropriate to tell him. And it is a marked tendency of physicians not to tell the truth to the terminally ill patient. It is my position that the terminally ill should be told the truth and that almost all attempts to establish exceptions to telling the truth in this situation fail. In what follows I will critically examine the reasons most often given by physicians to defend their decisions not to tell the truth.

Among ordinary persons as well as ethicists telling the truth is regarded as one of the most binding human obligations. Without truthfulness, communication between individuals would be impossible. But in the medical context, telling the truth to the terminally ill patient tends to be the exception and not the rule. This is not only an exception to the general, human obligation to tell the truth, but also contradicts the patient's purpose in consulting the physician, i.e., to learn about his condition, its diagnosis and prognosis. Why would the physician not tell the truth?

One reason is that many physicians feel that their patients would not understand the nature of their illnesses even if they

157

were told the truth. Therefore, these physicians conclude that even attempting to tell the truth would be fruitless.

While it is true that patients may have difficulty grasping medical information, I would point out that being truthful does not require that the patient be made to understand every last detail of his illness. Truthfulness requires that the physician explain in language comprehensible to the patient the nature of his condition. The discharge of this obligation does not require a mini-course in medicine. Ironically, in the case of the terminally ill patient, it is precisely the aspect of the patient's condition which would be most comprehensible to the patient—the fact that it is terminal—which physicians most often refuse to reveal to their patients.

Another reason given for not telling the terminally ill the truth about their condition is that to tell a patient that he is terminally is to be cruel. Let the patient live out his last days thinking that he is going to recover eventually. A terminally ill patient, especially a cancer victim, would probably go to pieces if told the truth. A bit of conventional wisdom that makes the rounds of medical schools and that is learned by young interns is not to tell a patient near an open window that he has terminal cancer. Many physicians give as their reason for not telling the terminal cancer victim the true nature of his condition their fear that the patient might commit suicide. When pressed, these physicians find it difficult to cite even one such incident which they themselves have verified. The point is that the physicians themselves simply cannot acknowledge that terminally patients would want to be told the truth.

Such widespread evasion would be understandable, even if not justifiable, if patients themselves expressed the wish not to be told. But studies show that terminally ill patients, even those with cancer, wish to be told the truth. But in spite of these findings, physicians generally persist in the belief that patients do not wish to be told the truth. Even direct requests by patients to the physician for the truth are almost always ignored unless the physician is satisfied that the patient "can take it."

Several years ago, I saw a short film which brought this point home to me. Actually, it was a film within a film. First, Elizabeth Kübler-Ross, who of course has written extensively about the terminally ill, interviewed a young man who had been told that he had cancer and would probably be dead within the year. In the interview, he showed calmness and serenity in the face of his own death. This filmed interview was then shown to a group of young physicians and their reactions were filmed in turn. All of them expressed utter disbelief that the young man could be so unruffled. I seem to recall that one of them even suggested that the interview had been staged. These physicians could not accept the fact that the man did not go to pieces or lapse into a state of hopeless depression. Like other physicians, they could not believe that a terminally patient would be able to take being told the truth.

Reflecting on these reactions, it became increasingly clear to me that physicians, who otherwise pride themselves on being rational and dispassionate, are governed by emotional predispositions in dealing with terminally ill patients. There are, I think, two sources of this emotional response of physicians to terminal illness. First, it has been found that physicians tend to have a greater fear of death than laypersons, sick or healthy. Therefore, it is easy to understand that physicians, like most of us, are liable to project their own response to death onto others. They assume that others fear death with the same intensity as they do. But of course this assumption is not supported by studies which show that most individuals want to know the truth. Most patients are not so paralyzed by fear of death that they refuse to face unpleasant facts.

The second source of the physician's emotional response is that the prognosis of death represents a wrenching defeat for them. The physician's training has been to stave off death, training shaped by the central imperative of modern medicine: cure. If the physician cannot cure he is admitting personal and professional failure. The terminally ill patient mocks the powers claimed by the physician.

The only way to overcome the attitude that death represents defeat for the physician is for him to affirm, or better reaffirm, that the central imperative of medicine is care not cure. Cure is subsidiary, care is primary. The physician cannot always cure, but he can always care.

The hospice approach to terminal illness embodies this affirmation. Cure is not an issue. The hospice physician does not feel defeated by his inability to cure. He, along with the rest of the hospice staff, stresses care. I recall Cicely Saunders' reply to someone who expressed surprise that there was no Intensive Care Unit—which more accurately should be called an Intensive *Cure* Unit—at St. Christopher's Hospice: all we have here, she said, is intensive care.

I have stressed the emotional source of the physician's reluctance to tell the truth to the terminally ill patient because this reluctance cannot be justified on practical grounds. For example, the anxiety which physicians claim the patient would feel upon receiving news of terminal illness is matched by the anxiety the patient suffers when he is uncertain as to his condition. What I mean is that physicians determined not to tell the truth will either lie to their patients or speak evasively. The patient who is told a direct lie obviously expects to recover. When his condition worsens, which it must, he will begin to doubt what the physician has told him. The patient who is spoken to evasively will also recognize that he is not getting better and any suspicion about the seriousness of his condition will be confirmed. Moreover, in both cases, others— family, hospital staff, and counselors—will most likely know the truth and the patient will eventually pick up hints and slips which will lead him to the truth. Therefore, I would argue that on practical grounds, it is debatable whether attempts to deceive the terminally ill patient are ever that successful.

Meanwhile, this deception can be counterproductive. As more and more patients and would-be patients begin to recognize that they will not be told the truth if they are terminally ill, the medical profession begins to lose its credibility. It is assumed that physicians will not tell the truth. This has two negative consequences. First, the widespread perception that physicians do not tell the truth erodes the trust and cooperation which physicians need in order to perform their tasks efficiently and effectively. Without the trust and cooperation of the patient the physician's ability to treat him will be seriously hindered. Second, it is interesting to speculate about how many people suffer acute anxiety or even, in extreme cases, attempt suicide because they believe that they are terminally ill even though their physicians have assured them that they are not. In other words, if physicians are thought not to tell the truth, then patients who have symptoms which are compatible with the presence of terminal illness, but which actually indicate a less serious, non-terminal condition might easily think that they are suffering a terminal condition because they do not believe the assurances from their physicians to the contrary.

In sum, physicians who do not tell the truth cause harm in two ways. First, they lower the overall credibility of the medical profession, making patients more mistrustful of physicians. Second, undue anxiety and uncertainty on the part of the non-terminally ill patient is likely to occur because, lacking confidence that physicians routinely tell the truth to terminally ill patients, patients may suspect that they are terminally ill and that the physician is simply lying when he says that the patient is not terminally ill. Since I do not know of any studies of how many patients might react in this way, I cannot even estimate the number of patients so affected. But I would suspect that the number is not insignificant.

However, I have saved what to me is the most decisive argument against not telling the truth until last. The basic assumption behind not telling the truth is that the physician knows better than the patient himself how the patient would react to news of his terminal illness. But the physician is not ethically justified in withholding from the patient the vital information that his process of dying is underway. The decision how to die is just as crucial for a person as the decision how to live. The physician who refuses—for selfish or unselfish reasons—to inform the terminally ill patient of his approaching death robs that patient of the ability to make his own choices about how he wishes to live during the time left to him. A religious person, for example, most definitely would want to know in order to make his peace with God.

In attempting to spare the patient harm by not telling the truth, the physician is, I believe, allowing another and even greater harm, the one which inevitably will occur when the patient finally realizes that he has not been told the truth and that he is going to die. And by then the patient's ability to make meaningful decisions, let alone the ability to act on them, will most likely to seriously impaired, if not impossible.

Cicely Saunders relates the story of a woman who was dying with metastic breast cancer. She was not told the truth and was implicitly encouraged by those who attended her to hope for some new treatment. After a few weeks she died. Another patient who witnessed what happened felt that she should have been told the truth because her last days should have been spent "on something more important than false hope." The patient went on to say that "I can face dying. I can face pain, but what I can't face is being treated as less than a person." To be a person, even if one is a dying person, means to make decisions which affect one's life and this cannot be done if one does not have true knowledge of one's condition.

The hospice approach to the terminally ill patient is an excellent illustration of this point. This approach is based on open communication with the patient, involving the patient in the decisions made about his care and treatment. The hospice is set up to help the patient to discover his own way of coping with and making meaningful his death. And this is impossible to accomplish without telling the patient the truth. Without knowledge of his terminal condition, the patient would not be able to decide, on the basis of his values and value-priorities, how his last days will be spent. We owe the dying person the opportunity: to exercise his decision-making for the last time. We ought not to decide for him, which is exactly what we do when we do not tell him the truth about his condition.

Unless the patient has explicitly asked not to be told the truth, I feel that he should be routinely told the truth. To do otherwise is to prevent him from choosing his own way of dying, the last choice he is called upon to make. We cannot live another's life for him, nor can we die his death. But in not telling the truth we are substituting our own decision for his, opting for a dying process characterized by deception, illusion and false hope. Dying, like living, can be full of surprises: death-bed reconciliations, attainment of blinding insights which give meaning to one's life and unexpected serenity. The mystery of human individuality is at the heart of the matter. To suppress this individuality by enmeshing it in a web of lies, deceptions and evasions about its impending end, is to banish the possibility of such surprises, to deny it the chance to cope in its own way with its death. We help that individuality and show it respect by sensitivity to its needs, by care, by accompanying it on its journey to death and most of all by being open and truthful with it.

10
Some Aspects of Psychotherapy with Dying Persons

Edwin S. Shneidman

From the psychosocial point of view, the primary task of helping the dying person is to focus on the *person*—not the biochemistry or pathology of the diseased organs, but a human being who is a living beehive of emotions, including (and especially) anxiety, the fight for control, and terror. And, with a dying person, there is another grim omnipresent fact in the picture: time is finite. The situation is dramatic, unlike that of psychotherapy with an essentially physically healthy person, where time seems "endless" and there is no push by the pages of the calendar. One of the main points of this chapter is that just as psychotherapy is, in some fundamental ways, clearly different from "ordinary talk," so working psychotherapeutically with a dying person involves some important differences from the usual modes of psychotherapy.

I

At the outset it is only reasonable that I indicate some issues that are fundamental to understanding any list of therapeutic suggestions. The "rules" for psychotherapy are rather easy to comprehend but their more meaningful application within the context of a stressful dying scenario has to take into account certain subtleties that lie behind the obvious and visible drama. We must look behind the apparent dying scenario if we wish to encompass the powerful and poignant psychological richness inherent in the dying drama. To be specific, I

164

shall suggest that there are three aspects of the dying process that need to be kept in mind.

A. Philosophic (Moral-Ethical-Epistemological) Aspects of the Dying Process

One can begin with the assertion that, typically, a death is a dyadic event, involving the chief protagonist (the dying person) and the survivors—basically an I-thou relationship. Toynbee (1969) has stated it succinctly:

> The two-sidedness of death is a fundamental feature of death
> . . . There are always two parties to a death: the person who
> dies and the survivors who are bereaved . . . the sting of death
> is less sharp for the person who dies than it is for the bereaved
> survivor. This is, as I see it, the capital fact about the relation
> between living and dying. There are two parties to the suffer-
> ing that death inflicts: and in the apportionment of this suffer-
> ing, the survivor takes the brunt.

Often the situation is even more complicated, involving several persons as in the two vignettes below.

1. A physician asks me to see one of his patients. He tells me beforehand that her numerous physical pains and complaints have absolutely no organic basis. I see her and talk with her. As much as I try to eschew simplistic diagnostic labels for a complicated human being, the tag of "agitated depression" seems to describe her rather accurately. She is complaining, pain filled; she wrings her hands; her brow is furrowed; she is restless; fidgety, tearful, woebegone. She looks older than her forty years.

   The story is this: Her wealthy husband has a terminal disease. He may very well be dead in a few years or even much sooner. He has told her that she makes him nervous and that he cannot stand her. He has placed her in a private nursing home. She hates that nursing home and wants to return to her own home. Coincidentally, he has employed a practical nurse to massage his muscular pains and also to act as chauffeur and "keeper" for his wife.

At the end of my session with the wife, the nurse comes into the office to take her back to the nursing home. She is rather heavily made up and has a striking figure. The picture is suddenly clear to me. The practical nurse is the husband's mistress. The wife has been evicted from her own home. "But, after all," says the doctor, "the poor man is dying."

2. A seventy-year-old man has cancer of the esophagus. He received a course of chemotherapy, which made him excruciatingly uncomfortable—nausea, vertigo, vomiting. Several weeks after the treatment he began to show memory loss, some confusion, and uncharacteristic irritability. A thorough neurological examination disclosed a malignant brain tumor. Another course of treatment was suggested. His son—a physician (neurologist) in another city (who was in daily telephone communication with his parents)—asked his father's doctor to forgo the treatments. To me, on the telephone, the son said: "What is the point of an unknown amount of possible good compared to an onerous treatment of absolutely uncertain benefit imbedded in a procedure which will give him a substantial amount of certain torture?" The local treating physician was incensed. The wife was in a quandary. The treating physician demanded that the patient be told "all the facts" and be permitted to make up his own mind. The physician-son retorted that his father, not being medically trained, was in no position to evaluate "all the facts," and more than that, his mind—specifically his brain—was no longer able to make the ordinary judgments of which he had been previously capable. As the mother's psychotherapist, I marveled at the sad game of what I called "Who owns the body?"

Toynbee raises the question of who, in the total suffering a death inflicts, is hurt the most? The two criteria are comfort and dignity—their opposites are pain and humiliation (degradation).

Imagine for each of the two vignettes cited above a chart in the shape of a circle. In each there seem to be four characters: in the first, the husband, the wife, the mistress, and the doctor; in the second, the father, the mother, the son, and the doctor. The second case is compounded by the fact that we do not know, from day to day, what the father can think or experience. How should the calculations of the percentages of dignity, self-esteem, well-being, comfort, sense of accomplishment, freedom from pain, and so on be made? Who should be given the largest percentage: who the least? Should, in the first case, the wife be scapegoated—given electric shocks for her "depression?" In the second case, should the treating physician's wishes—who may have the patient on some research protocol as part of a grant—supersede, in the name of science and possible help for future patients (not to mention the physician's narcissistic and professional investment in his research), the physician-son's emotional feelings about his father's dignity and comfort?

Far from being esoteric abstractions, these philosophic points touch on the deepest questions relating to death: Who have become the priests of death? What are the citizen's rights to "death with dignity"? When can a spouse or grown child say for a loved one, "Enough"?

B. Sociological (Situational) Aspects of the Dying Process

Inasmuch as nowadays, the majority of terminally ill persons die in institutions—hospitals or nursing homes—it is appropriate to ask: What are the constraints of the social environment? The recent observations and reports of field sociologists such as David Sudnow, author of *Passing On* (1967) (an intriguing description of "what actually happens" in hospitals, especially in emergency rooms and the various uses to which fresh corpses are put), and Barney Glaser and Anselm Strauss, authors of *Awareness of Dying* (1965) and *Time for Dying* (1968) (with their enlightening concepts of "mutual pretense" and "dying trajectory"), teach us that a great deal "goes on" in the institutional interplay that is neither in the organizational chart nor in the brochure given to visitors.

Whether or not a person is resuscitated; how many minutes doctors and nurses spend in a dying person's room; whether a person will be "pronounced dead" on this hospital shift or that; whether or not interns will practice surgery on the dead body—all these occurrences, and others, are what realistic sociologists tell us about—and it behooves us to listen. In an understanding of the dying person, we need to include a keen situational view of the events.

Glaser and Strauss's concept of "the dying trajectory" deserves our close attention. In *Time for Dying* they say:

> When the dying patient's hospital career begins—when he is admitted to the hospital and a specific service—the staff in solo and in concert make initial definitions of the patient's trajectory. They expect him to linger, to die quickly, or to approach death at some pace between these extremes. . . . Since the definition of trajectory influences behavior, these differing definitions may create inconsistencies in the staff's care of and interaction with the patient, with consequent problems for the staff itself, family and patient.

When ordinary, well-functioning individuals are asked about what they consider to be most important to them if they were dying, they usually list "control"—having some measure of "say" over their own treatment and management—as the most important item (followed by relief from pain, which can, in the last analysis, also be subsumed under control). But we see that there are often conflicting agendas between the dying person and his or her fight for dignity (self-control, autonomy) and the hospital staff and their interest in assigning that person (called "patient") to certain roles, including even the pace or rate at which those roles are to be played.

In order to be a "good patient," one has to die on schedule, in accordance with the dying trajectory mapped by the staff. To die too early, unexpectedly, is an embarrassment to hospital staff; but what is more surprising (and of psycho-social interest), is that to linger too long, beyond the projected trajectory, can be an even greater embarrassment to hospital staff—and a great strain on the next of kin who may have premourned and set their mind's clock for a specific death date, which, if not met, becomes painfully overdue.

C. Psychological (Characterological) Aspects of the Dying Process

For the terminally ill person, the time of dying is a multi-scened drama, with elements of Shakespearean tragedy and historical (introspective) pageant. It is probably true that each person dies idiosyncratically alone, "in a notably personal way," but nonetheless there are generalizations that can be made about the dying process. From a psychological point of view, the most interesting question is what are the psychological characteristics of the dying process.

In the current thanatological scene there are those who write about fewer than a half-dozen stages lived through in a specific order—not to mention the even more obfuscating writing of a life after death. My own experiences have led me to rather different conclusions. In working with dying persons I see a wide range of human emotions—few in some people, dozens in others—experienced in a variety of orderings, reorderings, and arrangements. The one psychological mechanism that seems ubiquitous is denial, which can appear or reappear at any time. (See Avery Weisman's *On Dying and Denying* (1972).) Nor is there any natural law that an individual has to achieve closure before death sets its seal. In fact, most people die too soon or too late, with loose threads and fragments of agenda uncompleted.

My own notion is more general in scope; more specific in content. It borrows from Adolph Meyer and Henry A. Murray in its spirit. My general hypothesis is that a *dying person's flow of behaviors will reflect or parallel that person's previous segments of behaviors, specifically those behaviors relating to threat, stress, or failure.* There are certain deep *consistencies* in human beings. Individuals die more-or-less characteristically as they have lived, relative to those aspects of personality which relate to their conceptualization of their dying. To put it oversimply: The psychological course of the cancer mirrors certain deep troughs in the course of the life—*oncology recapitulates ontogeny.*

What is especially pertinent is how individuals have behaved at some of the most stressful, least successful times in their lives—whether those incidents relate to stress in school, job, marriage, separations, loss, or whatever. The hypothesis further holds that people's previous macrotemporal patterns and coping mechanisms will give clues about their patterns of behavior when dying—fighting illness or surrendering to it, despairing, denying, and their combinations, as they become increasingly aware of the life-threatening situation.

II

I believe that working intensively with a dying person is different from any other human encounter. The main point is that when a clinical thanatologist (physician, psychologist, nurse, social worker, or any trained person) is working with a dying person, he or she is not just "talking." (There is, of course, an enormously important place for mere *presence*—which, after all, may be the most important ingredient in care—or for sitting in communicative silence, or for seemingly just talking about what may appear to be trivial or banal topics.)

Working with the dying person is a special task. A person who systematically attempts to help a dying individual achieve a more psychologically comfortable death or a more "appropriate death"—given the dire, unnegotiable circumstances of the terminal disease—is either a psychotherapist or is acting in the role of a psychotherapist. That role cannot be escaped. (This is not to say that many others—relatives, church members, neighbors—cannot also play extremely important roles). But the distinction between a *conversation* and a *professional exchange* is crucial; more than that, I now believe that working with dying persons is different from working with any other kind of individual and demands a different kind of involvement; and I am willing to propose that there may be as important a conceptual difference between ordinary psychotherapy with individuals where the life span is not an issue and psychotherapy with dying persons as there is between ordinary psychotherapy and ordinary talk. The following paragraphs outline what I feel are some of the important nuances of these differences.

1. Ordinary talk or conversation

    In this kind of exchange which makes up most of human discourse, the focus is on the surface content (concrete events, specific details, abstract issues, questions and answers of content). The individuals are talking about what is actually being said: the obvious, stated meanings, and the ordinary interesting (or uninteresting) details of life. Further, the social role between the two participants is one of essential equality, sometimes tempered somewhat by considerations of age, status or prestige. But each of the two parties has the social right to ask the other the same kind of questions which he or she has been asked. Some examples of ordinary talk might be two friends conversing with one another about the events of the day, or two lovers whispering intimate thoughts to one another, or two businessmen closing a deal, or two neighbors simply chatting.

2. A hierarchical exchange

    In this kind of exchange the entire focus (like in a conversation) is on the manifest content—on what is being said—but the situation is marked by an explicit or tacit acknowledgment by the two parties that there is a significant difference of status between them; one of them is "superior" to the other. Questions asked or suggestions made or information transmitted or orders given by one would seem inappropriate if attempted by the other party. Examples would be the verbal exchange between a supervisor and subordinate, between an army officer and enlisted man, or between an oncologist and a patient in the doctor's office. The officer can order the enlisted man, but not vice versa; the doctor can examine the patient, but not vice versa. The doctor-patient relationship is an hierarchical one in that a doctor and a patient do not exchange roles.

3. A professional (e.g., psychotherapy) exchange

Here the focus is on feelings, emotional content and unconscious meanings, rather than primarily on what is apparently being said. The emphasis is on the latent (between-the-lines) significance more than on the manifest and obvious content; on unconscious meanings, including double entendre, puns and slips of the tongue; on themes that run as common threads through the content rather than on the concrete details for their own sake. Perhaps the most distinguishing aspect of the professional exchange (as opposed to ordinary talk) is the occurrence of "transference"— wherein the patient projects onto the therapist certain deep expectations and feelings. These transference reactions often stem from the patient's childhood and reflect earlier patterns of reaction (of love, hate, dependency, suspicion, etc.) to whatever the therapist may or may not be doing. The therapist (like the doctor) is often invested by the patient with almost magical healing powers, which, in fact, can serve as a self-fulfilling prophecy and thus help the interaction become therapeutic for the patient. The roles of the two participants, unlike those in a conversation, are not coequal. The situation is hierarchical but the focus is not on the manifest content.

4. A thanatological exchange

A person who systematically attempts to help a dying individual achieve a psychologically comfortable death (or a more "appropriate" death or an "ego-syntonic" death)—given the dire, unnegotiable circumstances of the situation—is acting in a special role. (This is not to say that many others—doctors, nurses, relatives, dear friends, specially trained volunteers—cannot also play extremely important roles.) If the distinction between a conversation and a professional exchange is crucial, certainly the distinction between working with dying persons as opposed to working with any other kind of individual is a vital one. Working with a dying person demands a different kind of involvement. My position is that there may be as important a conceptual difference between ordinary psychotherapy and working with dying persons as there is between ordinary psychotherapy and ordinary talk. Below, I have attempted to limn out some of the important nuances of these differences.

III

I believe that every physician should be a clinical thanatologist, at least once (preferably early) in his or her career, dealing intensively (five or six days, for an *hour* each day) with the personal-human-psychological aspects of a dying person. This means sitting unhurriedly by the bedside and coming to know the dying person as a person—over and above the biochemistry, cytology, medicine, and oncology of the "case." This also means not avoiding the dying and death aspects of the situation, but learning about them, sharing them, being burdened by them, (and their enormous implications)—in a word, to share the intensity of the thanatalogical experience. It also means (1) working with the survivor-victims to help them survive better; (2) interacting with ward staff personnel (doctors and nurses) to help them cope better; and (3) being mindful of one's own countertransference so the thanatologist can survive better.

The reward of this onerous event—treating one person intensively as a paradigm of how one might optimally (if there were unlimited time and one had infinite psychic reserves) treat every dying person—is an enrichment experience that will illuminate all the rest of one's practice and will enable admittedly busy physicians to be enormously more effective in the necessarily briefer encounters with all their patients, terminal or otherwise. The proper role of the physician in the twentieth century is not only to alleviate pain and cure the sick but, when the situation requires it, to help people die better. And how can the physician really know "on the pulses" unless he or she carves out the time to gain the *intimate* experience of the psychological details of at least one or two intensive dying experiences?

Let me now list some of the specific characteristics of working with dying persons—as opposed to those who are "only" critically ill, sick, diseased, injured, or disturbed. What these add up to is the prefiguring of a new specialty—of import to all care givers and not limited to physicians—called thanatology.

What is special about thanatological work?

1. *The goals are different.* Because the time is limited, the goals are more finite. The omnipresent goal is the psychological *comfort* of the person, with, as a general rule, as much alleviation of physical pain as possible. With a terminal person, addiction is not the issue—yet many physicians are niggardly or inappropriately moral about the use of pain-relieving substances. We have much to learn from Dame Cicely Saunders, founder of

St. Christopher's Hospice (near London), about the humane uses of morphine, alcohol, and other analgesics. Nor is psychological insight the goal. There is no rule that states that an individual must die with any certain amount of self-knowledge. In this sense, every life is incomplete. The goal—fighting the calendar of the lethal illness—is to "will the obligatory"; to make a chilling and ugly scene go as well as possible; to give psychological succor; to permit the tying off of loose ends; to lend as much stability to the person as it is possible to give.

2. *The rules are different.* Because there is a foreseeable (although tentative) death date in the finite future—a matter of months or weeks—the usual rules for psychotherapy can realistically be modified. The celerity with which the relationship between therapist and patient is made and the *depth* of that relationship can be of a nature that would be totally appropriate for a dying person, but, with an ordinary (non-dying) patient might appear unseemly or even unprofessional. But the "love" that flows between patient and therapist (and in the opposite direction also) when the patient is a dying person can be sustaining, even ennobling. One might ask what would happen if the patient were to have a remission, even recover. That is an embarrassment devoutly to be wished; in that rare case, the therapist would simply have to "renegotiate" the "contract" or understanding between the two of them. But intensive work with a dying person generally permits a depth of transference and countertransference that should not be done or countenanced in perhaps any other professional relationship.

3. *It may not be psychotherapy.* Obviously, working with a dying person should, for that person, be psychotherapeutic. (Anything that might be iatrogenic should be avoided). But the process itself may be sufficiently

different from ordinary psychotherapy that it might very well merit a label of its own. What is important is that the process be flexible—which is somewhat different from eclectic—and be able to move with the dying person's shifts of needs and mood, efforts toward control, detours into denial, and so on. Working with a dying person contains elements of rather traditional psychotherapy, but it also is characterized by other kinds of human interaction, including rapport building, interview, conversation, history taking, just plain talk, and communicative silences.

4. *The focus is on benign intervention.* In thanatological work, the therapist need not be a *tabula rasa;* nor need the therapist be inactive. There can be active intervention, as long as it is in the patient's interests. These interventions can take the form of interpretations, suggestions, advice (when asked for), interacting with doctors and nurses on the hospital ward, interacting with members of the family, arranging for social work services, liaison with clergy, and so on. The notion that any intervention is an incursion into the patient's rights and liberties is rejected as a blunt idea that does not make the distinction between benign and malign activities. The clinical thanatologist can act as the patient's ombudsman in many ways—on the ward, in the hospital, and within the community.

5. *No one has to die in a state of psychoanalytic grace.* Putting aside the Jehovah or "savior complex" that is understandably present in many psychotherapists, there is underlying concern with "success" in the motivational system of any effective therapist. With a dying patient, therapists must realign their notions of what they can realistically do for that person. It is a process that no matter how auspiciously begun or effectively conducted always ends in death. We hear phrases like "death work," but we need to appreciate that very few in-

dividuals die right on psychological target with all their complexes and neuroses beautifully worked through. The therapist needs to be able to tolerate incompleteness and lack of closure. Patients never untangle all the varied skeins of their intrapsychic and interpersonal life: to the last second there are phychical creations and recreations that require new resolutions. Total insight is an abstraction; there is no golden mental homeostasis.

6. *"Working through" is a luxury for those who have time to live.* It follows from the above that people die either too soon or too late with incompleted fragments in their life's agenda. The goal of resolving life's problems may be an unattainable one; the goal of an "appropriate death"—Avery Weisman's felicitous concept—of helping the dying person to "be relatively pain free, suffering reduced, emotional and social impoverishments kept at a minimum . . . resolving residual conflicts, and satisfying whatever remaining wishes are consistent with his present plight and with his ego ideal." The best death is one that an individual would choose for himself or herself if the choice were possible (even though the disease remained unnegotiable). Dying people can be helped to put their affairs in order—although everyone dies more-or-less intestate, psychologically speaking.

7. *The dying person sets the pace.* Because there are no specific substantive psychological goals (of having this insight or coming to that understanding), the emphasis is on process and on the thanatologist's continued presence. Nothing *has* to be accomplished. The patient sets the pace. This even includes whether the topic of death is ever mentioned—although, if permitted, it almost always will be. The therapist will note the usefulness of "the method of successive approximations," in which a dying person may say, over the course of many days, "I have a problem, an illness, a tumor, a malignancy, a

cancer, a terminal metastasis." This is not a litany that needs to be recited. Different individuals get in touch with their illness at various points of candor. Any one of these points is equally good, as long as it is comfortable for that person.

8. *Denial will be present.* We have already characterized the notion of a half-dozen stages of dying as being oversimplistic and not true to life. In the most popular explication of this approach, denial is listed as the first stage ("No, it can't be me!"). But our disavowal of the idea of a half-dozen fixed stages of dying should not lead us into the error of neglecting the importance of the psychological mechanism of denial itself. Denial is not a stage of dying; it is rather a ubiquitous aspect of the dying process, surfacing now and again (at no predetermined regular intervals) all through the dying process. It is only human for even the most extraordinary human beings occasionally to blot out or take a vacation from their knowledge of their imminent end. It is probably psychologically necessary for dying people intermittently to rest their own deathful train of thoughts on a siding, off the main track that leads only to blackness or mystery. This means that the clinical thanatologist must be prepared for the dying person to manifest a rather radical change of pace. If the therapist will only ride with this transient denial, the dying person will—as surprisingly as he or she began it—abandon it and come back to some of the realities of the present moment.

9. *The goal is increased psychological comfort.* The main point of working with the dying person—in the visit, the give-and-take of talk, the advice, the interpretations, the listening—is to increase that individual's psychological *comfort*. The criterion of "effectiveness" lies in this single measure. One cannot realistically be Pollyannish or even optimistic: the therapist begins in a grim situation

that is going to become even grimmer. The best that the therapist can hope to accomplish is to have helped the ill person in whatever ways it takes to achieve some increased psychological comfort. However, hope should never be totally abandoned.

10. *The importance of relating to nurses and doctors on the ward.* If the dying work is done in a hospital—or wherever it is done—it cannot be conducted as a solo operation. It is of key importance that relatives and personnel on the ward be kept informed of the dying person's condition and needs, and more, that they be kept informed as to the guiding concepts that underlie this special therapeutic exchange. Like clinical research on a ward, thanatological work often goes best with the full cooperation of the chief nurse. It is understood that no one approaches a patient as a "patient care specialist"—the euphemism for clinical thanatologist—unless he or she has been asked to do so by the physician in charge of the case. Then such a person—who has been introduced to the patient by the regular doctor—acts as any consultant would act, the difference being in the frequency and duration of the visits.

11. *The survivor is the victim—and eventually the patient: the concept of postvention.* Arnold Toynbee wrote eloquently about his view that death was essentially a two-person event and that, in the summation of anguish, the survivor bore the brunt of the hurt. All that has been said above should now be understood in the context of advocating that almost from the beginning of working with the dying person, the clinical thanatologist ought to become acquainted with the main survivor-to-be, to gain rapport with that person, and to have an explicit understanding that the survivor will be seen in the premourning stages and then for a while, at decreasing intervals, for perhaps a year or so after the death. *Postvention*—working with survivor-victims—ought to be

part of any total health-care system. It is not only humane; it is also good medical practice, for we know—especially from the work of Colin Murray Parkes (1972)—that a population of survivors (of any adult age) is a population at risk, having elevated rates of morbidity (including surgeries and other hospitalizations) and mortality (from a variety of causes of death) for at least a year or so after the death of a mourned person. Postventive care relates not only to "losses" in the survivor's life but also to other aspects of stress from which that mourner may be suffering.

12. *Just as the role of transference is paramount, the place of countertransference bears careful watching, and a good support system is a necessity.* A terminal person's dying days can be made better by virtue of "the joys of transference" that are projected on the thanatological therapist. The therapist, if able, should work for an intense transference relationship. But there is a well-known caveat; where there is transference, there is also countertransference—the flow of feeling from the therapist to the patient. The therapist is invested in the patient's welfare and is thereby made vulnerable. When the patient dies, the therapist is bereaved. And during the dying process, the therapist is anguished by the prospect of loss and a sense of impotence. Dealing with a dying person is abrasive work. The therapist is well advised to have good support systems in his or her own life: loved ones, dear friends, congenial work, and peer consultants.

The other side of these injunctions is that a physician needs to take vacations from death. A gynecological oncologist, for example, might intersperse his or her practice with obstetrical cases, delivering babies as a balance for those patients who are dying of cancer of the uterus. Moreover, a physician in oncological practice should not fail to seek our psychological or psychiatric consultation for patients if they are significantly depressed or otherwise disturbed about dying and for *himself* (or herself) if there is any sense that one's own equanimity has been touched. This type of psychotherapeutic help might well be made a routine part of a physician's dealing with dying persons, lest the physician fall prey to the predictable consequences of the unusual psychological stresses that come from working constantly around and against death. (Shneidman, 1974, 1980)

References

Glaser, Barney G., and Strauss, Anselm. *Awareness of Dying.* Chicago: Aldine Publishing Company, 1965.

Glaser, Barney G., and Strauss, Anselm. *Time for Dying.* Chicago: Aldine Publishing Company, 1968.

Hinton, John. *Dying.* Baltimore: Penguin Books, 1967.

Parkes, Colin Murray. *Bereavement: Studies of Grief in Adult Life.* New York: International Universities Press, 1972.

Shneidman, Edwin S. *Deaths of Man.* Baltimore: Penguin Books, 1974. (First published by Quadrangle Books, 1973.)

Shneidman, Edwin S. Aspects of the Dying Process. *Psychiatric Annals* 7, no. 3 (March 1977).

Shneidman, Edwin S. *Voices of Death.* New York: Harper & Row, 1980.

Sudnow, David. *Passing On.* Englewood Cliffs, N.J.: Prentice-Hall, 1967.

Toynbee, Arnold. *et al. Man's Concern with Death.* New York: McGraw-Hill Book Company, 1969.

Weisman, Avery D. *On Dying and Denying.* New York: Behaviorial Publications, 1972.

Part IV

The Funeral

11
The Funeral and Ministry
Roger Branch and Larry A. Platt

It is impossible to overemphasize the importance of the funeral. Because of the associated grief, funerals are usually painful events, but if properly done, they are healing, restorative, victorious, and worshipful.

Funeral rituals are universal. According to anthropologists, this means that they perform for all societies some vital functions in social life. We have identified four basic functions of the funeral (Irion, 1986).

1. It provides a framework of supportive relationships for mourners.
2. It reinforces the reality of death.
3. It encourages the expression of grief.
4. It provides a fitting conclusion to the life of the deceased.

Effective funeral ministry will be linked to these and will contribute to their accomplishment.

Providing a Framework of Supportive Relationships for Mourners

Death is a time when people "circle the wagons" in defense against that ancient foe—mortality. The funeral draws together family and friends in an expression of unity and caring. This supportive network is critically important in dealing with grief both during the funeral and afterward. The minister can make significant contributions to the successful accomplishment of this function.

FIGURE 2

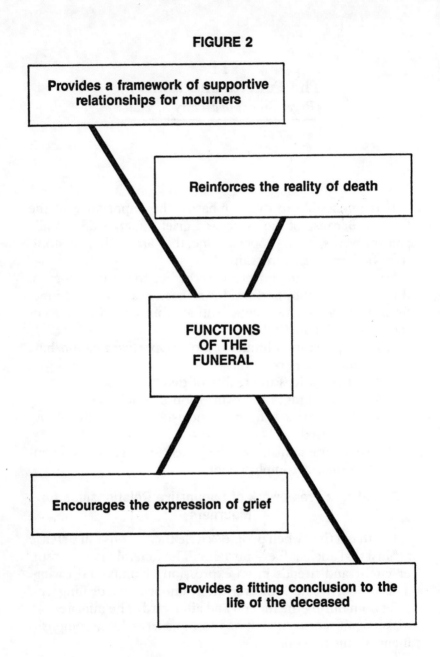

Provides a framework of supportive relationships for mourners

Reinforces the reality of death

FUNCTIONS OF THE FUNERAL

Encourages the expression of grief

Provides a fitting conclusion to the life of the deceased

Quality versus Quantity

Understand that large numbers of people present at a mourner's home, the funeral home, and the funeral service do not necessarily constitute social support. In fact, the management of a large number of mourners may pose a variety of problems which tend to erase the comfort that their presence provides.

Order in Confusion

The period between death and the funeral, and just afterward, is intermittently filled with people, noise, and confusion. Be ready to help manage the situation by assisting the mourners to find places of relative seclusion and quiet as needed. Some will feel guilty about a desire to slip away from those who have come to express their condolences. They need to know that their need to be alone with immediate family or one or two close friends is acceptable and natural. At points of deep distress, the minister might ask if the mourner would like to be alone or who the grieving person would prefer to have present to help during a time of seclusion.

Part of a Network

The minister must be aware that he is not the entire support network (Weizman and Kamm, 1985). Others might be more helpful, at least at certain points. Old, deeply established ties of kinship and friendship may touch the mourner in ways that the minister cannot. Funerals sometimes draw to the side of the bereaved trusted friends who have been away for years. Being alert to the question of who really meets social support needs best enables the minister to encourage those linkages that are obviously most desired by the mourners.

Need for Support Is Continuous

A number of visits to the bereaved during the time from death notification through burial may be necessary. Some people find themselves overwhelmed when the process of making funeral arrangements and preparations is added to a burden of grief. The minister can offer information and guidance, as well as spiritual and emotional support. Although the need for ministry is ongoing, it is not necessarily all-consuming. A series of relatively brief visits and/or telephone contacts during the two to four critical days surrounding the funeral allows the minister to meet the needs of most bereaved families.

Reinforcing the Reality of Death

Individual and social adjustment to death requires that the bereaved family, friends, and community accept the reality of the death itself (Worden, 1982). There is a tendency toward denial as a mechanism to avoid or postpone the pain of grief. The funeral forces attention upon and public acknowledgment of the death. The minister can do a number of things that help the bereaved come to grips with the reality of death (Jackson, 1957).

Avoid Euphemisms for Death

In speaking of death and the deceased use the terminology that affirms the reality of death. The person has not "passed away"; he has died. He is not "no longer with us"; he is dead. Simplicity, dignity, and good taste in word choice make for communication that is both accurate and humane.

Incorporate an Obituary Statement in the Funeral

Some ministers incorporate the obituary notice from the local newspapers. Others compose their own from information supplied by the funeral director and family. The latter approach avoids the errors that crop up in newspaper obituaries and permits a fuller, more personalized statement.

Inclusion of an obituary statement provides an element of structure, of ritualized finality, to the funeral. It personalizes the service because it clearly identifies the event with the deceased. By naming survivors and their relationships with the dead person, it asserts the reality of death to specific mourners.

Revisiting the Grave Site

There is something particularly final about the grave. It bears mute witness that physical death is permanent. Many families customarily return with an intimate circle of friends to the grave site after the grave has been closed and floral offerings arranged around it. This is typically a time of quiet reflection and individual leave-taking from the deceased. If the minister will arrange to return with those who reassemble at the grave site, he will find opportunities to help mourners understand and adjust to the reality of death.

Placing of the Headstone

The event of the placing of the headstone, when one is used, provides a little-explored opportunity to reinforce the reality of death. It often is done by a monument company with little or no notice. Typically family members then assemble to inspect the result.

With cooperation from the monument contractor to provide some advance notification, the family could arrange a brief, simple, private ceremony of remembrance. Its value in reinforcing the reality of death and in helping to work through grief is obvious. Inclusion of the minister at such an event, if not in some official role then as a fellow mourner, would provide further opportunity for individual and group ministry.

Making Possible Expressions of Grief

Grief is a normal, necessary reaction to loss. If it does not find expression in normal channels, it will affect the bereaved in other ways, in some cases for a lifetime (Parkes and Weiss, 1983). The funeral is society's therapeutic mechanism for bereavement. It encourages the expression of grief. The minister can play a valuable role in this process.

Do Not Assume that a Grieving Funeral Service is Unchristian

The apostle Paul instructed the Thessalonians about the resurrection (1 Thess. 4:13-18, RSV) in order "that you may not grieve as others do who have no hope." He did not say that they should not grieve at all but that they should not grieve as do those who have no hope. The resurrection certainly assures the bereaved that the loss of the loved one is temporary, not permanent. However, present loss brings present pain—a natural part of the human condition for which Christ was deeply sympathetic. "Blessed are those who mourn for they shall be comforted" (Matt. 5:4, RSV).

Some people hold the false notion that the expression of grief is undignified. In the first place, the reasonable expression of honest emotions of pain and loss is rarely undignified. Moreover, the funeral is not a show or performance but a public worship service of leave-taking from the dead, primarily serving the needs of the bereaved.

Some people are concerned that strong expressions of grief will somehow "get out of hand." They usually are people who think that there is something wrong or distasteful about anything more than a modest tear or two. Bluntly stated, they are wrong (Pine et. al., 1976). Grief must be expressed, and the funeral is supposed to be an event in which this happens. In fact, emotional contagion leading to general hysteria, fainting, and obvious excess is a rare occurrence, seen mostly at open-casket funerals involving sudden and dramatic deaths.

The skilled, well-informed minister can work with the family to avoid conditions leading to such events.

Use the Name of the Deceased

A depersonalized funeral suggests that the minister does not know the deceased or that he relies on a "canned" ceremony for virtually all funerals.

If the funeral does not relate specifically to the deceased, it will not speak to the bereaved. They will feel no grief because they are hearing nothing that touches the object of their grief, their dead loved one.

This is not to say that the minister should try to create emotional distress. Rather, a personalized funeral service that recognizes the deceased and acknowledges that the business of the hour is to mourn his dying and honor his memory has long-term effects (Margolis et. al., eds., 1975).

Involve People in the Service

When mourners have active roles in the funeral, the grief therapy function is strengthened (Davidson, 1984). The more a funeral service is a worship service with full congregational participation, the more positive will be its impact. Hymns, responsive readings, unison prayers, doxologies, and the like encourage the general expression of grief and other emotions. They also underscore the religious character of the service and the Christian message of eternal life and God's presence with His people in time of trouble and sorrow.

Provide a Role for Children

Children are often victimized unnecessarily by death because they are denied participation. Frequently they are given no information or misinformation or inadequate information. They may never be taken to the funeral home to view the body or even the casket. They often are not allowed to participate in the funeral.

When the circle of bereaved family and friends includes

children, it must be remembered that their basic needs are very similar to those of adults. They must come to grips with the reality of death, experience the pain of the loss, effectively grieve, and restructure their lives without the lost loved one (Wass and Corr, 1984).

A carefully guided visit for the children to the funeral home in a small group of family or other trusted adults should be considered. Make it a time for honest answers and deeply shared grief.

Children should participate in funerals. They are indeed sad ceremonies, but it is appropriate that a child who has lost a parent, grandparent, or other loved one be sad. Funerals are also services that help to heal and restore the brokenhearted. It follows that brokenhearted children should not be denied the funeral's healing influence (Rando, 1984).

Providing a Fitting Conclusion to the Life of the Deceased

The period of lying in state, the funeral, and burial ritual compose a set of public events that focus upon the deceased, just as they also affect the bereaved. These are events of leave-taking and of affirmation of the significance of the dead person. They also constitute the first step in restructuring the social world from which the deceased is absent. All of this requires that this final chapter be a fitting one for the life of the one who has died.

Christians Should Be Educated About Funerals

Family members often make bad choices about funerals because, under the impact of strong emotions, they fail to consider what would be appropriate to the life and character of their dead loved one. Ministers need to teach their congregations about funerals. Options about types of funerals, burial arrangements, and costs should be explored. Many variations and economic considerations are difficult for grieving people to understand. Mid-week or Sunday evening services could be devoted to a series of educational sessions on how to prepare for a funeral. Our experience and the experiences of others have consistently confirmed the benefits of this approach.

Church members should be encouraged to plan many of the details of their own funerals in advance. It is a good idea to write down choices about funeral and burial arrangements. These issues should be discussed within families to make certain that everyone is aware of others' desires or preferences. This practice makes the decision-making tasks of survivors much easier when death comes. It also helps to ensure that the funeral will be in accord with the wishes of the deceased.

Unfortunately ministers are not always well informed about potential considerations in funeral planning. Before you teach, you must learn. Funeral directors can provide volumes of information about options in types of funerals, burial arrangements, and matters of cost. Funeral directors generally do not deserve the image of exploiters of the grief stricken with which they have sometimes been saddled. The people who spend more than they should, sometimes contrary to the advice of their funeral directors, are those who feel compelled to "do right by Mama" instead of doing what Mama would say is right. In any event, funeral directors can provide plenty of useful information about practical decisions that must be made concerning funerals.

The final section of this book contains materials intended for practical application. They should have immediate value for preparing church members to shape their own funerals in a manner that reflects their definition of the lordship of Christ over all their lives.

The "Wake" Is a Significant Observance

The term *wake* is no longer widely used. Nor is "sitting up with the dead." However, there is usually some public event during the period of lying in state when people assemble and interact with survivors. Typically this involves a period of three or four hours when survivors receive visitors at the funeral home, usually near the casket of the deceased. Exact details vary from case to case. Two points should be remembered: The character of the individual should be reflected in this observance, and there should be ample opportunity for people to express themselves about the deceased.

Funeral Arrangements Should Be Carefully Considered

Again the issue is a fitting conclusion to the life of the deceased. The choice of funeral and burial arrangements should be weighed carefully with an eye both to the enduring needs of survivors and to the wishes of the dead person. Something as simple as inappropriate burial clothes (She would never wear a thing like that.) can seriously detract.

One family recently experienced the tragic death of their teenage son and were faced with the task of selecting the desired funeral arrangements. Because their son had once mentioned, in the most indirect manner that he might like to be cremated should he die, the parents reluctantly chose this type of funeral service. Once their son's ashes were scattered over the Atlantic Ocean, the parents realized how desperately they needed a permanent place to visit and reflect upon their son's life. The cremation funeral they selected was soon understood by both the mother and the father to have been a terribly inappropriate choice. Upon reflection they realized that a cremation service was not the clear preference of their son; nor, in fact, was the question ever fully discussed by any member of the family. Even more tragically, the cremation robbed the parents of solace for their enduring needs following the funeral.

Although cremation may be an excellent choice for some, it was not a fitting conclusion in this case. The memory of the son was not honored in any particular way by the service. The form of funeral was not especially representative of the character and life of the deceased. The cremation also failed to meet the special needs of the survivors. The funeral, then, was not a fitting conclusion to the life of their son. It was a mistake born of haste, confusion, and misguided intentions. The errors of their haste, however, live on as a problem the parents must endure each day. Although it has been over five years since the death of their son, the parents still deeply lament the inappropriateness of the funeral.

Obviously the help of a minister who was alert to the special needs of the family and reasonably versed in the nature and function of the funeral process would have been invaluable. The calm and sensitive guidance of a minister could have helped the survivors to analyze their choices more clearly and understand more fully their long-term needs after the funeral.

Tailor the Funeral Service to the Person

Most of the content of the service lies in the hands of the minister. Its effectiveness depends largely upon how hard he is willing to work on its preparation and presentation. Some ministers avoid eulogies completely. While it is true that lengthy, overstated, insincere outpourings of praise are repugnant, the reason for the funeral is the person who has died. Thus, a brief, truthful, carefully crafted eulogy is central. It provides opportunity to acknowledge the reality of death and affirm an appreciation for the life of the deceased. Through it the funeral provides a fitting conclusion to the life of the deceased.

The funeral is, of course, an ending point, an important event that celebrates the life of the deceased and ritualizes the real mourning evoked by the ending of that life. The funeral is also a beginning point—for the survivors who must now build new relationships and ways of life and for the one who has ended earthly existence to move on to eternal life. Whether the funeral effectively fulfills its functions as a life-enhancing religious observance depends largely upon the knowledge, insight, sensitivity, and spiritual depth of the minister. He will minister fruitfully if the funeral provides a

framework of supportive relationships for mourners, reinforces the reality of death, encourages the expression of grief,
and provides a fitting conclusion to the life of the deceased.

References

Davidson, Glenn. 1984. *Understanding Mourning.* Minneapolis: Augsburg Publishing
House.
Irion, Paul. 1986. "The Funeral and the Bereaved." In Larry Platt, et al., eds.
Encounters with Death, Grief and Bereavement.
Jackson, Edgar. 1957. *Understanding Grief.* Nashville: Abingdon.
Margolis, Otto, *et.al.,* eds. 1975. *Grief and the Meaning of the Funeral.* New York: MSS
Information Corporation.
Parkes, Colin and Robert Weiss. 1983. *Recovery From Bereavement.* New York: Basic
Books, Inc.
Pine, V. R. ed., 1976. *Acute Grief and the Funeral.*
Rando, T. A. 1984. *Grief, Dying and Death: Clinical Interventions for Caregivers.*
Wass, Hannelore and Charles Corr, eds. 1984. *Helping Children Cope with Death:
Guidelines and Resources.* New York: McGraw-Hill Book Company.
Weizman, Savine and Phyllis Kamm. 1985 *About Mourning: Support and Guidance for the
Bereaved.*
Worden, J. W. 1982. *Grief Counseling and Grief Therapy: A Handbook for the Mental Health
Practioner.*

12
The Clergy on the Firing Line
Regina Flesch

For a number of years I was the Principal Investigator in a research project supported by the National Institute of Mental Health, (originally through the Center for Studies in Suicide Prevention) designed to study the process of mourning in families bereaved either by vehicular accident or by suicide. Without unnecessary detail about our research plan, it should be noted that family members of hospitalized terminally ill patients suffering from known physiological illnesses are relatively accessible for interviews, and have been the focus of recent research studies. Family members whose bereavements are unexpected are less readily accessible and, therefore, have been studied and written about less. Survivors of major disasters are not alone in their tragedies; they have a feeling of sharing, as have families who lose loved ones in their country's service. Our work has been with interviewees who feel, and in many respects actually are, isolated and alone. Their loved ones often have died alone, in automobile accidents on the highway or through means of their own choosing, leaving survivors who feel abandoned.

My interest in the clergy's work with the bereaved began almost simultaneously with my exploratory interviews with these bereaved respondents. From interviews, it appeared to me that persons with a religious orientation somehow met an unexpected loss with greater resilience than individuals without a religious orientation, however that is defined. By "resilience," I mean the ability to continue daily functioning at least in the initial period of loss, the period of acute grief. This observation persuaded me to enlist as co-workers in interviews professional persons who traditionally worked with the bereaved, and who could be expected to have a continuing interest in bereaved individuals. Almost all bereaved families eventually must turn to clergymen to conduct the funeral service. Therefore, I began work with members of the clergy but I soon learned that many clergymen are as poorly equipped as other people to work with the bereaved.

In our research interviews, the first of which we conducted as soon as possible after the funeral, we heard directly about some clerical blunders. One respondent complained that the local rabbi really ought not to have mentioned to members of his congregation that the decedent, our interviewee's wife, had committed suicide. Another respondent, who had had no connection with any church prior to the accidental death of a family member on the highway, related that a local minister had paid him a condolence call to invite him to hold the funeral service in his church. However, during this visit the minister also informed him of the poor financial state of his church, and asked the bereaved family for future financial support as parishioners. His effort was understandably unsuccessful. Another example came from a grieving mother whose only child had committed suicide through the ingestion of drugs. Beyond child-bearing age, and at bitter odds with the boy's step-father, this woman had closeted herself in the house with her boy's belongings and with bottles of gin, but she had opened her door when the clergyman called. He exhorted her to combat her grief, giving her an example from his own life. He said he had lost his beloved wife of many years and was in despair, but he had trust in the Lord. He "kept on," and after a time, he had remarried. He now had a loving wife and a fine new family, so she, too, could remake her life. The woman related this story with a steady look and mirthless laughter.

These examples may be termed clerical "sins of commission." Clerical "sins of omission" can be mentioned more briefly. We have visited many individuals whose clergymen have failed to make even the most superficial condolence call after the funeral service.

In the single funeral that I had to arrange, the rabbi whom I telephoned initially objected to conducting the funeral service in a local church, although there was no synagogue in the village to which he was summoned, and although he on occasion had preached in that church. He suggested instead that the funeral service be held in his synagogue, over 20 miles away, to which the funeral party would have had to drive over the most heavily trafficked stretch of vacation highway in the country, on one of the two most active holiday weekends of the year. His ecumenism may have been stirred by my comment that no funeral party could drive that highway on the third of July, and he finally reluctantly accepted the original plan. Neither the rabbi who had conducted the funeral service nor the rector of the church where the service was held paid a condolence call, although both had promised a call within the week.

A Roman Catholic friend related a similar experience. Her lovely teen-aged daughter had collapsed without warning in school and had died in the mother's arms on the way to the hospital. The distraught parents telephoned their previous parish priest to conduct the funeral service. As he now served in another parish, he referred these heartbroken people to his successor with whom they had had no personal contact. To this day the mother feels bitter because the referral could have been avoided or else handled differently and because their previous priest neither attended the funeral nor paid a condolence call.

A few fortunate interviewees have told us, with pride and pleasure, of condolence calls by their clergymen. Without exception these calls have occurred within the first week after the funeral, and were perfunctory, brief, and final. After the first ten days the bereaved typically are left alone by laity and clergy alike. Clergymen often excuse their failure to keep in touch with parishioners on the grounds of heavy duties, but few clergymen attempt to enlist parishioners in visiting the bereaved. Unable to ask for help and also unable to mobilize themselves to attend a church which could help, bereaved people are neglected by busy clergymen, and thus lose contact with their church and church community. Yet our respondents have been pathetically grateful for any condolence call by a clergyman, and we often have heard how much a single short call by a clergyman has meant to a mourner.

Essentially the above failures in ministry to the bereaved can be subsumed under three headings:

1. Failures in heart—that is, failure in charity and loving kindness.

2. Failures in mind—that is, failure to comprehend the problems of bereavement and grief.

3. Failures in role—that is, failure to fulfill the clerical role as representative of an organized religious faith.

Let us now consider these clerical failures and what may be done about them.

Failures in Heart

Grief as an emotion is poorly understood, partly because there have been few nonretrospective studies (Averill, 1968). I believe it safe to say that most people, even those who have sustained a loss, have little appreciation of the need for patience and understanding with those in grief. Possibly if we consider the psychology of bereavement briefly, the problem will become clear.

Psychologists tell us that man's basic anxiety stems from the first separation anxiety, the separation of the child from its mother. The finality and permanence of separation through the death of a deeply loved person arouses enormous anxiety in the bereaved, so great, in fact, that it has been noted by more than one author that people in grief often fear loss of their sanity. The "work of mourning," (Freud, 1959) must proceed slowly, piecemeal, as the bereaved gradually tries to separate himself from the deceased. While the lost relationship is retained psychologically by the bereaved, he repudiates current reality and clings to the past.

It is easy to become impatient with people in grief, particularly with their reiterated complaints about their loss. Impatience is expressed through comments such as, "You've already told me twice about the day he died," or through nonverbal body language, shifting in the chair and obvious lack of interest, or through actual absence. When the clergyman visits, his impatience may find expression in narration of a personal loss—perhaps not as gross as the example cited earlier, but like the interjection of one young clergyman to an interviewee whose husband recently had committed suicide, "I *know* how you feel because my sister's husband just died." Such responses are correctly perceived by the mourner as signifying lack of understanding. Feeling abandoned and severely anxious, the bereaved person is highly sensitive to the least hint of rejection from others. He reads such signs with accuracy.

It is not necessary to know fully the nature of the lost relationship or the personality pattern of the mourner to understand the need of the grieving individual for support and simple human kindness *over a period of time*. This means not a single, perfunctory condolence call, but a sustained expression of understanding, acceptance and concern, despite the mourner's aversive behavior. Above all, the bereaved need charity, that inestimable gift which traditionally is associated with religious action.

A fine example of clerical charity was provided by a non-Catholic interviewee whose Catholic husband had been killed in a vehicular accident. This decedent's priest came to call after the funeral. When the widow saw him, she let forth a verbal attack against the Lord. I asked what the priest had replied, and she related: "Even when I said I denounced Him, the priest replied: 'He's always the first One that takes it between the eyes.' He said: 'Everybody had a bitter feeling towards God. He's the first One and the only One that takes it all. But He's got broad shoulders; He can take it. And He's forgiving.' " The priest added: "If you can find it in your heart to forgive Him, He'll forgive you." Grief stricken as she was, our interviewee responded to the charity of this reply and spoke of the help she received from that visit.

Failures in Mind

The current literature emphasizes, and the author's clinical experience documents, that one important element in the process of mourning is the disruption of normal patterns of activity. For example, a mother typically will have organized her life around certain routine tasks in relation to a child even after that child is grown and out of the home. She may look forward to weekend visits, to occasional suppers at home, or to contacts with the child's friends who stop in for a meal. Such contacts may be infrequent but are a source of happiness to parents and give *pattern* and meaning to the mother's activity. Even if no longer at home, when the child is removed through death, the mother's entire pattern of life is disrupted and may be destroyed permanently.

Typically, the bereaved mother starts to follow her old routines, but fails to carry them through to completion. The routines are no longer purposeful because the person who gave them meaning is no longer among the living. Sociologists term this "role loss" as distinct from "object loss" (Volkert and Stanley, 1966), the loss of the person. After a time, the mother may realize that she should try to do something about her lapses in activity. Recognizing that she should change her routines and develop entirely new areas of activity, she may even be able to accomplish a few changes. However, many bereaved people, by no means in the minority, simply are unable to initiate new activities or to find new roles. As a rule, the initiation of new friendships and new interests, or even the resumption of old patterns, are beyond the capacity of the individual in grief. The duration of this incapacity varies with the individual, with the closeness of the relationship and with other factors, but apathy, lethargy and withdrawal are commonly noted characteristics of grieving individuals. Nevertheless, once someone else starts a bereaved person on something, he may be able to carry through, particularly if the activity involves other people. The clergy can perform very helpful functions during this time, when old patterns of behavior are no longer operable for the individual and when he lacks the capacity to initiate new tasks. Brief condolence calls, even of ten minutes' duration can be enormously reassuring if during these visits there is a simple recognition of the individual's problem. In a brief call, the clergyman can convey understanding of this disruption of daily activities and without exhortation or pressure, he can offer help through the church or through other parishioners for the resumption of former activities and establishment of new roles. What is suggested is first, verbalized recognition of the disrupted life pattern by the clergyman who makes a condolence call, and that this problem be accepted as natural, a matter of course. Second, we suggest that the church community be enlisted in keeping the mourner in contact with the church, and thus, in contact with the community.

There are experimental programs in which lay visitors have been used effectively with the bereaved and, of course, there are church groups which rely on lay contacts to maintain their membership, i.e. the Church of the Lord Jesus Christ of the Latter Day Saints. However, in a large urban community, the enlistment of lay members for this kind of work has been rare. Many of our bereaved interviewees fall away from their church but would continue there if their clergyman had enlisted a church member's aid in their return (I mean not merely transportation, although that may be a factor).

Parishioners who themselves lack meaningful occupation outside their homes could be given basic instruction in how to call on bereaved individuals and how to help them to a religious service. The clergyman who thus coordinates human needs would strengthen the total membership of his church while bringing the bereaved back into the mainstream of life. Thus, this clergyman may build a unified congregation in which all members have a meaningful role.

Clerical Failure in Role

In addition to loss of a beloved object and loss of a valued role, we have mentioned a third type of loss, the loss of meaning in life that may follow a major bereavement. This may well be the most painful aspect of grief. Meaning in daily life underlies all action and unless one's life has meaning, there is no point in continuing. Our respondents have stated this openly, saying that they take tranquilizers, or drink, or do both, courting oblivion. One of our interviewees, deeply despondent since her husband's death in a vehicular accident, lost all interest in her remaining family, her daughter, her grand-children, and also in her daily existence. She developed some alarming physical symptoms which she described rather casually. When I asked her if she thought much about dying, she gave me a long, slow look and replied, "I have no business here anymore."

Other interviewees have shown that they too need to find meaning in life, but more than this, meaning also in death. From the bereaved one hears again and again the anguished cry of "Why?," and because the need for meaning is so compelling, the listener may be tempted to engage in the search for an answer. In my interviews, I have heard of clergymen who, in an effort to be helpful, have been drawn into the question of, "Why?" and have replied that the loss may "have been for the best," or that it was "God's will," or that the answer would come through prayer. The problem with such answers is that they engender no communication and no rapport with the bereaved. I must confess that I have no simple answer to this question of providing new meaning in the life of the bereaved, but I have the conviction that this is the role *par excellence* of the clergyman. The ultimate meaning in life and death is not a problem which can be referred to the psychologist, psychiatrist or social worker; traditionally it is a problem for religion. In meeting this problem with a bereaved person, it has occurred to me that we may look profitably at some of the principals involved in psychotherapy.

In a typical psychotherapeutic situation, a patient comes in complaining of certain human problems in his life—relationship problems with his wife, his staff, or his children. He usually is absorbed in these complaints which he regards as external, and he is apt to review them without initial willingness to examine his own part in the problem. The good therapist listens quietly and tries to clarify in his own mind how the patient has contributed to the problem. He hopes that the patient eventually can be helped to see this contribution himself—will, in other words, develop "insight" into his difficulties. However, if the therapist tries to inject "insight" into the discussion before the patient himself is ready for it, the patient is apt to terminate treatment prematurely. A bridge must be built for the discussion of the patient's contribution to the situation, and that bridge is the *relationship,* the *rapport,* between the patient and therapist. That rapport also is the *vehicle* for the patient's emotional reorientation. As Alexander and French (1946) put it, "In many cases it is not a matter of insight stimulating or forcing the patient to an emotional reorientation, but rather one in which a very considerable preliminary emotional readjustment is necessary before insight is possible at all." This readjustment may be accomplished only through a foundation of rapport and trust.

Religious faith is similarly the outgrowth of trust directed toward a Supreme Being, as Martin Buber (1959) explains in "I and Thou." Religious faith cannot be engendered by pressure or exhortation, anymore than can insight. The psychotherapist is neither obligated nor able to inject insight where this is lacking nor is the clergyman obligated to inject faith where absent. An active listening to the complaints of the bereaved and an active acceptance are essential to building up that *trust* which must lie at the heart of faith. Like the psychotherapist, the clergyman's obligation is not to answer questions but to supply a nonjudgmental atmosphere in which questions may be raised. This means also a supportive relationship in the context of the example of his own faith, a faith strong enough to withstand the mourner's hostility and doubt. Thus, the clergyman, through his own faith, provides to the bewildered mourner a witness to what that can mean in time of crisis. Father Meissner (1969) says, "Faith provides illumination, direction and meaning to life." "If one cannot be the rose, one can live near it," goes the old saying. Here may lie the clue to why even atheists, despite their own disbelief, acknowledge that they have received solace from the words of a clergyman at the funeral.

Actually, more than providing an example, this means *sharing* the powerful force in life that faith is. Here is the real role of the clergyman, to testify to the bereaved that faith can give meaning to life when object and role are gone.

An example of the kind of meaning that comes through such faith was provided from personal experience. Some weeks before my husband died, when he (but not I) must have realized his time was short, I asked him while I was preoccupied with other matters if he believed in God. Without hesitation the reply came: "Oh, yes." With my attention immediately focused, I questioned again, "Now, how can you, a scientist, believe in God?" He reflected for a moment and, smiling gently, replied: "I will tell you. When I pat a dog on the head and he licks my hand, I think how little he understands of the food I give him, or of the world in which he lives, or of me. As his understanding is of me, so is mine of God. But I believe."

The real role of the clergyman is to share that kind of faith.

References

Alexander, F., and French, T.M.: *Psychoanalytic Therapy: Principles and Practice.* New York, Ronald, 1946.

Averill, J.: Grief: its nature and significance. *Psychol Bull,* 70:721, 1968.

Buber, M.: *I and Thou.* New York, Scribner's, 1959.

Freud, S.: Mourning and melancholia. In Riviere, J. (Translator), *Collected Papers.* New York, Basic Books, 1959, vol. IV.

Meissner, W. W.: Notes on the psychology of faith. *Journal of Religion and Health,* 8:47, 1969.

Volkert, E. H., and Stanley, M.: Bereavement and mental health. In Fulton, R. (Ed.): *Death and Identity.* New York, Wiley and Sons, 1966.

13
The Funeral and the Bereaved
Paul E. Irion

The literature of cultural anthropology indicates that nearly every culture has developed some sort of ceremonialized patterns for marking the death of a member of that society. Such ceremonies seem to have two major functions: to separate the body of the deceased from the community of the living and to assist the mourners in adjustment to their loss.

It is my intention to describe in some detail, according to our psychological understanding, the major needs of the bereaved and then to point ways in which the funeral, rightly understood and conducted, can meet those needs.

The funeral is part of a process in which the mourner restructures his life without the presence of the person who has died. This process recognizes changes in the status of both the deceased and the mourners. It is obvious that the deceased has changed because he has died and is no longer a part of the aspect of existence which we call life. The mourner has changed because his life is now lived without the relationship to the deceased as he has known it. There is movement along a continuum from a relationship of presence (i.e. living, interactive, responsive relationship) to a relationship of memory.

The funeral also is part of a pattern through which the mourners interact with the social groups of which they are a part. In its optimum expression the funeral is a social event in which mourners are surrounded by a group which shares something of their loss and joins them in marking the end of the relationship of presence with dignity.

Then follows a period of transition during which life is reorganized without the deceased. When this transition is completed, there is reunion or reincorporation of the mourners into normal social relationships with the group. This process is much more apparent in a society which observes formal mourning periods. Modern American social practices no longer follow such a pattern. Within a day or two following the funeral, most behavior unique to mourning is abandoned. Individuals have little or no social guidance for the reorganization of life without the deceased. This means that the brief period, in which the funeral is one of the major focuses, is extremely important because it contains a condensation of experiences which were formerly prolonged. If one views mourning as a painful, abnormal experience, this brevity is cause for rejoicing. If one sees mourning as a therapeutic process which inevitably requires time, there must be concern that the brief period allotted be utilized with maximum effectiveness. A part of the vital function of the funeral is to assist in all three of the phases in the rite of passage of the mourners (to use van Gennep's term [1961]) during these days: the separation or isolation, the transition to life without the deceased, and reunion with the group.

Loss which comes through the death of a significant other produces in mourners psychological needs that can be met in the funeral. Lindemann (quoted in Jackson, 1963), who pioneered the modern psychiatric understanding of grief, stated: "The funeral service is psychologically necessary in order to give the opportunity for 'grief work.' The bereaved must be given the capacity to work through his grief if he is to come out of the situation emotionally sound. Finally, we need to see to it that those whom we serve are left with comforting memories. Some will argue this point. I think, however, it is psychologically sound." The funeral is an integral part of the series of experiences through which persons pass in the course of bereavement.

The funeral has several fundamental psychological functions: to increase the acceptance of the loss, to sanction and encourage the expression of one's feelings toward the reality in which one finds himself, and to participate in the process of working through these feelings.

The funeral is helpful psychologically by enabling mourners to confront realistically the crisis of loss. Anthropological studies indicate that there is some basis for assuming that one of the points of origin for the funeral was the need to cope with the reality of death. A mourner who is unwilling or unable to face the fact of death encounters difficulty in coping with the loss. The person who accepts as reality that death has taken place is aided because there is then a reasonable explanation for the profound feelings which sweep over him in bereavement. He knows why life seems so empty, why he seems to be resentful of other people whose lives are untouched, why he wants to pull away from contact with others. But even more important, the individual is motivated to begin the painful process of mourning, the process of reorganizing life without the presence of the deceased.

The funeral underscores the reality of the bereavement situation as it offers realistic interpretation of what has taken place. It provides a kind of consensual validation because the mourner is joined by others in the group who are experiencing a similar loss. The separation from the body of the deceased by burial or cremation affirms further that the relationship as it has been known has really been severed.

Acceptance of reality demands a response which is seen in the various feelings evoked by bereavement. Each individual response is unique, but all have in common the need for expression. This ventilation of feelings of the bereaved serves a variety of purposes. It is a healthful catharsis, giving release to pent-up feelings, making available for more constructive use energy which has been devoted to denying or avoiding such strong feelings. The need for catharsis is followed by the need for developing insight. While catharsis is helpful, its healing capacity is limited without a growing awareness of the nature of the feelings that are released and some understanding of their origin. Although the funeral itself will very probably not be an occasion for such insight, it can be an event in which catharsis is enabled, opening the way for the development of insight.

Another psychological value of the funeral is seen in the way in which it supports the process of remembering the deceased. Freud's (1959) early discussion of mourning begins to illuminate this task. "Reality passes its verdict—that the object no longer exists—upon each single one of the memories and hopes through which the libido was attached to the lost object, and the ego, confronted as it were with the decision whether it will share this fate, is persuaded by the sum of its narcissistic satisfaction in being alive to sever its attachment to the nonexistent object." Lindemann's research built on this foundation and pointed to the necessity for "learning to live with memories of the deceased." This is a matter of delicate balance. It would not be healthful for the mourner to try to recall the deceased from the dead by his memories, trying neurotically to perpetuate the relationship through illusion. Neither would it be healthful to seek to extinguish all memory of the deceased because of the painfulness of such recall. The deceased must be remembered in a context of finality as one who has lived *and died.* The remembrances are a point of contact with the life of the deceased which are radically different from the relationship of presence during life.

The funeral itself is only one part, sometimes even a small part, in the whole psychological process of meeting bereavement. Yet, because of its public nature it is extremely important. It represents the response of the communitgy or the church to the emotional experiences of the mourners. Thus, it cannot be regarded as either irrelevant or contradictory to the psychological processes of acceptance, release, expression and assimilation that enable the mourner to endure and overcome the tremendous disorganization of his life which has taken place.

Form follows function. Design must, therefore, be related to usefulness and efficiency. But, even more, design seeks to integrate usefulness and beauty. The designer's problem is to find forms which meet diverse and complicated needs.

Several assumptions are basic to this effort to lay out an effective form for the funeral. First, the rationale of the funeral is fundamentally sound. I believe that the psychological, social and religious principles for helping those who are bereaved are well enough established to enable us to describe with some adequacy the function of the funeral. Rightly understood and conducted, the funeral has the potentiality for providing the form by which these functions are fulfilled.

Second, elements of the funeral practice of many ages, including our own, have not followed this rationale. It is undeniable that some forms have developed which have not been related to the major purposes of the funeral, or which may represent minor functions that disregard or even contradict more significant function.

A third assumption is that the existence of forms which do not follow the real function of the funeral has only damaged, but not destroyed, the validity of the funeral. I cannot share the view of some that the funeral is anachronistic and should be discarded. I believe that full value can be reclaimed for the funeral by bringing together function and form.

What, then, are the functions the funeral can fulfill for those in acute grief?

One of the functions of the funeral is to provide a framework of supportive relationship for mourners. This support is operative on two rather different levels: the support of religious or philosophical meanings and the support of a concerned group of family and friends.

As thoughtful man confronts death, he is driven by age-old

questions. What is death? What happens when a person dies? What causes death? Is there any justice in death? It is not only the meaning of death in general that is being probed, but mourners also struggle to fit the death of a loved one into their total picture of existence. The religions of the world and various philosophies of life have sought to provide some answers, hypotheses, articles of faith. The major goal is to support the mourners with a context of meaning which will be helpful in working through some of the intellectual problems associated with bereavement.

Since bereavement is a shared experience, the group (family, congregation, neighborhood) stands ready to support each of its members, particularly those who are most deeply involved in this individual loss. One of the ways in which the group fulfills this function is by just standing by to sustain the mourners until they have sufficient strength to assimilate their loss. Not only is this done through thoughtful giftgiving, flowers, memorials, food, favors, it is also done through attendance at the funeral. Here family and friends gather for the public occasion in which a life is commemorated, common meanings for death are affirmed and there is separation from the body of the deceased. On most occasions these are painful experiences for mourners and they are sustained by the presence of others in an act of community.

The funeral fulfills the function of providing supportive relationship most adequately when maximum participation by the community is enabled. This means that it is best when the funeral can be so arranged that a maximum number of the community can be present and participating. It also means that those in attendance should be participants rather than merely observers. Opportunity should be provided for readings in unison or, where possible, for some of those in attendance to speak of the loss which is shared by all. The public, corporate dimension of the funeral can be an effective channel for supporting those who have sustained the heaviest loss.

A second major function of the funeral grows out of the need for reenforcing the reality of death. The funeral is a means for enabling the individual to acknowledge his loss in a public setting. Not only does it provide a way of dramatizing the loss and what it means to the individual, it also, as we have said, affords a supportive relational framework in which the weight of reality can be tolerated and the painful process of reorientation begun.

To follow this function, it is necessary that the form of the funeral have a note of authenticity. It would probably be naive to insist that everything appear exactly as it really is. Life is just not lived that way. However, it is possible to strive to reduce to a minimum the disguises of reality and to work toward full recognition that disguises are involved. It would probably be expecting too much to propose the removal of all the accoutrements of the funeral that are provided to make it more aesthetically pleasing: the cosmetics provided to make the corpse more presentable, the simple flowers which relieve the starkness of the occasion, the artificial turf covering the excavated grave. Such things do damage only when they are taken seriously, when they complete the illusion of unreality, when they participate in a grand disguise of death as life. If that is their purpose, they should be resisted.

The funeral should not lend itself to any *serious* attempt to disguise reality. In a way, what is required here is what Kierkegaard called humor. This he defined as the capacity to see inadequacies and imperfections in something and still to maintain the capacity to hold it in high regard. Applied to the reality of the funeral, this would mean that one could see the imperfections manifested by the efforts made to approve appearances: removing the pallor of the corpse, of covering a pile of dirt. But such minor embellishments must *never* be used to hide the fact that death has occurred, that relationships have been severed, that a new focus for life must be found by the bereaved.

There should be no effort to disguise the fact that we are dealing with the *dead* body of a loved one, with an open grave.

Careful evaluation must be made to see whether practices are merely minor aesthetic touches or major attempts to deny the reality of death. Probably the central point in this whole issue is the corpse, the body of the deceased. On the one hand, it often has been regarded as a means for creating the illusion of life instead of facing the reality of death. It has been regarded as asleep rather than dead, it has been treated to give the illusion of imperishability, it has been the object of feelings which will not admit that death has changed relationships. So there have been proposals, many of them thoughtful, that getting rid of the body from the funeral entirely would avoid these illusions.

But one can also argue that, surrounded by the proper meanings, the presence of the dead body can be a significant means for reenforcing the reality of death and loss. If we have regard for the wholeness of man, his body, now dead, cannot be sloughed off unthinkingly. It provides tangibility, a physical object, which all the mourners see and consensually validates the fact of death.

Another function of the funeral is to make possible the acknowledgment and expression of the mourners' feelings. A mourner needs to be freed to release the great variety of feelings which may be welling up in him. Some of these feelings may well be verbalized or acted out in the funeral. Of course, not all feelings will emerge fully at the time of the funeral. But it is one of the functions of the funeral to provide a pattern of freedom and acceptance which will permit the emergence and assimilation of feelings as the mourning process goes on.

One can see the funeral as a means of creating a climate of acceptance within which the feelings that a person already has within him can be recognized and accepted. The content of the funeral should convey understanding of the feelings of the mourners, e.g. the sorrow which accompanies many deaths, the pain of separation. It is important not to dictate what feelings the mourner should be having.

Too often in the past one of the important criteria for

judging elements of the funeral was: will it cause an expression of feelings? On this basis some funerals have been made coldly impersonal because references to the deceased brought tears to the eyes of mourners. Others have proposed eliminating the body of the deceased from the funeral because it becomes a focus for the feelings of the bereaved. Still others want the funeral to be very brief, to the point of being perfunctory, as a way of reducing the emotional involvement of the mourners.

It is more helpful for the funeral to permit and even encourage the mourners to accept their feelings toward their situation, toward the deceased and toward themselves. The funeral can affirm the willingness of the community to understand and accept the feelings of the mourners. So any effort to screen the bereaved family from the community, to privatize the funeral, carries the implication that this community is unable or unwilling to accept and share in the expression of the mourners' feelings.

One other function of the funeral is to mark a fitting conclusion of the life of the one who has died. It may be thought of as a ritual of separation. There is a sense in which the radical discontinuity of death from life makes itself felt in sensing the ending of the relationship as it has been known.

There are a number of ways in which the funeral can accomplish this purpose. The realistic way in which the funeral faces death is involved. Realism is supported by the presence of the body of the dead and the separation from the body. It is sustained by a disavowal of the goal of long-term preservation. It is supported by the practice of concluding the funeral by disposing of the body of the deceased, whether by burial or cremation.

Death should be portrayed in terms of *both* the continuity and discontinuity it involves. To overbalance either of these poles renders the funeral less effective in carrying out this function. If the funeral rests solely on the theme of existence after death, as resurrection, social immortality or the ongoingness of the life-process, the finality of death from the standpoint of human experience may be regarded as illusory. The funeral is not designed to affirm that death has no effect upon man, that death is circumvented rather than endured.

The function of fittingly marking the conclusion of life also involves ways in which honor and respect can be shown for the one who has died. This does not mean an extravagant display of esteem by planning an unduly lavish funeral or through expansive memorials. This is no effort to deify the dead. Rather it is a recognition that death is an intensely personal thing. A person has died. Man's death is as distinctly individual and personal as his life. To pay no attention to his demise is a depersonalizing measure, just as much as it is to pay no attention to his living. Sophocles in his *Antigone* bore ancient witness to this fact. In a real way, marking the death of a person is a means of testifying to the worthwhileness of his living.

Obviously, it is clear that I regard the funeral as a valuable experience when it is rightly understood and conducted. I am not oblivious to some of its present shortcomings, but I am unwilling to accept the thesis that the funeral no longer can fulfill useful functions. There are elements of the funeral which have brought value to individuals and groups for many centuries. It can be shown that, even though some of the values may have been obscured by some contemporary patterns, the values persist and can be restored to full effectiveness.

References

Freud, S.: Mourning and melancholia. *Collected Papers.* New York, Basic Books, 1959, vol. IV.

Jackson, E.: *For the Living.* New York, Channel Pr, 1963.

Lindemann, E.: Symptomatology and management of acute grief. *Am J Psychiatry, 101:*141, 1944.

Van Gennep, A.: *The Rites of Passage.* Chicago, U of Chicago Pr, 1961.

Part V

Grief and Bereavement

14
Why You Should Understand Grief:
A Minister's Views
Edgar N. Jackson

IT IS IMPORTANT for us to know what grief is and how it works, for we have discovered that it is a major source of illness and distress to body, mind, and spirit. Research in psychosomatic medicine shows that some forms of illness are the means by which the human organism acts out its grief. Admissions to general hospitals are higher among the grief-stricken than among the general population. Admissions to hospitals for those with mental and emotional ailments clearly indicate a form of depression that is related to grief. Among the grief-stricken, spiritual crises develop marked by a loss of meaning for life and active despair. The percentage of suicides, both actual and attempted, among the grieving is above average. These things emphasize the importance of understanding what takes place in grief.

Grief is often camouflaged. This in itself presents a problem as the grief may not be expressed through the usual and more easily identified forms of behavior. In some it may appear as a subtle change of character. In others it may take the form of increased dependence on sedation, tranquilizers, or alcohol. In still others grief may be acted out as aggression and hostility or dependency and indecision. It is important to realize the variety of ways by which grief may manifest itself, for the human being is complex and brings into each new experience all that he is and has been in the past. With his response thus modified, variations, as numerous as the individuals involved, are produced.

221

The problem of coping with grief in contemporary culture is also somewhat different from what it was in the past. In the first place, grief is an experience of acute deprivation. In an affluent society, there is less experience in adjusting to deprivation, and thus there is less preparation for the injured personality to manage the new and disrupting experience of death.

In the second place, our culture is not only affluent but also largely death-denying and death-defying. It tends to isolate and leave the grief-stricken emotionally unsupported; the natural and usual feelings that come with grief seem to be rejected as inappropriate. Even the social devices which support the sound expression of emotion are being modified to conform to the death-defying mood and thus the bereaved person is doubly denied at the time when his need is most acute.

An implication of the general mood of denial is that it limits the opportunity both to talk out and to act out the deep feelings. If the general level of the nature and impact of acute grief could be understood, it would make significant communication more prevalent, and this in itself would have therapeutic value. And the importance of acting out deep feelings through rites, rituals, and ceremonials has special value when dealing with emotions too intense to be put into words.

It is important to understand that some emotions are often misinterpreted because there appears to be no direct relationship between the effect and the cause. Some of the unfortunate emotional responses show up in the unwise "falling in love," which is the way some people try to handle the emotional capital they are obliged to withdraw from the lost love object, but cannot wisely reinvest. Thus persons establish unwise or ill-advised love or dependency relationships to physicians, pastors, or others who happen to be on the scene during a period of emotional crisis.

With grief there is almost always guilt—real, neurotic, or

existential. This grows from the ambivalent nature of love itself, with its balancing of responsibility and privilege, sorrow and joy, benefits and deprivations. When death comes, life is rethought, and the bereaved tends to think of what might have been if he had been different. Some persons are overwhelmed by their feelings of guilt and try to punish themselves by using a variety of techniques of self-injury, self-deprivation, and self-rejection. Remorse is as unfruitful an emotion as self-pity, and when understood can often be relieved.

Wisely, funeral practices provide methods by which people can quickly work through their guilt feelings. Sometimes this is done by the final gift for the deceased, a casket, or by gifts to the bereaved. Gift-giving is a generally employed device for acting out guilt feelings, for it serves as a symbolic form of retribution when real retribution is no longer possible because of death.

On the more positive side, it should be noted that the person in grief needs a philosophical base from which to operate in sustaining the value of life. The whole idea of the rites and ceremonials at the time of death is to verify these ideas in the grieving individual and in the supporting community, which needs to assert its viability.

Other positive ideas are found in certain concepts—a concept of purpose that is adequate to give a significant meaning to a person's life and the lives of others; a concept of man as a being with sustaining spiritual value; a concept of God as essential goodness; a concept of death as relative; a concept of historical continuity; and a concept of an undying quality of some portion of what he may call his own soul. These ideas would be an achievement of the individual and would bear the marks of his own needs and the qualities of his own personality. For all practical purposes, these would be the elements of the faith he would live by. Often confrontation with death stimulates the building of a more positive philosophy of life.

Sometimes the person in grief is so puzzled by the feelings

and physical symptoms that possess him that he feels he is becoming emotionally disorganized. It is important to realize that grief has the characteristics of a normal neurosis; hence, for a short period of time the bereaved may well show symptoms and suffer feelings out of the ordinary.

Physically, these symptoms may involve the breathing apparatus, with shortness of breath, choking up, sighing, crying, and sometimes hysterical reactions. On a short-term basis this is quite normal and nothing to be alarmed about. The digestive system may also be affected by nausea, loss of appetite, loss of sphincter control, or compulsive eating and drinking. These symptoms, too, are quite within the range of the normal on a short-term basis. Also, there may be generalized responses, with weakness of the large muscle systems, dizziness, faintness, and an over-all feeling of distress. This, too, is quite within the range of the normal on a short-term basis.

The abnormal tends to show up when the normal responses are prolonged over extended periods of time, or when they do not show up at all. The person who shows no feeling may be in more difficulty than the one who does. We do not choose whether or not we have feelings, but only how they will be managed. When feelings are so powerful that they cannot be coped with, they are apt to be repressed, denied, or detoured into other behavior forms that act out the feelings through the body in illness, through the emotions in personality change, or through the mind in disruption of the basic value structure of the individual.

The seriously disturbed person, who is unable to function normally in meeting his own needs or in his basic relationships with others, needs special help and should have the benefits of treatment by those who are qualified according to accepted professional standards. Grief can be a most painful emotion, and for people to remain in that state for long periods of time is unfortunate and usually unnecessary.

Grief work is the natural process by which the emotions reorganize themselves to cope with the loss and re-establish healthful relationships. The essential processes of grief work are, first, the facing of the physical reality with all of its implications; second, the recognition and expression of the emotions that are relevant to the physical event; third, the process of working through the emotions by talking them out in visitations and family events or with trusted counselors, and also by acting out the deep feelings through appropriate rites, rituals, and ceremonials. These tend to create an atmosphere of acceptance of the emotions at the same time as they confirm the reality of the event. Fourth, is the acceptance of emotional support from the general community, the religious or spiritual community, and the supportive family. The grief-stricken are probably more dependent emotionally than at any time since early childhood. To deny this may create emotional hazards. To accept the fact and the feelings as well as the emotional support provided may be a major resource in hastening the process of wise grief-management.

Grief work may have its negative manifestations, and thus there are some things to guard against. We may try to blot out the natural pain by drugs. This usually does not serve a therapeutic purpose, but only postpones feelings that will then have to be dealt with at a less appropriate time and place. Unless there is a special medical problem, it is usually best to face the painful facts as quickly as possible and let the wisdom of the organism work itself out. Perhaps one of the soundest of the procedures for resolving psychological denial is the traditional practice of "viewing the remains." Here the basic facts of death are spelled out so that there is no longer any basis for psychological denial. This often produces a breakthrough of denied feelings and hastens the grief work.

An understanding of the meaning of grief as a profound emotion, and the other side of the coin of love, gives a sounder base for interpreting the meaning of life itself as well as for a significant structure of values for living. Furthermore, an understanding of grief supports a kind of courage that is not afraid to live because it is not afraid to recognize that life must be lived within mortal bounds. A wise reexamination and an imaginative development of resources may make it possible for us to understand clearly and to manage wisely the powerful emotions of grief so that life grows through the process rather than being destroyed by it.

15
Sudden Death: Pastoral Presence with the Bereaved

Irene Moriarty

When Mary came to the place where Jesus was seeing him, she fell at his feet and said to him, "Lord, if you had been here my brother never would have died." When Jesus saw her weeping, and the Jews who had accompanied her also weeping, he was troubled in spirit, moved by the deepest emotions.

John 11: 32-33

To be weeping, troubled in spirit and moved by the deepest emotions characterize one who is in grief. In approaching Lazarus' tomb, Jesus and Mary evidence the pain of those who mourn.

This article explores the pain of those who mourn, singling out the concerns of those who are suddenly bereaved. Building upon insight gained from counseling families in which an infant has died suddenly, it also offers suggestions for appropriate pastoral care of those who mourn a sudden death.

It traces the pastor's role in sharing the family's experience of discovering the death, in providing calm in the whirlwind of resuscitative and investigative activities, and in offering healing through the services that bring closure to the relationship, in counseling the family during this bereavement and in discerning spiritual dimensions of their grief. The pastoral role it espouses is that of allowing the situation to call forth one's own centeredness, sharing with the bereaved one's quiet presence, vulnerability and feelings.

Sharing the Experience of Discovery

Finding a person dead is an experience of such depth and intensity that the human psyche is overwhelmed. For many people, the cushion of denial and panic wrests them from this encounter almost immediately. Others, however, remain in the encounter for awhile, as this bereaved mother describes:

> I was dozing on the couch, but then I got up and went in to wake Mark so that we could have lunch and I could take the boys shopping afterwards. I knew something was wrong when I walked into the room. I could see the back of his head, and it was a funny color. I went and turned him over. I started giving him mouth-to-mouth resuscitation, but I was getting sick. I stopped I knew he was dead. I had just seen a talk show on SIDS so I knew that's what it was.
>
> The apartment got cold and clammy. I just backed out of the room and stood in the hall. It was horrible. It was like — you know that TV ad for that movie where there's a man just talking and they show a bassinet from the back so you can't see what's in it. And as he talks in a creepy voice, the bassinet slowly is turning around so you can see what's in it. All of a sudden a monster claw reaches out of it.
>
> I don't know how long I just stood there before I called the paramedics. But then I called, and everything started happening, and my neighbors took me and Jimmy to their apartment while they worked on the baby.

During the bereavement period, the moment resurfaces at unexpected times such as dreaming, the state between waking and sleeping, lovemaking, prayer or waiting at a stop light. Some bereaved people have found that looking at photos taken while their loved one was alive or the sight of him or her lying peacefully in a coffin help to erase this image. The incident becomes manageable in the retelling of it to a sensitive listener. Pastoral counseling requires encouraging such retelling, listening and assuring the family that moments of re-living the event are normal and eventually subside in intensity and frequency. Telling the story dredges up the feelings of the time, however, so family members may both recoil from talking about it and compulsively relate the details. This approach/avoidance toward anything that provides contact with pain is manifest throughout bereavement. The pastor can gently guide the bereaved to approach centering experiences (e.g. prayer, some types of fantasy, deep conversation, lovemaking, being touched by music or literature) and to be open to the feelings that surface. The bereaved person's ability to communicate the depth of the experience of finding the child is contingent upon his or her achieving sufficient distance from the event and developing a relationship of adequate trust with the listener. This may be months or years after the death, and it is the shedding of a heavy burden.

Creating Calm in the Whirlwind

During the first hours and days after the death, the family is caught up in a whirlwind of intervention to which they are very emotionally vulnerable. Their emotional condition is one of shock, confusion, numbness, pain, anger and bargaining. Moreover, they are caught up in a series of events that are unfamiliar to them, and they are interacting with professionals who are reacting to a crisis situation. It can be difficult for the professionals not to speak out of their own denial or bargaining, inadvertently excerbating the family's pain and guilt. The family is often avoided, and made to wait alone while no one provides a clear statement on their loved one's condition. By creating a place of stillness and calm within this tempest, the chaplain transforms it into a more humane experience which eventually contributes to the family's healing from this death. The minister brings centeredness to this situation by providing presence, information and closure.

To sit with the family and say, "I'm sorry this happened. They're doing everything they can for your daughter," sounds simple, but in the actual situation one may find these very words sticking in one's throat. Nonetheless, this human *presence* and vulnerability is precisely the pastoral care that the family most needs at this time. Mindful of their shock and numbness, the chaplain might move them to a private, quiet area, offer to phone relatives, and their personal pastor or physician, or if appropriate, offer to baptize their loved one during this critical time. Remaining with them during police questioning and consultation with medical staff also manifests the presence. It is necessary to let go of the impulse to do or say things, and simply *be there*.

Information is another major need of the family at this time. As a parent entreats,

> Let you know *something* that's going on, because when you're sitting there, you're thinking, "Well, what are they doing? What are they finding? What's happening?" And you're feeling *guilty* also. And you're thinking, "Are they suspecting that we smothered the child? Are we suspecting that she choked and we didn't care?" And these feelings are going through your mind all at the same time. And it's a double thing. You're worried about is there something they could have done, or is it . . . what is it?

The minister can use his/her position to mediate between family and medical staff. From the beginning the family should be told that the situation is serious and be kept advised of what is being done to resuscitate. Once the medical staff determines that the person is dead, the family should be notified and allowed an opportunity to speak with the physician. They should be told the cause of death if known; if not known, an autopsy is *strongly* advised. The family also needs assurance that the police and coroner investigations are routine in sudden deaths lest they fear that they are being singled out with suspicion. The normal post mortem changes that account for the appearance of the body should be explained to them.

Finally, the chaplain can provide the family with an opportunity to say good-bye to their loved one, to spend time talking or holding her or him again. The family may then need help in planning what to do next, such as contacting a funeral director or going to a friend's house. The chaplain might phone the family the next day to assure them of continued concern. An emergency room nurse describes such a *closure:*

> After that, I brought Jimmy into the pediatric room, and I prepared him for viewing because this is what the family wanted. The mother and the father and the whole family went up and they just circled the stretcher and viewed him. The one who wanted to touch him touched him.
>
> After awhile, the mother and father began to walk away, but they stopped and turned around and saw the family still there. So the mother and father went back to the stretcher. That mother picked up that child, and the father reached out and put his hand on him and put his other hand on the mother's hand. And where the mother got the strength to say what she said, I don't know. What she said came from 'way down deep.' But she said a good-bye and a thank you for all of the family, that they were here, and that they had that child for seven months.
>
> And after that she said her prayer and goodbye and they put Jimmy's body back down, the family all turned around, and they all walked out.

The pastoral counselor who becomes involved with the family after the death should be aware that the events just described comprise a story that the family needs to re-tell in the ensuing months and years. Anger and blaming that accompany the story may be appropriate to the family's experiences of that day, or they may be the family's scapegoating of the professionals in their anger at the death itself. The pastoral counselor's primary role is to elicit the story, to listen and encourage family members to share their perceptions of that day with one another.

Healing Through Closure Services

Given the breadth of individual, family and cultural variables, to generalize about the kind of services that are most healing for families would be specious. In addition to the practical necessity of disposing of the body, families need the following of the services and method of disposition they select: reinforce the reality of death, say good-bye, gather their support community and begin their grieving. Other families require a public proclamation of the meaningfulness of death, communal prayer and opening of themselves to the healing presence of God. The pastor can use the process of planning the services as well as the services themselves to address these needs.

The pastoral counselor can use the *occasion of deciding about services* to encourage family members to relate the story of the death and the events that followed, to reminisce about the deceased and search for memorabilia to be a part of the ritual, to share their faith and meaningfulness of this death for them and to communicate with each other. The pastor can then support them in their decision. One couple describes the support that they received at that time:

> The one thing about the funeral director was that he followed all our wishes. Whatever we wanted, he did. He also brought up this: "Do you want an open casket or a closed one?" In our case, we had it open. I'm really glad that we went along with that because when I found Karen she was a little distorted compared to the way she was after they fixed her up. And it was a really big help to me in remembering what she looked like. If we had left it closed, I suppose it wouldn't have been that tragic to me, but it really helped a lot.
>
> I think it's great that they let you have your option. Take a few hours to think about it. Go home and talk with your family about it. If you want to hold your child, rock her, they let you.

The situation of deciding about the services may be emotionally intense. Dysfunctional dynamics of power and patterns of communication longstanding within the family may impede the process. If a family is minimizing the situation in order to protect one of its members, consult directly with the member being "protected." Family members are highly susceptible to suggestion and may be receiving pressure from other relatives or friends to minimize this event and reinvest in life. This pressure to minimize is particularly evident when the death is of an infant or young child. Although there are situations in which the needs for family re-inforcing, good-bye saying and support group gathering can be met in other ways and direct disposition of the body is appropriate, this choice is far more likely to be a manifestation of avoidance or denial and should be gently confronted.

The anxiety and inadequacy that a pastoral counselor may feel in this situation are appropriate to these strong feelings and dynamics and should not be construed as indicative of the actual efficacy in the situation. In addition to whatever skills of facilitation one may have to offer, the pastoral counselor's contribution to his/her own prayerful centeredness in this emotional whirlwind should not be underestimated.

Families commonly are uncertain the *role*, if any, that *children should play* in the services. The children in the family each had a relationship with the deceased and therefore need ritual as do adults. Moreover, the loss and separation are the simplest feelings of grief and may be all that younger children apprehend about the death. To exclude children from sharing this significant family experience can reinforce these feelings. To attend the service dispels some of the mystery and superstition with which children surround death; to be excluded raises questions that vivid imaginations seek to fill. Attending the services also expresses to the children the support of the extended family and friends. Older children can invite their own friends and schoolmates to bring their own support system to the services. Any child's reticence to attend should be honored, although their fears may be dispelled by describing to them what will happen and assigning an adult to leave with them should they become frightened. Some of the most moving ceremonies are those in which the children of the family are a part of the service itself. They embody the reality that life continues.

Services are a *painful confrontation with the reality of death*, but in that confrontation lies their healing power. Seeing the person lying in a casket, hearing him or her spoken of in the past tense, receiving the stammered expression of friends' condolences — these reinforce for the family, "Yes, it's really true. She is really dead, not just away for the weekend." This is of particular importance in an unanticipated death because these seem especially unreal. The memory of having gone through the movements of the service may be the only reality that family members have to hold onto months later when they wonder if the whole thing was a dream.

Services draw together the family's *support system.* This helps the bereaved family by giving them the support of a gathered community, perhaps a community who can publicly reinforce their shared faith. To encounter others who also miss their loved one and who care for them is invaluable to a bereaved family. They later recollect this experience in their times of feeling isolation. This drawing together also helps the friends and relatives by providing them with a structured system in which to make that first awkward contact with family, paving the way for their condolence calls in the weeks that follow and that continue supportive contact throughout the mourning. Considering their numbness at the time, families later evidence a remarkable recollection of who attends or does not attend the services. Finally, services allow the family to *say good-bye to their loved one* and to be touched by the *healing presence of God.* The good-bye is said to one who is never coming back and comes from so deeply within that it can be articulated only through ritual and symbol, the same vehicle that articulates and precipitates one's experience of God. The pastor who facilitates the saying good-bye and being touched is one who allows his or her spiritual centeredness and feelings to be called forth by the community, is personally present to the emotions and dynamics of the community gathered and builds upon these and upon their shared faith to move the community forward with faith. The mechanisms for distancing oneself from pain can be subtle as one mother indicated when she observed that her pastor never removed his coat. Healing takes place through the presence rather than the elaborateness of the ritual, as a bereaved father describes:

> But he didn't say anything there. He disappeared, and I didn't know where he went. And I thought, Ok, I guess he just couldn't handle it. So off to the cemetery we went, and we went to where they have a chapel; you don't go to the graveside. They had the casket, on a little pedestal, and Father showed up. He walked up to the front, turned, looked at the casket, and at us. And then he said, "Blessed are the pure of heart, for they shall see God." And he turned around and walked out. That gave me chills then, and it gives me the chills every time I repeat it. But I was so thankful, and I think, this was the beginning of my recovery. What I had lost three days before, this the beginning of my recovery. I didn't think he could be that soft, but when he was . . .

Ministry During Bereavement

Unlike the rapidity of events surrounding the death and services, bereavement stretches well past the time social conventions allows it. The intensity of the symptoms subside after the funeral service, yet commonly people are just freeing themselves of the burden of grief one-and-half to two years after the death. This section presents select dimensions of bereavement and their implications for pastoral counseling.

Bereavement is such that families are unable to act on their own behalf. Therefore, the pastor bears the *responsibility to initiate* and maintain contact with them during this time. The pastor is central to a family's support system, and even a little contact carries great weight with them.

A *minimal schedule of contact* would be a personal visit one to two weeks after the death and another visit about six to eight weeks after the death. Other contacts, whether personal or by phone, might include the first major holiday after the death, the deceased person's birthday, the anniversary of the death, and in the case of a child or infant death, the birth or adoption of another child. These occasions, as well as major family events such as a graduation or wedding, renew the grief.

The *time spent with the family* is one of listening, reminiscing about their loved one, facilitating communication among family members, evoking and sanctioning their grieving and identifying and building upon their sources of support. The pastor should encourage touching and expressing emotions particularly crying. In order to be effective, the pastoral counselor must be willing to reach into one's own times of loss and to share one's vulnerability with the family.

The pastor who reaches out to counsel bereaved families can *anticipate being rejected by some.* This rejection has a number of sources. The family may be in tension at the time of the pastoral contact. If this is a possibility, the pastor who is rejected should offer to call again. On the other hand some families are antipathetic toward religion and do not want pastoral intervention. Other families have sufficient inner support that there is no need of outside help, or strong cultural or familial patterns that allow them to resolve their grief in their own way. Still other families are adamant in their denial of the death or are firmly entrenched in patterns of interaction that not only are internally destructive but also highly resistant to intervention. To be rejected can be frustrating for a minister who sees the family's needs and know[s] that she or he has the skills to help.

Guilt that they may have caused the death is particularly strong with suicide, accidental death, parents whose child has died or young children who may believe that their fantasies caused the death. Other things about which families commonly feel guilty include: negative feelings they had towards the deceased, their own grieving (e.g. they are able to laugh or they feel jealous of those who have never suffered a loss) unfinished business in a relationship and that they did something to deserve this punishment.

A death can place great stress on the *relationships within a family*, both because of the withdrawal from relationships evidenced by some people in pain, and because of the restructuring of roles and responsibilities that follows the loss of one member. On the other hand, these relationships can be a primary source of support, nurturing, and healing as members take turns being strong and being dependent. In order to facilitate the latter, the pastor can encourage openness and communication and point out the ways the family is grieving differently. Family members benefit from knowing that the others are also hurting, and they may be unable to identify another's grieving.

Often parents are uncertain about what to tell their *children* about death and are too caught up with their own grieving to be able to respond to their children. They appreciate help in guiding their children through grief. The pastor can support the parents in speaking openly about the death with the children and in sharing together their experiences of bereavement. The pastor can also assist the parents in explaining the death to the children and reassure the children that their experiences are normal and will subside with time. Bereavement counselors have found that the family photo album is an effective vehicle for communicating with younger children.

Unresolved grief from previous losses often resurface with a subsequent death, compounding the grieving. This is particularly true of deaths that parents have suffered in childhood. It is also evident in the grandparents of an infant who dies who have themselves suffered an infant death a generation before and have not been allowed to grieve for it. Encourage grieving the former death along with the present one.

The approach/avoidance dynamic described earlier enters into the *sexual relationships* of the bereaved. This is in part attributed to the effect that grieving has on one's sexual appetite, causing some to lose interest in sexual activity while causing in others intense arousal. In addition, some people withdraw from relationships in pain while others reach out to them. These patterns are particularly evident in the intimacy of sexual relationships. The centering of making love, which can cause feelings of grief to surface, and the relationship of sexual intercourse to conception, if the death was that of a child, can also contribute to ambivalence toward sexual activity. Thus bereaved parents may emotionally withdraw from each other in their sexual relationship creating tension and reinforcing the isolation and pain of their grieving. On the other hand, they may embrace sexual intimacy precisely because it allows them to experience their feelings, to share support and help each other in their vulnerability, to be renewed in love and to experience the healing of physical touching.

Although the bereaved family's sometimes selfish sense of the uniqueness of their pain should be respected, talking with others who have undergone a similar experience is valuable for alleviating their loneliness, isolation and fear that they are going insane. *Grief support groups* provide this opportunity and a pastor would be wise to familiarize oneself with the resources already available in the community. If no such group exists, the congregation or cluster of congregations might start one. Many grief support services have originated in religious settings. The kind of support that families experience talking with other bereaved families simply cannot be had elsewhere, and this outlet for expression of grief alleviates some of the strain on the regular support system.

The pastor may strengthen the family's *support system* by encouraging friends and relatives or other concerned laity in the congregation to visit the family, helping with day to day things and listening to them. Families may or may not wish to share their grief with others. They may seclude themselves to avoid the awkwardness they feel around others who don't know what to say to them. They may avoid their favorite bar, church services, or other gatherings of folks they know.

A normal period of bereavement extends 18 to 24 months after the death. Most expressions of sympathy are given in the first two weeks with no outreach to the family after that time. The pastor can model an ongoing awareness of the presence of bereaved people in the congregation by addressing the alienation, pain and anger of grief during regular Sabbath or Sunday services.

One final observation about bereavement ministry is that the congregation's best interests are served by the *ministers who nurture themselves*, that is, ministers who are aware of their own limits, and able to say no and ask for help, who receive ministry from the laity and encourage congregation members to minister to them, who tend to their own families and support systems, and who take time to pray and play for themselves. Burned out, cynical pastors are ineffective in the support they can offer and in their modeling of a healthy investment in living.

Discerning Spiritual Issues

Another relationship that can be profoundly affected by the experience of grieving is a person's relationship with God, in which one can experience the gamut of alienation, guilt, blame, betrayal, anger and/or deepening of trust, nurturing and commitment. This is true for children as well as adults. In addition, to the extent that prayer and religious services are centering for the individual or family, they facilitate feeling the depth of the loss. Unfortunately, one's relationship with God and practicing of religion are often heavily weighted with moral values and one prohibits oneself from experiencing or articulating negative feelings towards God and religion. This can prevent a person from healing the loss. Although the individual who is overtly angry may be more uncomfortable for the pastor to be with, that person may move beyond the anger and blame more easily than one who does not acknowledge them. This section will briefly explore some of the religious concerns of bereaved and offers suggestions of pastoral intervention that can be effective in addressing these concerns.

There are five ways in which people respond to a death spiritually. The first is to choose faith, firmly, stead-fastly and blindly; the death was God's will, and that is that. The second is to equally firmly choose disbelief. A third is to incorporate the death into an ongoing, vital faith and wrestle through the feelings in prayers and dialogue. The fourth is to grieve the death within a disbelief system, not healing through an acknowledged opening of oneself to God, but through receiving the love of friends and family, being honest and experiencing and sharing the feelings of grief, resonating with the articulation of human pain of the arts and/or one's own ethnic heritage and enjoying the relief of transcendence that humor can provide. For each of these four, the belief system that preexisted the death is able to accommodate it. The fifth type of response, one that is very painful, is that the bereaved person is plummetted into a crisis of faith in which the old beliefs cannot accommodate the death.

In discerning the way in which people are handling the death, one should listen to the feelings that underlie what the bereaved is saying, listening for the fluidity of a relationship or feelings that are being processed versus the frozenness of denial or suppressed anger or guilt.

Most families appreciate hearing an articulation of their tradition's theology of afterlife. It allows them to let go of worrying about their loved one.

"Why did this happen" is the question that all families ask. For professionals in ministry, this questions touches into centuries of theological debate about the existence of evil, the will of God, divine intervention, and so on. It may also touch into years of one's own painful struggling with those issues. For the family member, however, the question is deeply emotional. It is wise to address this feeling level first. Individuals may be seeking of a minister not an answerer but a listener who will hear them through their questioning. The pastor's not having all the answers sanctions their not having all the answers, either. At times it is the bereaved themselves who are the teachers.

To allow the bereaved to call forth one's centeredness, sharing with them one's quiet presence, vulnerability and feelings takes many forms in the varied roles which a pastor has in relation to the family. In sharing the experience of the discovery of death, counseling bereavement and discerning spiritual issues, the pastoral counselor employs skilled listening, and presence to pain, elicits story-telling, encourages experiencing and expression of feeling, particularly through centering experience, and encourages communication among family members. During the whirlwind of professional intervention the pastoral counselor offers presence, provides information and facilitates closure. Through the funeral or memorial services the pastor can help the bereaved family to recognize the reality of death, say good-bye to their loved one, gather their support community, begin grieving, publicly proclaim the meaningfulness of death and open themselves to the healing presence of God.

16
How Do I Tell Them? The Gentle Art of Death Notification

Larry A. Platt and Roger Branch

High on the list of jobs nobody wants is the task of telling someone that a loved one or close friend has died. Although it is obviously necessary, no one is eager to assume the responsibility. W. J. Smith (1985: 7) reported a case where a father's pain over a stillborn child was magnified because he learned the bad news by hearing the obstetrician and pediatrician arguing loudly over who would tell the parents.

No doubt part of this reluctance to serve as the messenger of death is related to the inherent sadness of the experience. Moreover the unfamiliarity of death in modern society along with its death-denying tendencies adds to the difficulty of the task. As products of the same culture, ministers are not immune to feelings of uneasiness and avoidance tendencies. Not even a well-defined theology of resurrection and eternal life will make this duty easy. Indeed, nothing makes it easy. There is no formula, no set of correct phrases, that will ward off the shock and pain for those who must hear the bad news.

Yet death notification can provide an opportunity for significant ministry. Some people who are bereaved remember every detail of these early moments of grief while others retain only vague, general recollections. In either case they always recall with gratitude anyone who with sensitivity and compassion helps them through this dark moment of life.

Ministers, hospital and military chaplains, and Christian counselors often have passed to them the task of informing family members and friends of a loved one's death. The fol-

242

lowing suggestions will not ease the sorrow but they are valuable guides to a more effective ministry, providing as much help as possible for the bereaved.

Empathize

Before you speak, put yourself in the other person's place. The greatest barrier to effective service is the tendency to turn in on oneself in reaction to a stressful situation. When we focus upon ourselves, we fail to think of the other person and to anticipate conditions, needs, and probable reactions.

What is the present state of the hearer's physical and emotional well-being? What issues and concerns are already on his or her mind? Imagine the impact of what you are about to say. What things will the hearer want to know, both immediately and over time? Have some general strategy in mind and the facts organized.

Consider the Surroundings

Be aware of the physical environment in which you will be speaking to the bereaved. News of death is bad news, often physically and emotionally devastating. Some places are almost barren of structural resources to deal with crises that may emerge.

For example, hospitals are organized for the care of the living. They are poorly designed in terms of physical structure to meet the special needs of death notification in most cases. There is little privacy. Survivors often find themselves huddled in cold, sterile hallways that are empty and forbidding or full of bustling people.

Examine the place where you are. Try to get to a spot where there are chairs or benches. If prior arrangements can be made with staff members to secure a bed if it is suddenly needed, it is a wise precaution.

An example of a thoughtful approach to death notification was provided by Sergeant Smith, a veteran highway patrolman. After a man was killed in an auto accident, Sergeant

FIGURE 3

Points to Consider in Death Notification

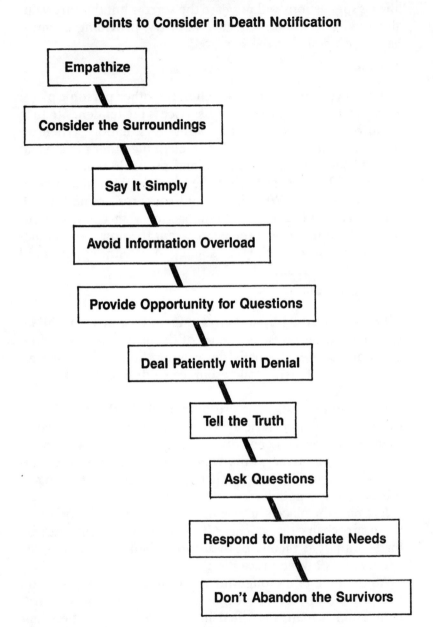

Empathize

Consider the Surroundings

Say It Simply

Avoid Information Overload

Provide Opportunity for Questions

Deal Patiently with Denial

Tell the Truth

Ask Questions

Respond to Immediate Needs

Don't Abandon the Survivors

Smith had the duty to inform the man's wife. He arrived at the home just as she was leaving her automobile carrying a large bag of groceries in each arm. Realizing that she might drop the groceries or collapse in public, he approached her and said, "Here, let me take those groceries into the house for you." Naturally the woman knew that something was wrong from the moment that the trooper arrived. However, he saved her from the harsh blow of the bad news until they were shielded from public view and in a location where she could sit down. If she had collapsed, couches or beds, water, and possibly medication were nearby. A telephone was at hand to summon family members and friends. Sergeant Smith steered the notification process into the best available environment.

Say It Simply

Communicate the message accurately. The experience is so stressful for survivors that shock can set in almost instantly, distorting perceptions and interfering with communication. Avoid long pauses while casting about for the right words to say the sad thing best. "Say it straight"—directly and simply.

Don't use technical jargon—medical terms that might sound learned and professional. Remember Cassell's (1979) contention that the application of these technical terms to death, which is a fundamentally moral event, is one of the reasons death is such a problem in modern society. More importantly, they fail to communicate, which is the central task of the moment. For example, physicians' use of "gestationally nonviable infant" (Smith 1985: 5) to refer to a stillborn or newborn child might make about as much sense to a parent whose child had just died as a sentence in Sanskrit.

Avoid euphemisms. Saying that someone has "passed away" in no way changes the stark reality that he has died. Unless the hearer is listening closely and is familiar with this colloquial way of referring to death, the potential for misunderstanding is great. Consider the case of the nurse who intercepted the wife of a man who had just died as she was going to his room, as yet uninformed of his death. Adopting a tone intended to be both professional and sympathetic, the nurse declared, "Mrs. Blank, your husband is no longer with us." "Well, where have you transferred him?" the still uncomprehending widow demanded. "Mrs. Blank, I'm sorry but your husband has just died" would have worked much better.

Avoid Information Overload

Relate the message in manageable units. It is not necessary to say everything in the first sentence. Prior planning will help you sort out the essentials, which should be set out as concisely, accurately, and clearly as possible early in the notification process.

One common reaction to anxiety is to talk too much, and death notification is stressful enough to generate anxiety. There is a tendency to avoid silence, filling every moment with words. However, once the essential information has been provided, silence can be valuable. It gives opportunity for the message to sink in and for the survivor to organize his thoughts.

Provide Opportunity for Questions

Questioning is a natural part of complex communication. No matter what you have said, no matter how well you have presented the message, people will ask questions. You should not think of it as doubting your truthfulness or as a measure of how well you have done your job.

Questions allow the newly bereaved to clarify and amplify their understanding of the death message. What happened? Where? When? How? Who was there? Did the dying person say anything? If so, what? Was the death very painful? In many cases, the questions will cover facts that have already been stated. Remember that under stress the mind does not operate quickly or accurately. Some of your statements may not be heard at all or may be heard incorrectly.

Questions help to establish reality. Part of the requested

repetition of facts is aimed at transforming painful, undesirable information into experimental reality.

Questions allow the survivor to deal with important issues of personal concern which might not be obviously significant to another. Details that might be omitted in the telling because they are not seen as important may be drawn out through questioning.

Deal Patiently with Denial

Outright denial of the death report is not an unusual response. Sometimes death seems so impossible that denial is almost automatic. "I was just with him an hour ago at lunch and he was in perfect health. He couldn't be dead of a heart attack." Denial is also a defense mechanism against an emotional blow that is too much to accept.

It is pointless to argue with this rejection of fact. Denial is an emotional response that short-circuits normal intellectual activity. It will pass, and you will probably be asked to restate the facts, although the requests may come hours, even weeks later.

Tell the Truth

While it is not always necessary, or perhaps even wise, to relate everything that you know at once, do not say anything that is not true.

Generally, people who report death events do not intentionally distort the facts. However, they sometimes fill gaps in their knowledge with conjecture or what they think the bereaved person wants to hear. Their motives may be good but problems almost always develop as a result of the inaccuracies.

Such statements as "I'm sorry I don't know the answer to that" or "I don't know and surely wish I had thought to ask that" are good examples of how to respond to questions when the point-of-fact answers are unknown.

Two of the most often asked questions are, "Did he say

anything?" and "Did he suffer much?" There is a powerful temptation to insert a "white lie" on behalf of the grieving survivor. What's the harm in inventing a last loving message from dying lips? What good is there in telling someone that a loved one died in agony? One problem is that falsehoods usually are detected. For example, another witness will give a conflicting report. Legal actions may be taken which require truth telling. If your integrity as a messenger is destroyed, your role as comforter will be compromised. It makes good sense to limit gory details, but don't deny the existence of suffering if a direct question is asked. Something like, "Yes, he was in some pain, but not for long" is both accurate and sensitive to the emotional distress of the bereaved.

Ask Questions

Use questions to test whether the person receiving the death notification has adequately understood what you have said. Try to get him or her to repeat to you the essential information. Sometimes genuine confusion exists. Grief and shock distort mental functioning. Questions can help you check the accuracy of communication. They also help to reveal the physical and emotional conditions of the hearer, including needs that require immediate attention.

Respond to Immediate Needs

Be prepared to help deal with immediate problems and issues. In some instances this might include calling for medical assistance. Strong physical and emotional grief reactions are not uncommon and may require quick response. One valuable service is to help assemble an interpersonal support system by calling family members and friends who live nearby. Notification of kin who live farther away is usually done by the family or an intimate friend who knows the family well. However, in some cases survivors may need help with this task. Often there are minor children at home, school, or play with whom the bereaved needs assistance. Just assuming the responsibility for picking up a child from school can be extremely helpful. It is probably best in most situations for a parent to inform a child about the death, but a minister may also play a significant helping role, especially if he has a strong positive relationship with the child.

The survivor might seek guidance about what to do next. Many people have made no plans for dying and few know much about what to do when it happens.

Don't Abandon the Survivor

If the survivor is alone, at least stay until other aid arrives. Try to be there regularly as a source of help and consolation. Ministers are, or certainly can be, critically important members of the caring circle of family and friends who offer special assistance.

Raleigh is a strong man with scores of friends. But he was shattered by the death of his wife of over thirty years. A steady stream of earnest friends sought to offer consolation during funeral home visitation and at his home. However, he turned again and again to a minister for help, and they repeatedly found strength through prayer.

The most important thing that a minister can do for the bereaved is be there.

References

Cassell, Eric J. 1979. "Dying in a Technological Society." In Larry A. Bugen, ed. *Death and Dying: Theory, Research, Practice.* Dubuque: William C. Brown Company Publishers. pp. 291-298.

Smith, W.J. 1985. *Dying in the Human Life Cycle.*

17
Grief and Grief Management: Some Reflections
Erich Lindemann

Physicians and psychiatrists are now practitioners in the field of grief and bereavement, and they, too, have had to acquire a philosophy regarding death and its meanings. On a very simple level, physicians need to understand grief and bereavement because studies show that many people become sick following the death of a loved person. A great many more hospital patients have had a recent bereavement than people in the general population. And in psychiatric hospitals, about six times as many are recently bereaved than in the general population. So it is somewhat of an urgent medical problem.

Furthermore, in a great many conditions, both physical and psychological, the mechanics of grieving play a significant role. I am talking about bereavement in a functional and operational way rather than in an existential way; and I am drawing on information furnished not only by patients but also by bereaved persons who were not patients but who offered themselves as subjects when psychiatrists found it necessary to study the process of grieving in normal people.

I think of the processes of grieving as constructive processes which deal with a significant transition from one combination of roles and action sequences to a new one. Death is one form of social change, in which a member of a social group departs and cannot be restored. There are other changes in which somebody leaves and might come back. There are some changes where he definitely will come back and one would not like him to come back. Not all departures

250

of people by death or otherwise are departures which one mourns. Some departures are necessary, highly wished for. We kill a few people once in a while, both outside and inside the country. We have discussions about capital punishment, whether or not we should put people to death. So death seems not just to be an inexorable thing that befalls all of us, but also an instrumentality of social life. People have to get out to make room for others, and people have to be rearranged with each other to maintain a viable network of social relationships.

Now saying that, I bring something quite positive to death in the sense that perhaps the departure and the concern with the departure might include a component of resurrection: i.e., a new situation in which this person is not completely absent because what he had to give stays in the system even though he might have died in the flesh. And one of the interesting aspects of our working with bereaved people, even as a secular physician or psychiatrist, seems to me to be the theme of resurrection. The problem is, however, that the resurrection cannot take place in terms of the individual now mourned. The resurrection has to take place in terms of the functions which this person had in the life of the survivors. And work with bereaved people, which we started some twenty years ago and gradually have learned to do better and better, has turned out to be a search for a proper allocation of the functions of the now-deceased person in the network of surviving people, including the one who happens to be the patient.

If that is so, we ought to look at some of the features of the bereaved state. Very clearly the mourner goes through a phase of great perplexity, emotional paralysis, preoccupation with his own condition, vivid preoccupation with the image of the person who has departed; and gradually begins to ask certain questions. The first questions may be, "Where is he? Is he in heaven? Is his presence still tangible, for example at the breakfast table in the morning? Can I hear him speaking to me?" Or is he perhaps in some way going to live on in the roles and functions which he had which some other people might take over? And the core of what we call "grief work," which we can teach, which we can support, and which we can learn from patients who do it best, seems to be that the various components of the now-deceased person will be reviewed, scrutinized, rearranged so that the particular unique constellation which the loved one had which seems at first irreplaceable can now be replaced by a number of people who can take on this load of meaningful participation in the survivor's life orbit.

Now this is difficult to do because it hurts. And why it hurts so much puzzled Freud, has continued to puzzle our psychoanalysts, and is puzzling us as physicians who deal with such patients. And if one looks closely, one might find that some of the recent developments reported in the literature regarding experiments on behavior in general—both animal and human behavior—instead of focusing as they used to on drive satisfaction, on instincts and their vicissitudes, now focus on sequences of action which may be programmed in a satisfying way by a given person, provided he can look ahead to an undistrubed opportunity for further acting in these routines. As soon as he anticipates that his programming may be upset, for example by an impending death, he becomes anxious. However, if somebody actually has died, one finds a situation in which one has to look backward; and there has to take place a momentary stopping of one's whole program of actions; and these actions now have to be reordered in such a way that they are fitting the new system in which one lives, which is without the person who died. Now this phase of retrospective rehearsal of past events, reallocating the specific patterns which belonged to the shared life—this is called "grief work."

We also notice that quite often the job of redistributing the related activities is extremely difficult, and cannot be done by one mourner alone. There is usually a collectivity of mourners, and the mourner whom we, as doctor, psychiatrist or counselor meet, is one of them, unfortunately often separated from the others and prone to consider grieving as a solitary business. Such a patient may retreat into a psychological cave and be very busy with what the deceased meant for him. The constructive step is being busy with situations involving the interaction of a number of people, of whom the person who departed was only one. And if one does that, one is likely to find that the redistribution is much more possible than one thought.

Particularly severe forms of grieving occur if the mourner was excessively dependent on the person who died. In such instances, the deceased may have accounted for supervision, for love, for support, for participation, for initiation of action, and so on. If this person is gone, it is extremely hard to reconstruct one's program. But even in the more usual situation of loss of parent or spouse or close friend, the more intimate aspects of the relationship cannot easily be transferred to anyone else. The point is that in every bereaved state there comes, during the time of counseling, a review of the possibility that there will emerge a feasible life, a feasible role which is cherished in some manner by the others as it used to be cherished by the now-deceased, so that one's self-worth is re-established.

The second significant aspect of the "resurrection" of the deceased is the internalization, or more precisely the unconscious fusion, of some part of his image with the self of the survivor. This means that some of the operations which the deceased person used to do previously now are enacted and felt to be part of the survivor. This is one of the most common experiences, probably occurring at least briefly in every severely bereaved person. In most counseling this is likely to be underplayed because it is difficult and confusing to understand, in the first place, and hard to alter, particularly if the person is so busy with the change within himself that he doesn't do the work of grieving which we have described above. In other words, sometimes the resurrection of the deceased within the confines of the survivor serves the purpose of evading grief work because it falsifies the situation. Just how this operates has been the topic of a number of recent articles: this problem of internalization, of temporarily sharing the roles which the deceased person previously had and executing them for him, so to say, after he is gone. It seems to have somewhat of the function of a moratorium, so that one can postpone most of the grieving, and through enacting the role of the deceased, can scrutinize intensely his unique style of interacting with the human and non-human environment. How effective this psychological process of role-playing can be is well illustrated in psychodrama, where, however, the assumption of other peoples' roles is intentional, while in the case of bereavement it is unconscious. Now for the counselor, the important task is to understand this process and share it with the patient or counselee in such a way that you allow him to do it, but lead him step by step to the insight that this is a temporary phase of the readaptation, and that this form of "resurrection" cannot replace the work of mourning.

Now the third point is this: that we see a great many grievers who grieve not for another person who died, but who grieve for themselves. And when you have an incongruity between the future operations of your own self in terms of what it used to be and its future operations in terms of what it can be now, you are likely to find a remarkable process of grieving which has come to light recently in work on the rehabilitation services. A great many people come to our attention after losing a leg, losing an eye, after crippling arthritis, after accidents in which they incurred a marked deformity. And if you look carefully, you will see that they are "hung up" on the grief work. Namely, the roles which they used to play when they still had their leg, or before they were blind have now to be replaced by a new set of roles vis a vis others with complementary roles and with new expectations and satisfactions. And this is just as painful as losing another person. As a matter of fact, one loves oneself somehow just a little more than almost anybody else; and the difficulty of dealing with severe, drastic change in one's own self is one of the core problems which one finds on the rehabilitation ward.

One finds it also in many depressed people who are stuck with depression because they, or an important other person, did something which shattered their self-image as a person who can always be expected to live up to a particular social or moral code. If a dear friend, or one's beloved self, dramatically fails to carry out an expected role, then one might find a very interesting form of grieving for the lost self, which now has to be reinstated in some new network of activities and expectations about oneself. Many of the people who come back from jail have a terrible time, as you know, and the problem is both within themselves and with the others who take them back. Similarly, a great many people who have been in the mental hospitals cannot be reintegrated into their families because it is not understood by either party that there is a new role relationship. They cannot simply step into the old role they used to have before they became sick. The patient is a new person now. Also in the meantime, while he was gone, particularly if he stayed in a state hospital some distance away, his family accidentally did some grieving about him; so that when he comes back they have emancipated themselves from him and figured out a new role network.

Consider also the contemporary community mental health effort. The central maxim is: never take disturbed persons out of the home if you can possibly help it; let them stay there while one learns instead how the home works; have teams which go out into the homes and assist them in this setting. This is an example of how inclusion of states of grief in medical and psychiatric research and practice has led to some significant changes in the organization and distribution of health services. In no small measure, these studies of bereavement contributed to the development of the contemporary

program in community mental health, which has greatly increased the scope of psychiatric activities in the community.

Psychiatrists are trying to solidify the styles of counseling
which are appropriate for them, while learning how to be
effective as consultants to the other helping professions.
Mourners do not readily accept consolation and counseling.
When one visits a bereaved person, one may get the feeling,
"I am really not wanted here." Under these circumstances,
the counselor has an impulse to withdraw; but to hang on just
at this time may be most helpful. He must accept as a basic
issue that he is justified in asking the bereaved to tolerate his
presence.

The period of confrontation with the loss begins after a
week or ten days, when all the business of the ceremonial is
over, and is mixed with hostility and depression. And it is only
then, when the sorrow is really felt, that there gradually
emerges what we call grief work. I have referred to resurrection: a fervent effort to resurrect or make permanent what the
deceased person had to offer; and one way of doing it is by
enacting it oneself. Usually, however, this cannot be enacted
in toto, but little things which were part of the roles of the
loved one who died have to be picked up. The problem
becomes one of redistributing the activities of the deceased
person among other significant people in his orbit. And I
think that, for counselors, this whole string of specific piecemeal replacements of the functions of the person who died
becomes one of the major areas of counseling. For instance,
who makes the decisions in the family now? Who enforces
discipline? When the husband was alive, the mother could
say, "You just wait till Daddy comes home," or, hiding behind
his authority, "I have to ask Daddy if you can have the car or
not." In other words, a number of interactions with other
members of the family have been conditioned to the presence
of this lost member and now the griever has to take over some
of these responsibilities, not by morbid identification, but
simply because there are issues to be settled.

In this very important phase of grieving, it is difficult to know what the counselor should do and what part of the assistance should be shared among other helping professions. He is competent to make the problems explicit and to give hints regarding resources in the community which the person previously might not have used. There are books on how to prepare your wife to be a widow, and the insurance companies are interested in this problem. In churches and in groups like "Parents without Partners" one finds people who have recently gone through similar situations, are having the same predicaments, and can jointly mobilize these resources.

In other words, the resurrection, or the reaffirmation of the activities, of the now-deceased person can be done in effective ways, usually in collaboration with others, or can be done in a forced somersault way by the mourner himself, who eventually has to realize that this cannot work. The person who is outgoing and finds it easy to make contacts and reach out for help will do well, while the person who is shy and easily embarrassed, or who is preoccupied with all the love scenes which should have taken place and the quarrels which should not have taken place, who is very busy with the past, will need some time to work this through before the resurrection for the future can occur.

The counselor should realize that the surviving parent often feels perplexed as to how to speak about the death of the spouse to the children. One of the meaningful contributions of research has been to show that it's a different story at different age levels. For a child two or three years old, the failure of the person to return may be seen as an arbitrary act, because parents are considered as omnipotent: they can control the environment. So the death, for the young child, may mean that father or mother has deserted him, and often has the quality that it has for grownups if the person committed suicide. The youngster will often remember all the mischief he did or contemplated vis a vis Dad or Mother, and then get into this bind, "I have been a bad boy, or girl, and they have rejected me."

For children, particularly girls, to lose the mother before age five is often catastrophic. For boys, a particularly catastrophic event is to lose their father when they are in puberty, when they just begin to emancipate themselves and to think, "How could I do it alone, and get rid of this guy who is always blocking me?" And then if in fact father dies, there often ensue great complications of adolescent development. There is, of course, guilt about one's negative feelings toward him. Moreover, there is a void if he is not there to set and enforce limits and to provide direction. A good many of these youngsters who may previously have turned to uncles and other boys' dads and Scout leaders as substitute fathers, when father actually dies cannot at first use such substitutes very well. Hence it is a highly specialized counseling problem to help these boys go through this very difficult grieving, which is mixed up with emancipation problems at that particular stage of development.

Similarly, if a little girl's father dies while she is involved in relinquishing her abandoned, childish expression of affection in favor of more grown-up, reserved ways of behaving with him, she may also suffer a significant interruption of her normal development. When the parent dies suddenly, then the loss is not only bereavement but also being stuck in a developmental task. This may have the consequence that in this area no further development takes place. Psychiatrists find such developmental gaps in adults who are treated for neuroses and mental disturbances.

Bereavement refers to an objective state, a change in the network of social relationships which has been brought about by the departure of some person. Death is the most irretrievable form of this, but one can also discern elements of bereavement in other crises, in a whole variety of situations in which there is drastic social change. For example, a group of men works very nicely together for a number of years, and then one of the members is promoted to be the boss. The others are bereaved and he is bereaved and has a promotion depression, because he now has been removed from the opportunity for a style of give-and-take with a group which had become dear to him, and has to operate in a new way. Or, the marriage in which a young woman moves over into the orbit of the husband, so that the contact with her own family is greatly reduced, may go through a bereavement in the objective sense that the amount of interaction with those who used to be accessible to her is very much less. She may find herself depressed, in a grief state, when she least expects it. Obstetricians and pediatricians may encounter the puerperal depression which develops right after the first baby comes. And what is the bereavement there? Being a young mother in some way becomes an incarceration. Surely she has access to new experiences, new duties and activities; but particularly if she was a professional woman and had to give up her work when the baby arrived, many of her previous companions have been lost. Hence a bereavement exists which is often not acknowledged under these circumstances. Here, also, the grief work has to be done.

It is important for mental health counselors to be alert to these modified forms of bereavement and to the kinds of grief processes which one should expect, because knowing how grieving works, one can help these people accept that they have this feeling rather then being embarrassed about it; and secondly, one can make them come to terms with the fact that you cannot just lose contact with significant others without grieving about it. You have to do something about the resurrection side of it, to replace them in one way or another.

Now what are the things which might happen in poor grieving? I have mentioned the problem of misidentification, which is such a difficult and unexpected thing, where the enactment of the deceased person may function as a delay of the grief work. Another common problem is the excessive hostility and irritability which alienate the griever from others. Another type of poor grievers are persons who are so overwhelmed by their loss that they feel that they would disintegrate if they allowed themselves to grieve; and some of them do indeed commit suicide. The ever-recurring phrase is, "I couldn't live without him," or "without her." So the violence and hostility which is felt may turn against the self. It is important to sense this, and not to push the person to grieve under these circumstances. On the other hand, not to leave such a person but to keep up the contact is a very important, supportive thing to do.

The magnitude of the emotions which are either truly aroused or suspected by the griever may lead to other operations which we call neurotic defenses. A person mobilizes ways of dealing with the situation which would make the grieving unnecessary, such as putting all the belongings of the deceased into one room, locking that room and never going into it. Some people make abrupt decisions to leave the place where they used to live with their husband or wife and go into a new setting, as though they could leave behind the reminders of the person who died. This avoidance of the recollection of the way the loved one looked, the way he talked, which is quite contrary to the grief work, where one has a very vivid imagery along these lines, is quite characteristic of those people who are not ready to grieve or who cannot manage to do it.

It is among these people who have forgotten the image, repressing it, technically speaking, that one finds patients who are victims of illness or of peculiar psychological states of various forms. There may be an identification with the illness of the person who died. The survivor is then very busy going from doctor to doctor, getting angry with the doctor who does not concur with his diagnosis. Or, the griever may not be busy with grieving, but with finding and prosecuting a villain who he believes is responsible for the death. In each case, the mourner adopts a contemporary activity which is not grieving, but constitutes a very active program of "undoing" the death, as it were.

Then there is another form, which counselors might see and wish to refer. We use the term regression for this, namely, that a griever appears to be much younger in his behavior than formerly. A mother may lose her child and act as though she experienced the world as a child, not being able to do her ordinary chores. She develops a state of perplexity in which she needs expert help.

There are also the so-called anniversary reactions. Certain persons succeed in avoiding grieving; they go on with their daily business in a matter-of-fact way as though nothing had happened. These people do not need any counselors, and everything seems to be fine. This is often a problem with war widows: the wife whose husband went away to war was already required to make some provision for his absence, and already had some preoccupation with the possibility that he might die. If he is killed, she finds herself a hero's wife, so that grieving seems inappropriate. She may then just not feel anything, even though there may be a massive emotional response which is waiting to be expressed. And the difficulty is that at some inappropriate moment some stimulus or some story about a situation similar to the husband's will elicit this response. Another example might be a person who as a youngster of ten was bewildered by his mother's illness and death, and may develop comparable symptoms when he reaches the same age at which the mother's tragedy occurred. This is one of the particular situations which psychiatrists must know and recognize: that such an early loss may take place and be responded to years later, whereas with proper assistance at the time of the death the problem could have been avoided.

And this is one of the reasons which has motivated us, even if we do not counsel every grieving person, at least to be handy to review the circumstances which were prevailing at the time of death and the conditions under which these persons died, and somehow to let the griever know that there are knowledgeable, friendly people in the helping professions who can provide expert assistance. This is important at times of suicide and after accidental death. The nurse has an important role in preparing the family for death of the loved one during the terminal phase of illness.

The attrition of the human environment for the older person is a major problem in gerontology. Yet as one gets older, the grieving often happens in an expected situation. "We are both old; well, one of us has to go first. What will I do when you are gone? What will you do when I am gone?" And there is more prospective concern looking toward this aloneness and the possible solutions that one might find at this age.

How do counselors help people to bring out their grief feelings so that they can resolve and cope with them? It is something that has to be learned, and is an art and a skill which some people find easy. Some people find it natural to emphathize with others, to communicate to them that they are ready to receive their communications, that they will not reveal or take advantage of them, that there is no embarrassment ensuing. But most of us have to learn it the hard way—by supervised practice. Learning how to interview and counsel effectively is one of the technical skills which we hope will become very widespread in the whole program of mental health preparation for the helping professions.

Each helping profession has a prescribed style of counseling, and its practitioners are not to become pseudopsychiatrists. But within the framework of the values, the goals which your profession has, you still can learn the four essential things. First of all, not to come with a questionnaire and fire questions. Secondly, not to bring up topics which are so emotionally charged that it would be unwise for the person to mention them or even to think about them at that particular moment. That means to become alert to the degree of emotion that the person feels and can tolerate in their relationship with you. Thirdly, you must realize that you cannot just break in through the door and expect a communication before the person even knows you. You have to have a building-up of a human relationship in the framework of which the communication occurs. So you have to become more than just a funeral director, a minister, or a psychiatrist. You have to become Mr. So and So, who really cares, and for whom this sharing of a state of affairs is an important tool to be more useful to the griever. Fourth, you cannot run away after you have gotten a significant piece of information. You have to linger, and you must perhaps come back, because each bit of meaningful communication and self-exposure to another person includes a degree of heightened intimacy with you who are the listener. You have to give the griever an opportunity to return to the natural level which you had before his revelations, and somehow have to define what it means that you know this now.

Now these are hard things, which you have to practice. If any one of these four things go wrong, it would be better if you had never asked the questions, because to have the experience of a bad relationship with a person who should have been a helper may be an impediment to seeking help from others. So we are eagerly working in community health centers at finding opportunities to distribute these human relations skills; and I think most of us ought to know how to meet other people with basic psychological insight, just as we know how to use vitamins.

18
Weathering Widowhood: Problems and Adjustment of the Widowed During the First Year
Raymond G. Carey

The Widowed After One Year

Do you feel you know the problems of the widowed and what helps them through bereavement? Try the following quiz and compare your answers with those obtained from a recent study of 119 widowed persons interviewed after thirteen to sixteen months of bereavement [1].

1. Widows are: a. better adjusted than widowers; b. more poorly adjusted than widowers; c. about equally adjusted compared to widowers.
2. Forewarning about the death of a spouse will be an asset for adjustment during bereavement: a. for both men and women; b. for women only; c. for men only.
3. Age is related to adjustment so that: a. younger widowed persons are better adjusted than older persons; b. older widowed persons are better adjusted than younger persons; c. there is no difference between age groups.
4. Level of income is a prime factor in adjustment: a. for widowers only; b. for widows only; c. for both widows and widowers; d. for neither.
5. The best adjustment after one year is experienced by widowed persons: a. who live with independent children; b. who live with dependent children; c. who live alone.
6. After family members, widowed persons obtained the most help from: a. physicians; b. nurses; c. neighbors; d. clergy; e. funeral directors.

Answers: 1.(b) 2.(b) 3.(b) 4.(d) 5.(c) 6.(e)

Previous Research

Lindemann developed the concept of anticipatory grief, using the term to refer to the capacity to experience grief and come to terms with loss before the loss actually occurred [2]. When the loss actually occurred, grief would be diminished. Numerous authors, Pollack, Richmond and Waisman, Friedman et al., and Futterman, et al. have stated that anticipatory grief lightens the burden of grief after death [3-6].

Studies of bereaved spouses show divergent findings with respect to factors relating to adjustment and the length of time required to adjust.

Peter Marris studied the reaction to bereavement among a carefully drawn sample of seventy-four widows of men aged forty or under in London [7]. Although the majority of Marris's respondents had been widows for an average of two years, they had hardly recovered. Many felt their lives were futile and empty. They had withdrawn from earlier interests and social ties, had become dependent upon their immediate families, and seemed apathetic. Insomnia and loss of weight were commonly found.

Bornstein and Clayton, however, found that a large number (65%) of spouses who grieve, fortunately, begin to feel better within a month [8, 9]. Most are better at four to six months, and the majority (83%) are feeling well within a year. A small group (17%) continued to have a significant degree of psychological distress.

Lopata analyzed interviews with 301 widows, fifty years of age and over, who lived in metropolitan Chicago [10]. Many had been widowed for years. Her study shows that women with more income and education are hit hardest by widowhood, but also have more resources to build a satisfying new life. Forty-two percent of the sample (56% of the blacks) agreed that, "I feel more independent and free now than before I became a widow," and in spite of financial and health problems over one-third agreed that "this time of my life is actually easier than any other time." Lopata says that this does not mean they had an unhappy marriage. They are the same women who listed loneliness, rather than money or other worries, as the worst problem of widowhood.

Glick, Weiss, and Parkes did a longitudinal study of widows and widowers under forty-six years of age [11]. They interviewed them after three weeks, eight weeks, and thirteen months. Forty-nine widows (21% of the sample) and nineteen widowers (16% of the sample) completed the three interviews. The approach was mainly qualitative and descriptive. The report focused on widows. The main finding of their study was that forewarning of death had a salutary effect on the adequacy and nature of adjustment. Among widows, lack of forewarning of death was associated with a phobic response to remarriage. Although widowers without forewarning might remarry, they seemed more likely than other widowers to harbor tension and anxiety. Marked guilt or anger early in bereavement was also associated with unsatisfactory adjustment. Loneliness was a major problem for widows even a year later.

The Present Study

The purpose of this study was:

1. to develop a simple self-report measure of adjustment-depression;
2. to identify factors relating to adjustment so as to assist physicians, local clergy, and other helping agents predict which spouses would have the greatest difficulty during bereavement;
3. to identify problems of widowed persons;
4. to identify which people within and without the hospital helped widowed persons most and how they helped; and
5. to resolve some of the apparent contradictions in the previous research.

Every widow and widower seventy years of age and younger whose spouses died at an acute general hospital between

January 1, 1974, and November 1, 1974, were considered possible respondents (n — 161). Those over seventy years of age were excluded so that the effects of advanced age would not be confused with the effects of bereavement. Every widow and widower seventy years of age and younger whose spouse was pronounced dead on arrival (DOA) at the hospital from April 1, 1974, to November 1, 1974, was also included in the study (n — 60), because one of the main items under investigation was the effect of forewarning and anticipatory grief.

Of the 221 possible respondents, 119 (54%) accepted the invitation to participate in the study, thirty-eight (17%) refused to participate, and sixty-four (29%) were not able to be reached. Of those who could be reached, 76 per cent of widows and 75 per cent of widowers accepted the invitation to be interviewed. Respondents were from twenty-eight to seventy years of age, with a median age of fifty-seven for both widows and widowers. None of the widows had remarried, although 20 percent of widowers had remarried. All respondents were white. Other characteristics of the sample are summarized in Table 1.

Table 1. Description of Respondents

		WIDOWERS N = 41	Widows N = 78
Age	range	30-70 yr.	28-70 yr.
	median	57 yr.	57 yr.
	mean	56 yr.	56 yr.
Education	high school graduate or less	76[a]	93[a]
	BA or graduate degree	24	7
Living	alone	39	45
	with dependent children	34	33
	with independent children	22	15
Remarried		20	0
Income from all sources:	under $5,000	7	23
	$5,000 to $10,000	5	40
	$10,000 to $15,000	39	14
	over $15,000	46	12
Religious affiliation	Protestant	51	46
	Catholic	39	41
	Jewish	2	6
	Other	2	4
	No religious preference	5	3

[a] Numbers indicate percentages.

The widowed people were interviewed in their homes from thirteen to sixteen months after the death of their husband or wife.

A shortened version of the questionnaire was also given to 100 married people approached randomly in and around the hospital, the same area from which the widowed respondents came. Only those married people who appeared to be over forty years of age were invited to respond so that they would be of approximately the same age as the widowed. Of these, eighty-six responded. The age range for the widowed was twenty-eight to seventy as compared to thirty-six to seventy-seven for the married. The median age was fifty-seven for widowed and fifty-six for married. The married sample was 50 per cent male, as compared to 34 per cent male for the widowed sample. Of the married persons, 20 per cent had college degrees, as compared to 13 per cent of the widowed.

Results

Adjustment scale — An eight item self-report measure of adjustment-depression was developed that clearly differentiated widowed persons from married persons and widowed persons among themselves. This measure, called the Adjustment Scale, is a quantitative measure which can locate a person on a continuum between adjustment and depression. The Adjustment Scale correlated highly with the Bornstein-Clayton measure of depression [9], but is simple to administer and we feel provides a more exact measure of the level of adjustment.

As expected, married persons were significantly better adjusted than widowed persons as measured by the Adjustment Scale. This was true of both men and women. Only 3.5 per cent of married persons were in the depressed category as compared to 25 per cent of the widowed, and 82.5 per cent of married persons were in the well-adjusted category as compared to 50 per cent of the widowed.

Factors in adjustment — The clearest, and perhaps the most important, finding in the study was that widowers were significantly better adjusted than widows. This difference held up even when respondents were broken down by level of income, the amount of forewarning, level of education, and age.

The relatively better adjustment of widowers as compared to widows may be related to several factors. First, women are encouraged to build their identities around their husbands, as symbolized by taking the husband's name at the time of marriage. When a woman's husband dies, her life style is radically changed. This may be less true in the future because women today are more career oriented than in past years. Second, statistics show that women tend to live longer than men and men usually marry women who are younger than themselves. It is, therefore, easier for a man to remarry. Finally, the volunteered comments of respondents suggest that the difficulty widows experienced in making decisions and in handling financial matters alone, their concern about personal safety, and worry about dependent children outweigh the difficulty widowers experienced in maintaining their homes and handling the physical and emotional needs of children alone.

The second key factor in adjustment was the amount of forewarning about the death of a spouse. Widows who had forewarning about the approaching death of their husbands had a significantly higher level of adjustment than the widowed who had no forewarning. The critical amount of time was a minimum of two weeks; there was little difference between groups with longer periods of forewarning. Forewarning, however, was not a significant factor for widowers.

The reasons why forewarning was only a factor in the adjustment of women are not clear. The fact that 20 percent of widowers in this study had remarried as compared to none of the widows invites further study. Perhaps women do not work through their grief as quickly as men. Therefore, the opportunity for anticipatory grief would be more beneficial for women. Perhaps it is more important emotionally for women than for men to talk through their anxieties and grief. Widows more than widowers commented on the helpfulness of having their children, neighbors, or clergy act as sounding boards. Women may also have deeper emotional attachments toward their husbands than men do toward their wives. Another possibility is than men have somewhat more opportunity to remarry.

Age was a significant factor in adjustment. The widowed over the median age of fifty-seven were better adjusted than the widowed under the age of fifty-seven. The age factor, however, was more important for widows. Age may be positively related to adjustment because younger widowed persons are more inclined to feel cheated because their spouses had abbreviated life spans.

Widowed persons with college degrees were significantly better adjusted than those with a high school education or less. Education was a stronger factor in the adjustment of widows than of widowers. Education provides a person with more interests, more opportunities for meaningful employment, and more financial security. These advantages explain the positive relationship between education and adjustment and would be particularly important for women who were not working at the time their husbands died or who still had dependent children to support.

Widowed persons who received more than $10,000 annually from all sources were better adjusted than those who received less than $10,000. However, because 85 per cent of men had an annual income over $10,000 and 83 per cent of women had an annual income under $10,000, the effect of income largely reflected the influence of the sex variable on adjustment.

Widowed persons who lived alone were better adjusted than widowed persons with dependent children, and they in turn were better adjusted than those who lived with independent children. It is not clear from the study whether living with adult children beyond the first year of bereavement has a negative influence on adjustment, or whether living with adult children is a sign that the person has not yet made a good adjustment.

There was a curvilinear relationship between happiness in marriage and adjustment to bereavement. Those who reported that their whole marriage had been very happy were better adjusted than those who said that there had been some period of unhappiness in their marriage. However, those who had prolonged and serious problems (e.g., two women and one man who were married to alcoholic spouses and three widowers whose wives had committed suicide) appeared to be well adjusted. Apparently, where there had been a very severe problem, there was a great feeling of relief when it was ended. But, in general, married persons who are capable of working out a happy marriage are also those most capable of handling the period of bereavement.

Main problems of widowed persons — In response to the open-ended question: "What were the main problems you faced before your spouse's death (when anticipated)?" two problems were prominent. The first was the respondent's own difficulty in accepting the reality of the situation, that is, the slow deterioration and approaching death. The second problem was fear of what life would be like after the patient died, that is, how they would care for themselves and their children and what their goals in life would be.

Avoiding the subject of death also resulted in problems for many. Some women had no knowledge of the financial condition of their families because death was not discussed. One man said it was difficult to "fake for my wife that I had faith in a miracle when I knew there wouldn't be one." Another expressed his anguish about "keeping the knowledge that I knew she would die from my wife and also from the children."

With respect to the care of terminal patients, a few respondents said that medication for pain should be given to terminal patients as they want it, and that a spouse should be free to dismiss a physician's responsibilities regarding an overdose of drugs. Other respondents were opposed to continued testing on patients who were clearly dying. They felt such testing was not only futile, but caused unnecessary pain and discomfort.

When asked to name the main problems faced after the death of their spouses, loneliness was named by 27 percent of widowers and 54 per cent of widows as being a great problem. Loneliness was particularly difficult at certain times of the day, for example, at the time of the evening meal and later in the evening. The widowed also feel lonely doing things by themselves, for example, going to the theater and shopping. Indecision about the future and a lack of personal goals were also problems for many. There is a need to be needed by someone. The widowed, especially those without children, found it difficult to find someone with whom to share their feelings and the burden of their grief.

For widowers, learning how to run their houses without their wives and handling the emotional and physical needs of their children were frequent problems. Getting younger children off to school and helping them with their homework were difficult for widowers whose wives had taken care of these needs.

For widows, making decisions alone without their husbands was often a source of anxiety because they repeatedly questioned whether they had made the right decision (e.g., to move, to sell their house, to go to work). Some women were fearful regarding personal safety and security and had nightmares about people breaking into their homes. For women who were not accustomed to handling financial matters, the ordinary routine of paying bills and making purchases presented difficulties.

Who Helped Most?

Respondents were asked which people within and outside the hospital gave them help (little? some? great?). If the widowed responded "great help," they were asked their reasons.

Respondents who said they were disappointed in some person or group were also asked their reasons.

Physicians — Physicians were rated as offering great help by 47 per cent of the widowers and 40 per cent of the widows. They were considered of great help when they were honest, compassionate, available, not hurried, and comforting to the family. Some sample quotations from those who praised physicians were: ". . . he gave us all the information we wanted in language we could understand." ". . . he was honest, yet encouraging." ". . . he answered our questions kindly, with compassion." " . . . he called me to discuss taking my husband off the respirator. We made the decision together; the full responsibility was not mine." ". . . he took time with us; we didn't have to chase him."

On the other hand, 27 per cent of widowers and 33 per cent of widows expressed disappointment in their physicians. Most expressions of disappointment centered around allegations of failure to be honest with the patient and/or family, avoiding the family, lacking gentleness, having a "poor bedside manner." being cold, impersonal, unconcerned, and misdiagnosing patients.

Nurses — Nurses were rated as offering great help by 56 per cent of widowers and 55 per cent of widows. Usually they were praised for being solicitous and showing concern for the patient and/or relatives. People were also grateful for information regarding tests and equipment when this was not given by the physician.

Some quotations from those who were pleased with nurses were: ". . . they extended visiting hours." ". . . she put her arms around me." ". . . they gave me confidence that I could care for my husband when I took him home."

Only 12 per cent of widowers and 15 per cent of widows complained about nurses. It seemed that when relatives were not satisfied with overall hospital care, they vented all their feelings onto nurses. The major complaint was an attitude of coldness and unconcern.

Chaplains — Chaplains were rated as offering great help by 44 per cent of widowers and 71 per cent of widows. They were considered of great help when they consoled the widowed, helped patients talk about their approaching death, were available and attentive to patients and relatives. Only 5 per cent of widowers and 7 per cent of widows expressed disappointment in the chaplains.

Social workers — The majority of people had no contact with social workers. Some did not know they were in the hospital. This may explain why only 10 per cent of the widowed said they received great help from social workers. Some said they wished they had met a social worker because they would have appreciated having a non-religious counselor with whom to talk.

A number of different services were mentioned by those who found the social workers of great help. The widowed appreciated help in making accommodations for patients sent home. For example, social workers contacted the Cancer Society to get hospital equipment at home. They also helped with financial advice, for example, getting state aid to pay a hospital bill. Social workers arranged for transportation for patients who had to return for outpatient treatments and also found people to stay with patients at home during the day.

Only 4 percent of the widowed said they were disappointed in social workers. For example, some social workers allegedly failed to familiarize themselves with the case histories of patients (e.g., "I had to tell her over and over that my wife was terminal.").

Family — Of all non-hospital personnel, the family was rated as the most helpful group to the bereaved. The family was rated as a great help by over 80 per cent of both widows and widowers. Family members were praised for offering emotional support and understanding.

Before the death of the spouse, family members helped most by taking care of the patients when they were at home and visiting them in the hospital while their spouses were at work. The family members that helped most with these needs were both teenage and adult children. The siblings of both the husband and wife helped most in those families where there were no children.

After the death of the spouse, the family helped widowed persons realize that they were not alone, for example, by making them feel loved and cared for through phone calls and visits, by keeping them busy, or taking them to dinner. A frequent note was that the family helped by "just being there." Invitations to dinner were appreciated most of all because many people find it difficult to eat alone. For example, one man said that he cooked his dinner at home and then threw it out and went to a restaurant to eat so that he would not have to eat by himself. Finally, the widowed praised family members who came in from out-of-town or at some personal inconvenience to visit the patient, to attend the funeral, or to visit them during bereavement.

Funeral directors — Funeral directors were said to be of great help by 76 per cent of both widows and widowers. Funeral directors were second only to family members in receiving praise from the widowed. They helped to obtain social security benefits and insurance payments. They were praised for not pressuring people into expensive funerals and for not sending their bills immediately. They were frequently praised for being "courteous," "honest," and "professional." Only one respondent expressed disappointment in a funeral director.

Local clergy — The local clergy were rated as a great help by 56 per cent of widowers and 62 per cent of widows, while only 5 per cent of widowers and 15 per cent of widows expressed disappointment in the clergy.

The clergy helped in a number of ways. First, visits to patients both in the hospital and at home before the time of death were greatly appreciated by their spouses. Second, counseling the widowed both before and after the death of their spouses was also frequently mentioned with gratitude.

Third, many widowed commented on the conduct of the funeral. The family appreciated the local clergy allowing them or their friends to take part in the funeral service and for giving permission to clergymen from their old neighborhood to say a funeral mass or conduct the service in their new church. One woman was grateful when her parish priest conducted the funeral service for her non-Catholic husband. On the other hand, one Jewish woman wrote a eulogy for her husband and was irritated when her rabbi refused to read it at the funeral because it was his policy not to read anything that he did not write. A minister was criticized for revealing confidential aspects of the husband-wife relationship that were complimentary, but private. Finally, visits by clergymen to the widowed following the deaths of their spouses were rare, but greatly appreciated.

Neighbors — Neighbors were rated as a great help by 56 per cent of widowers and 68 per cent of widows. Before the death of the patient, neighbors helped by checking on the sick at home while spouses were at work, by driving children to school, and by bringing in meals. After the death of the patient, neighbors were praised for attending the funeral, for sending cards and flowers, and for bringing food to the home after the funeral. Widowers frequently had food brought in for themselves and their children during the prolonged illness of their wives and also for weeks after the deaths of their wives. Widows were grateful for neighbors who provided a sounding board for them and who kept them busy, for example, by taking them shopping, to dinner, or to places of entertainment.

Only about 2 per cent of the respondents expressed disappointment in the behavior of neighbors. However, a number of widowed people left old social groups and joined new ones to avoid accusations of being a "romantic threat" to other husbands and wives. Even a young widow in a wheelchair was subject to this accusation. An older widow was accused by her neighbor of flirting with her eighty year old husband. Another widow allegedly was propositioned by her neighbor (her husband's best friend) only five weeks after her husband's death.

Finally, while many neighbors would say, "Call me anytime," their availability usually only lasted a few weeks. Unless there is a visible need, neighbors stop offering help after a few months. For example, a young widow confined to a wheelchair continued to get a great deal of help from her neighbors.

Implications — Several major themes emerge from the findings of this study. First, physicians and counselors are well-advised to give special attention to the importance of anticipatory grief in women. This study suggests that a physician may assist adjustment in bereavement by clearly, gently, and tactfully informing a wife of the seriousness of her husband's condition as soon as this is evident. About 20 per cent of widows of hospitalized patients were upset because they allegedly were not so informed, although few widowers complained they were not informed. A physician might also promote contact with nurses, chaplains, social workers, and other counselors who can assist a wife to deal with her emotions while her husband is still alive.

Second, it is apparently not standard procedure for clergy to make follow-up visits to the bereaved after a spouse's death. Many widowed who are church-goers expected such a visit, were grateful when they received it, and were disappointed when they did not. Third, the non-technical, humanistic aspects of health care delivery are seen as having great value by the families of patients who are seriously ill. Both physicians and nurses are esteemed as much for their honesty, gentleness, availability, and unhurried concern as they are for their technical competence. The importance of humanistic concern to patients is underscored by the large percentage of the widowed, especially widows, who found the chaplains of great help.

References

1. R. G. Carey, The Widowed: A Year Later, *Journal of Counseling Psychology, 24,* pp. 125-131, 1977.

2. E. Lindemann, Symptomatology and Management of Acute Grief, *American Journal of Psychiatry, 101,* p. 2, 1944.

3. G. Pollack, Mourning and Adaptation, *International Journal of Psychoanalysis, 42,* pp. 341-361, 1961.

4. J. B. Richmond and H. A. Waisman, Psychological Aspects of Management of Children with Malignant Diseases, *American Journal of Diseases of Children, 89,* p. 42, 1955.

5. S. B. Friedman, P. Chodoff, J.W. Mason, and D. A. Hamburg, Behavioral Observations on Parents Anticipating the Death of a Child, *Pediatrics, 32,* pp. 610-625, 1963.

6. E. H. Futterman, I. Hoffman, and M. Sebshein, *Parental Anticipatory Mourning,* Mimeo Copy, 1970.

7. P. Marris, *Widows and Their Families,* Routlege and Kegan Paul, London, 1958.

8. P. E. Bornstein and P. J. Clayton, The Anniversary Reaction, *Diseases of the Nervous System, 33,* pp. 470-471, 1972.

9. P. E. Bornstein, P. J. Clayton, J. E. Halikas, W. L. Maurice, and E. Robinson, The Depression of Widowhood After Thirteen Months, *The British Journal of Psychiatry, 122,* pp. 561-566, 1973.

10. H. Z. Lopata, *Widowhood in an American City,* Schenkman, Cambridge, 1973.

11. I. O. Glick, R. S. Weiss, and C. M. Parkes, *The First Year of Bereavement,* John Wiley and Sons, New York, 1974.

19
Without Warning: The Impact of Sudden Death
Larry A. Platt

Adjusting to the death of a loved one is always painful. However, the process is especially difficult when the loss occurs suddenly and without forewarning. Weizman and Kamm in their recent book on mourning describe the unique problems posed by unexpected death:

> "There is nothing to compare with the impact and profound shock of sudden unexpected death. The assault is a jolt to the system. After a sudden death the period of shock and disbelief is long lasting. Those who have suffered the sudden death of a loved one will experience a long period of numbness and denial."

Therese Rando describes in more detail the differential impact of sudden death:

> "At least when a death has been anticipated, even though it puts tremendous emotional demands on the individuals involved, coping capacities are directed toward an expectable end. When the loss occurs, it has been prepared for. When this preparation is lacking, and the loss comes from out of the blue, grievers are shocked. They painfully learn that major catastrophic events can occur without warning. As a result, they develop a chronic apprehension that something unpleasant may happen at any time. It is this lack of security, along with the experience of being overwhelmed and unable to grasp the situation, that accounts for the relatively severe postdeath bereavement complications that occur in cases of sudden death."

279

Part of the explanation for the overwhelming and intense influence of sudden death on the bereaved lies in understanding the special circumstances that accompany an unexpected death. William Worden identified eight special features that surround sudden death which complicate the ability of the survivors to cope with the loss:

1. A sudden death usually leaves the survivors with a sense of unreality;
2. Sudden death promotes a strong sense of guilt on the part of the survivors;
3. In the case of sudden death, the need to blame someone is extremely strong;
4. Sudden deaths are frequently complicated by the involvement of medical and legal authorities;
5. Sudden deaths often elicit a sense of helplessness on the part of the survivors;
6. Survivors of sudden death often exhibit high levels of agitation;
7. Sudden deaths leave the bereaved with many regrets for things not said or activities not done with the deceased; and
8. In the case of sudden death there is an increased need to try to understand why the loss occurred.

The special elements that are part of the devastating experience of sudden death frequently lead to the development of an inter-related set of negative feelings, thoughts and behaviors unique to the survivors of an unexpected loss. Parkes and Weiss have labeled this constellation of destructive symptoms as the "Unexpected Loss Syndrome." They describe this phenomenon in their book, *Recovery from Bereavement*, as follows:

"It would appear that this syndrome is likely to occur following losses that are both unexpected and untimely. It is characterized by a reaction that includes difficulty in believing in the full reality of the loss, avoidance of confrontation of the loss, and feelings of self-reproach and despair. As time passes, the bereaved person remains socially withdrawn and develops a sense of the continued presence of the dead person, to whom he or she continues to feel bound. But this feeling does not protect the bereaved person from loneliness, anxiety and depression. These remain severe and hamper the person's ability to function socially and occupationally."

Beyond the distinctive features of the "Unexpected Loss Syndrome" noted by Parkes and Weiss, the impact of sudden death on the bereaved often manifests itself in a variety of behaviors. Lazare has developed a list of behavioral symptoms, which if present in survivors six months to one year following a death, are suggestive of the presence of unresolved grief:

(a) A depressive syndrome of varying degrees of severity since the time of the death, frequently a very mild, subclinical one often accompanied by persistent guilt and lowered self-esteem;

(b) A history of delayed or prolonged grief, indicating that the person characteristically avoids or has difficulty with grief work;

(c) Symptoms of guilt and self-reproach, panic attacks, and somatic expressions of fear such as choking sensations and shortness of breath;

(d) Somatic symptoms representing identification with the deceased, often the symptoms of the terminal illness;

(e) Physical distress under the upper half of the sternum, accompanied by expressions such as "There is something stuck inside" or "I feel there is a demon inside of me";

(f) Searching that continues over time, with a great deal of random behavior, restlessness, and moving around;

(g) Recurrence of symptoms of depression and searching behavior on specific dates, such as anniversaries of the death, birthdays of the deceased, achieving the age of the deceased, and holidays (especially Christmas), that are more extreme than those anniversay reactions normally expected;

(h) A feeling that the death occurred yesterday, even though the loss took place months or years ago;

(i) Unwillingness to move the material possessions of the deceased after a reasonable amount of time has passed;

(j) Changes in relationships following the death;

(k) Diminished participation in religious and ritual activities that are part of the mourner's culture, including avoidance of visiting the grave or taking part in funerary rituals;

(l) An inability to discuss the deceased without crying or having the voice crack, particularly when the death occurred over a year ago; and

(m) Themes of loss.

In his text, *Grief Counseling and Grief Therapy*, William Worden amplifies on Lazare's listing by adding the following symptoms of unresolved grief:

- A relatively minor event triggering major grief reactions;
- False euphoria subsequent to the death;
- Overidentification with the deceased leading to a compulsion to imitate the dead person, particularly if it is unconscious and the mourner lacks the competence for the same behavior;
- Self-destructive impulses;
- Radical changes in lifestyle;
- Exclusion of friends, family members, or activities associated with the deceased; and
- Phobias about illness or death.

A number of clinicians and researchers have proposed a broad range of intervention strategies which are of therapeutic value for individuals with unresolved grief. Therese Rando in her book, *Grief, Dying and Death,* provides a useful outline of such clinical intervention techniques. While space does not permit a complete discussion of these therapeutic strategies, a representative sampling of her listing does offer some valuable insights into the various approaches that may be of benefit to survivors of sudden death who are experiencing unresolved grief:

1. Be present physically, as well as emotionally, to render the griever security and support;
2. Do not allow the griever to remain socially isolated;
3. Remember that you cannot take away the pain from the bereaved;
4. Do not let your own sense of helplessness keep you from reaching out to the griever;
5. Expect to have to tolerate volatile reactions from the bereaved;
6. Make sure you view the loss from the griever's unique perspective;
7. Let your genuine concern and caring show;
8. Do not tell the griever to feel better because there are other loved ones who are still alive;
9. Do not forget to plant the seeds of hope that someday the pain will decrease;
10. Listen nonjudgmentally and with permissiveness and acceptance;
11. Allow the bereaved to cry and cry, talk and talk, review and review without the interruption of your sanity;
12. Do not be amazed if the griever talks about many of the same things repeatedly;
13. Do not be afraid to mention the dead person to the griever;
14. Encourage the griever to realistically review and talk about the deceased and their mutual relationship;
15. Help the griever maintain good physical health;
16. Help the bereaved to deal with practical problems that develop as a consequence of the death;

17. Help the griever to understand that a healthy new relationship with the deceased must be formed;
18. Ask the griever in what appropriate ways will he keep the deceased's memory alive and continue to relate to her;
19. At the appropriate time, encourage the griever to find rewarding new things to do and people to invest in; and
20. Do not push the bereaved into new relationships before they are ready.

Often we can do little to alter the tragic circumstances which surround sudden death. The forces which are at work in unexpected deaths due to accidents, homicides, suicides and a variety of natural causes are frequently beyond our control. As we develop a better comprehension of this special type of loss, we will become more effective in aiding and comforting the bereaved. While more research is certainly the key to increasing understanding, willingness to reach out to one another in the midst of great sorrow will always be the most essential element in responding to loss.

Notes

1. Weizman, S. G. and Kamm, P. *About Mourning, Support and Guidance for the Bereaved.* Human Science Press, Inc., New York, 1985, p. 101.
2. Rando, T. A. *Grief, Dying and Death, Clinical Interventions for Caregivers.* Research Press Company, Champaign, Illinois, 1984. p. 52.
3. Worden, J. W. *Grief Counseling and Grief Therapy. A Handbook for the Mental Health Practitioner.* Springer Publishing Company, New York, 1982. p. 84-85.
4. Parkes, C. M. and Weiss, R. S. *Recovery from Bereavement.* Basic Books, Inc., New York, 1983. p. 93-94.
5. Lazare, A. "Unresolved Grief," in A. Lazare (Ed.) *Outpatient Psychiatry: Diagnosis and Treatment,* Williams and Wilkins, Baltimore, 1979. p. 507.
6. Worden, p. 62-63.
7. Rando, p. 79-103.

Part VI

Resources for Death-Related Ministry

20
Planning a Funeral: A Checklist
Larry A. Platt and Roger Branch

Many families are amazingly unprepared to deal with a funeral. They simply do not know what steps to take or they are so distressed by grief that they function poorly. In either case the pastor may be called upon for guidance. Since ministers should not be expected to know everything about everything, the following checklist is offered as a useful, practical reference. It can also be used as an educational tool in teaching church members about how to cope with death. Only rarely will the minister find it necessary to help the family carry out more than a few of these steps. The funeral director normally assists with many of these activities.

1. Notify your funeral director.
2. Notify your pastor.
3. Make list of immediate family, close friends, and employer or business colleagues. Notify each by phone.
4. Decide the day and hour of the service.
5. Decide where the service will be held.
6. Decide upon the cemetery, marker, casket, and vault.
7. Select the pallbearers.
8. Arrange for transportation (including police escorts for procession).
9. Arrange for music to be used in the service.
10. If flowers are to be omitted, decide on appropriate memorial to which gifts may be made (as a church, library, school or some charity).
11. Notify lawyer and executor.

12. Write obituary. Include age, place of birth, cause of death, occupation, college degrees, memberships held, military service, outstanding work, list of survivors in immediate family. Give time and place of services. Deliver in person or phone to newspapers.

13. Arrange for members of family or close friends to take turns answering door or phone, keeping careful record of calls.

14. Arrange appropriate child care.

15. Coordinate the supplying of food for the next days.

16. Consider special needs of the household, as for cleaning, etc., which might be done by friends.

17. Arrange hospitality for visiting relatives and friends.

18. Collect all sympathy cards and notes of floral tributes.

19. Prepare list of persons to receive acknowledgments of flowers, calls, etc. Send appropriate acknowledgments. (These can be written notes, printed acknowledgments, or some of each.)

20. Check carefully all life and casualty insurance and death benefits, including Social Security, credit union, trade union, fraternal, military, etc. Check also on income for survivors from these sources.

21. Notify insurance companies, including automobile insurance for immediate cancellation and available refund.

22. Check promptly on all debts and installment payments. Some may carry insurance clauses that will cancel them. If there is to be a delay in meeting payments, consult with creditors and ask for more time before the payments are due.

23. If deceased was living alone, notify utilities and landlord and tell post office where to send mail. Take precautions against theft.

21
Profiles of Helping Organizations

As with so many other aspects of the ministry, efforts to meet the needs of the dying and the bereaved require an enormous amount of time and energy. Those who seek to effectively serve the dying patient or a grieving family quickly realize that there is only so much that any one person can do. When we look beyond ourselves to find others who can help in this special death-related ministry, most often we turn to trusted friends and dedicated members of our church families. Given the unique demands of death ministry, however, the number of individuals who possess the needed skills is quite limited. The simple fact is that there is a critical shortage of people who are capable and willing to serve in the demanding world of the dying and the grieving.

Beyond the circle of the church family, there is a variety of secular and nondenominational voluntary organizations designed to address the vital needs of the dying and the bereaved. Many of these groups have been established for a number of years and maintain an effective pool of professional, paraprofessional, and volunteer counselors and facilitators. Following is a list of helping organizations selected by the authors as being particularly useful to those who are a part of the death ministry. The groups included were chosen on the basis of their record of integrity and achievement and their inventory of essential resources, such as personnel, educational materials, and facilities.

Most of the organizations are national in scope and have

affiliated chapters throughout the United States. As with any resource group, local chapters can vary in quality and capabilities. Some local units may be composed of highly skilled, seasoned volunteers, while others may be newly formed chapters consisting of staff members who have received minimal training and possess little or no field experience. Given such variations, it would be wise for any person who might wish to use these groups as referral resources to first contact the local chapter representative and conduct a personal assessment of the group's professional standards, capabilities, and quality of personnel.

While caution and thorough evaluation are always advisable when personally referring individuals to outside sources, the organizations contained in this listing have earned the reputation of being dedicated and talented groups especially trained to deal with a variety of death-related needs. They can serve as a vital addition to your death ministry.

American Cancer Society
    National Office: 90 Park Avenue
                  New York, N.Y. 10016
                  (212)586-8700
A rich source of information, pamphlets, reports, audiovisual materials, and educational program services, the American Cancer Society is an invaluable liason with a variety of health professionals. The society operates several programs including Reach for Recovery, a self-help group that uses specially trained volunteers who have had mastectomies to serve as counselors for those women and their families facing similar procedures.

American Heart Association
    National Office: 7320 Greenville Avenue
                  Dallas, Texas 75231
                  1-800-527-6941
One of the most well-known of the national disease-

oriented organizations, the American Heart Association raises funds for research and various health education projects. It also maintains several self-help support groups through its Stroke, Heart, or Coronary Clubs. With major chapters in every state, the association is also a useful source of information and audiovisual resources.

The Candlelighters Childhood Cancer Foundation
   National Office: 2025 Eye Street, N.W.
                      Suite 1011
                      Washington, D.C. 20006
                      (202)659-5136

The Candlelighters is an international network of support and counseling groups for children with cancer and their parents and families. With over two hundred chapter groups, the Candlelighters also provides a broad range of information services and educational programs. Through its national offices it lobbies for the rights and needs of children with cancer. The organization produces a newsletter and circulates a list of recommended publications. The Candlelighters is an excellent resource group that maintains an impressive array of information resources. Their parent-to-parent letter-writing program is an effective source of counseling.

The Compassionate Friends
   National Office: Executive Director
                      P.O. Box 1347
                      Oak Brook, Illinois 60521
                      (312)323-5010

Originally founded in England by the Reverend Simon Stephens, this voluntary organization is designed to help bereaved parents. Through its 475 local chapters established throughout the United States, the members of Compassionate Friends seek to provide individual and group support to parents of children who have died. The organization offers a periodic newsletter and a list of audiovisual resources available for purchase. It provides an especially useful environment for bereaved fathers who lack adequate role models for expressing their grief.

Forum for Death Education and Counseling
      National Central Office: 221 Arthur Avenue
                                 Lakewood, Ohio 44107
                                 (216)228-0334

The forum is a nonprofit national organization composed of educators, researchers and counselors engaged in death-related activities. The forum maintains a number of regional chapters and holds an annual meeting of its membership. The organization sponsors workshops and seminars during the year and publishes a monthly newsletter. The forum currently produces an annual volume of some of the best scholarly papers presented at its annual meeting. Its membership directory identifies highly qualified professionals engaged in death education and counseling. The forum newsletter is a useful publication that includes a diverse collection of letters, poems, research reports, and reviews of new books in death and dying.

Leukemia Society of America
      National Office: 733 Third Avenue
                         New York, New York 10017
                         (212)573-8484

In addition to its national information service regarding leukemia, the society also publishes a variety of brochures concerning the emotional aspects of the disease and its effects on family members. Through its fifty-eight state and regional chapters, the Leukemia Society also maintains a Family Support Group program which offers counseling and support to patients and their families as they seek to cope with the realities of leukemia, Hodgkin's disease, lymphoma or multiple myeloma.

Make Today Count
    National Office: P.O. Box 303
                      Bulington, Iowa 52601
                      (319)754-7266
Founded by Orville Kelly, a cancer patient, this organization has grown to over two hundred chapters in the United
States. Local chapters provide help to those persons who have
life-threatening illnesses as they seek to cope with their conditions. Support for the family members is also provided. The
organization produces a periodic newsletter and promotes
professional education concerning the emotional needs of the
dying person. The national office publishes a packet of information detailing how to start a local chapter.

The Mended Hearts, Inc.
    National Office: Executive Director
                      7320 Greenville Avenue
                      Dallas, Texas 75321
                      (214)750-5442
Founded in 1951, this self-help organization is endorsed by
the American Heart Association and offers help, support, and
encouragement to heart disease patients and their families
through 174 chapters across the United States. Members of
The Mended Hearts visit homes or hospital rooms of heart
disease victims to provide personal counseling. Primarily
using volunteers who themselves have had heart disease, the
program seeks to help patients and their families cope with
the life-threatening illness.

National Center for the Prevention of Sudden Infant Death
Syndrome
    National Office: President
                      330 North Charles Street
                      Baltimore, Maryland 21201
                      (301)547-0300
This organization serves as a national clearinghouse of

medical and scientific information about SIDS. In addition to its national activities designed to promote public awareness about SIDS, it also provides referrals to local medical and counseling support groups. The National Center produces a pamphlet, "Facts On Sudden Infant Death Syndrome," containing current information about this condition. An allied group that should also be contacted regarding this disease is the National SIDS Foundation, 2 Metro Plaza, 8240 Professional Plaza, Landover, Maryland 20785, (301)459-3388.

National Hospice Organization
    National Office: President
                        Suite 902
                        1901 North Fort Myer Drive
                        Arlington, Virginia 22209
                        (703)243-5900

The national-level organization of over 1200 individual hospice programs located in the United States, the National Hospice Organization produces a monthly newsletter and a variety of useful materials on the hospice concept including the pamphlet, "The Basics of Hospice." This organization can provide a broad range of informational services on how to start a local hospice, the standards of hospice care, and the necessary training for hospice staff and volunteers. The National Hospice Organization is an invaluable source of technical assistance for new hospice groups and is a good communication link with other community hospice programs around the country.

National Save-A-Life League
    National Office: 815 Second Avenue
                        Suite 409
                        New York, New York 10017
                        (212)736-6191

Organized in 1906, this is one of the oldest suicide prevention and follow-up self-help groups in the United States. The league offers personal counseling, family guidance, and public education regarding suicide. They maintain a twenty-four-hour hot line (212)736-6191 for immediate assistance and referral anywhere in the country. The league also offers a speakers' bureau for various public education activities.

National Self-Help Clearinghouse
      National Office: Graduate School and University Center of the City University of New York
                         33 West 42nd Street
                         Room 1227
                         New York, New York 10036
                         (212)840-7606

   As a central clearinghouse for self-help groups of all types, the National Self-Help office is an invaluable resource. It is notable for its records of helping organizations throughout the United States and as an effective referral resource for concerned groups and individual caregivers. The organization produces a monthly newsletter and a variety of brochures and directories.

Parents of Murdered Children
      National Office: Executive Director
                         1739 Bella Vista
                         Cincinnati, Ohio 45237
                         (513)242-8025

   Through its national office and local chapters, this organization offers emotional support and counseling to parents who have lost a child through murder. A nondenominational group, Parents of Murdered Children (POMC) produces a number of informative brochures and offers educational programs on this acute type of loss. Since deaths of children due to offenders who were operating a vehicle while under the influence of alcohol and/or drugs are included, this organization offers help for thousands of deeply grieving parents. Its special familiarity with the criminal justice system and its impact on survivors makes PMOC an unrivaled source of guidance as parents go through the legal process of resolving their child's murder.

S H A R E
National Coordinator: SHARE Program Facilitator
St. John's Hospital
800 East Carpenter
Springfield, Illinois 62769
(217)544-6464

SHARE was established in 1977 as a social support group for parents who have lost a baby, through miscarriage, stillbirth, or early infant death. Through a collaborative network of several hundred SHARE chapters and other similar organizations, SHARE provides a variety of follow-up support services. The organization produces a newsletter and a useful pamphlet, "Starting Your Own SHARE Group." An often neglected category of the bereaved are the mothers, fathers, siblings, and other family members who experience the loss of a baby in its early stages of development. This organization serves this special and often overlooked target group.

THEOS Foundation
National Office: Suite 410 Office Building
Penn Hills Mall
Pittsburgh, Pennsylvania 15235
(412)243-4299

THEOS, which is an acronym for "They Help Each Other Spiritually," has over one hundred sixty chapters throughout the fifty states. The group serves as a source of support and comfort for young and middle-aged widowed people. THEOS publishes a newsletter and a collection of publications entitled, "Grief Steps I and II: The Journey Through Grief," as a helping resource for the recently widowed. As a nonsectarian Christian ministry to the bereaved, THEOS is an effective organization that can provide a forum for the widowed to share their feelings with others who have experienced similar losses.

Widowed Persons Service/American Association of Retired Persons

> National Office: Program Department, AARP
> 1909 K. Street, N.W.
> Washington, D.C. 20049
> (202)728-4370

With nearly five hundred chapters located in the United States and Canada, the AARP's Widowed Persons Service is one of the largest of its kind. Founded in 1973, this program provides personal counseling, support groups, telephone referral services, and public education on the realities of widowhood. Although the program is affiliated with the AARP, the Widowed Persons Service is open to widowed men and women of all ages. The program maintains a national directory identifying its various local groups and produces a pamphlet "On Being Alone." Technical assistance in starting a new chapter program is also available.

Audiovisual Sources of Death-Related Ministry

The annotations that follow offer a sampling of the best in films, filmstrips, and videotapes designed for teenage through adult audiences on the topics of death, dying, and grief. The two dozen audiovisuals recommended in this section were chosen following a detailed analysis of nearly eleven hundred media resources. The guiding criteria applied during this rigorous selection process included: (a) the overall quality of the production; (b) the accuracy of the death-related content of the material; (c) the type of audience targeted; and (d) the affordability of the rental or purchase price of the audiovisual.

The following listing provides a source of educational materials that could serve as excellent tools in any church program which focuses on death and dying. Each citation includes an identification of the type of medium involved, its running time, year in which it was produced, rental or purchase price and the name of the distributor of the material. Business addresses for all of the distributors, including telephone numbers, are listed at the end of this section as a service to those who want to order some of these teaching aids.

A Time to Cry
Color film or videotape; 28 minutes; 1979; rental
Mass Media Ministries
The reactions of two different families to the loss of a loved one and the role of their religious faith in helping them cope

with the tragedy are effectively presented. The therapeutic benefits of sharing one's own grief with others are also stressed.

But He was Only Seventeen: The Death of a Friend
Color filmstrip w/audiocassette; 3 parts, total running time 37 minutes; 1981; purchase only
Sunburst Communications
Finalist—National Educational Film Festival
   This three-part program designed for high-school students surveys three topics: "The Stages of Grief," "Learning to Mourn" and "Reinvesting in Life." The grief-related feelings and behaviors of several teenagers are explored following the accidental death of their high-school friend. The filmstrip series analyzes the various facets of grief and stresses the essential coping skills needed to deal realistically with death.

Children in Crisis: Death
Color filmstrip; 40 minutes; 1975; purchase only
Guidance Associates
   Produced by *Parents* magazine, this five-part series analyzes the topic of children and death, including these issues: "Death as a Reality of Life," "Expressing Grief," "Ages of Understanding," "Explaining Death to Children," and "The Importance of Funerals." Each of the five segments is about eight minutes in length and offers a brief overview of each topic area.

Chillysmith Farm
Color film or videotape; 55 minutes; 1981; rental
Filmakers Library
Blue Ribbon—American Film Festival
CINE—Golden Eagle Award
   An excellent film about aging, dying, and family life through four generations. Based in part on the book *Gramps*, the film picks up with recollections of Gramps and his death

and chronicles the life and death of Nan, Gramp's wife. A positive portrayal of the strengths of family life today amidst the realities of aging and death.

Death and Dying, Closing the Circle: Part 5 - Dealing with Loss and Grief
Color filmstrip or videotape; 20 minutes; 1977; purchase only, five-part series
Award Winner, National Council of Family Relations
   One of an excellent five-part series on death, dying, and grief; part 5: "Dealing with Loss and Grief," focuses on the experiences of several families who have suffered a loss and their search for meaning in life. Good photography and a solid script make this an outstanding teaching program.

Death and Grief
Black and white film; 16 minutes; 1971; rental
University of Michigan Medical Center
   Dr. Edgar Jackson, recognized theologian and expert on grief, discusses various aspects of grief and bereavement. He explains individual responses to bereavement and the nature of abnormal grief. He also offers an overview of the functions of funerals.

Dying
Color film or videotape; 97 minutes; 1976; rental
Audio Visual Department, Pennsylvania State University
   Available in three parts or one continuous presentation, this is one of the most revealing films on the subject of death. Through a careful examination of how four families cope with the gradual process of dying, the unique power of love, faith, and social bonds are dramatically revealed. This is one of the most valuable teaching tools available.

Grief
Color film; 28 minutes; 1980; rental
University of Southern California

This film presents the varied feelings of grieving individuals by portraying the experiences of a widow, Katie, during the months following the death of her husband. Katie expresses anger, guilt, despair, and the loneliness which is a concern of many grieving spouses. Through the social support of her friends and the counseling of a widows' group, Katie resolves many of her grief-related anxieties and begins to build a new life.

Gramps: A Man Ages and Dies
Black and white filmstrip w/audiocassette; 21 minutes; 1976; purchase only
Sunburst Communications
Based on a best-selling book, the filmstrip depicts the last months of an aging grandfather and the caring circle of family love that surrounded him until his eventual death. The photography is both explicit and dramatic and the dialogue is most poignant. A good case study of a dying individual and the beneficial role the extended family plays in the process.

Grief Therapy
Color film; 18 minutes; 1976; rental
Pennsylvania State University
Originally a part of the CBS television "60 Minutes" series, the film features Dr. Donald Ramsey who conducts on-camera therapy sessions, including a mother who has been grieving for her dead daughter for nearly three years. The film offers a powerful account of the nature of grief and its debilitating effects. A moving documentary that illustrates the effectiveness of counseling in aiding the bereaved to accept the "letting-go" process essential to grief resolution.

Jocelyn: Facing Death at 17 with Strong Faith
Color film on videotape; 28 minutes; 1980; rental
Filmakers Library
Award—American Film Festival
Award—National Hospice Association

The true story of a teenage cancer victim whose struggles to face her terminal illness are aided by her strong religious beliefs. A moving personal account of faith and love in the midst of dying.

Living with Dying
Color filmstrip; 29 minutes; 1973; purchase only
Sunburst Communications
The first of this two-part presentation focuses on death as part of the natural life cycle and man's various attempts to achieve immortality. The second part of the series describes how children learn about death in our society and reviews the major psychological stages by which individuals react to the dying process.

Parents' Responses to Their Children's Illness
Color videotape; 27 minutes; 1977; rental
University of Michigan Medical Center
Produced by the Association of American Medical Colleges, the film examines parental responses to the terminally ill child and the eventual death of a child. A number of parents are interviewed and the social psychological mechanisms by which they seek to cope with this family tragedy are discussed.

Picking Up the Pieces: One Widow Speaks
Color videotape; 29 minutes; 1975; rental
Public Television Library, WNED TV, Buffalo, New York
This film presents highlights of an interview with Lynn Caine, author of the best-selling book, *Widow*. Ms. Caine discusses the shock and pain that followed the death of her husband and her struggle to build a new life for herself and her family.

The Long Valley: A Study of Bereavement
Color film; 2 parts, 59 minutes total; 1976; rental
Pennsylvania State University Audio Visual Services

Internationally recognized grief expert, Dr. Colin M. Parkes, interviews clergy, doctors, social workers, and six bereaved people about the process of grief. Dr. Parkes explains the basic stages of grief and the effects of unresolved grief. A good introduction to the nature of grief on a general adult level. However, some might find the lecture orientation of Dr. Parkes distracting.

The Pitch of Grief
Color videotape; 28 minutes; 1985; rental
Fanlight Productions
National Hospice Organization Film of the Year
An excellent portrayal of the emotional character of grief. The film profiles four men and women as they seek to deal with their personal grief. Through intimate interviews, the film documents the broad range of emotions related to grief and mourning. The videotape provides a good overview of the symptomology of grief and the role of social support groups in helping the bereaved deal with their loss.

To Die with Dignity: To Live with Grief
Color videotape; 29 minutes; 1978; rental
University of Michigan Media Resources Centers
The film explores the issue of how people cope with death. The views of a minister, a doctor, a terminally ill patient and a couple who have recently lost their son are shared through brief interviews and comments.

Understanding Death
Color filmstrip w/audiocassette; 6 parts with total running time of 45 minutes; 1975; purchase only
Eye Gate Media
A six-part series designed for middle school children covers the following topics: "Life-Death," "Exploring the Cemetery," "Facts About Funerals," "A Taste of Blackberries," and "Children and Death." The series surveys feelings and

behavior of children about death and includes a parent/teacher resource booklet. The last part of the filmstrip package, "Children and Death" is designed as a teaching guide for adults using the filmstrip with children.

Valley of the Shadow: A Journey Through Grief
Color film or videotape; 38 minutes; 1980; rental
Creative Marketing/Human Services Press
   The powerful true story of Jim and Jan Kunzman, who lost their five-year old and eight-year old children in an auto-train accident and the pain and suffering of their resultant grief. The focus of the film is on the father and how his sorrow was intensified by the lack of social support he experienced from his friends and neighbors. The role of Jim's mismanaged grief and the resulting physical and mental effects are also stressed.

Widows Are You Listening?
Color film or videotape; 1979; 28 minutes; rental
Martha Stuart Communications
   The anger, loneliness, and humor of widowhood are discussed by several widows who share their experiences. The needs of the widowed and the process of their adjustments to the loss of a spouse are also depicted.

With His Playclothes On
Color filmstrip w/audiocassette; 47 minutes; 1976; preview fee; purchase only
OGR Service Corporation
   Dr. Glen Davidson, Chief of Thanatology in the Department of Psychiatry at Southern Illinois University School of Medicine, analyzes the grief behavior of parents and siblings in a family following the sudden death of its youngest member —twenty-one-month-old Jerry. Dr. Davidson deals with the various grief responses of the individual family members and illustrates how counselors can aid in the process of mourning.

You See—I've Had a Life
Black and white film; 32 minutes; 1973; rental
University of California, Berkeley

A moving account of the life of Paul Hendricks, who at age thirteen must learn to live with the fact that he has leukemia. A frank and positive look at family life and personal courage in the face of adversity. The film depicts Paul and his family's attempts to fill their remaining days with faith, life, and love.

The Mourning Process: Mrs. Kelly
Color videotape; 51 minutes; 1979; rental
St. Louis University Medical Center Audio Visual Department
Recommended for staff education by the Association of American Medical Colleges

Mr. Kelly has died of a chronic, long-term illness, and this film depicts the grief responses of his wife through extensive follow-up interviews. The interviews show the basic stages of grief including shock, denial, emergency and resolution, and illustrates effective communication patterns in grief counseling. Although the videotape is somewhat long, a viewing of selected segments is very effective.

Bibliography

1. Anderson, H. The Death of a Parent: Its Impact on Middle-Aged Sons and Daughters. *Pastoral Psychology*, 1980, 23(3): 151-167.
2. Arkin, A. M. "Emotional Care of the Bereaved." In O. Margolis, et al., eds. *Acute Grief: Counseling the Bereaved.* New York: Columbia University Press, 1981. pp. 40-44.
3. Ball, J. F. "Widow's Grief: The Impact of Age and the Mode of Death." *OMEGA*, 1976-77, 7(4): 306-333.
4. Bendiksen, R. "The Sociology of Death." In R. Fulton, ed. *Death and Identity.* Maryland: The Charles Press Publishers Inc., 1976. pp. 59-82.
5. Berlinsky, E. B. and H. B. Biller *Parental Death and Psychological Development.* Lexington, Mass: D. C. Heath, Lexington Books, 1982.
6. Blanchard, C. G., et al. "The Young Widow: Depressive Symomatology Throughout the Grief Process, *Psychiatry*, 1976, 39(4), 394-399.
7. Brister, C. W. *Pastoral Care in the Church.* New York: Harper and Row, 1964.
8. Bugen, L. A. *Death and Dying: Theory, Research and Practice.* Dubuque: William C. Brown Company, 1979.
9. Carr, S. and B. Schoenberg. *Grief: Selected Readings.* New York: Health Sciences Publishing Company, 1975.
10. Carse, J. P. and A.B. Dallery, eds. *Death and Society: A Book of Readings and Sources.* New York: Harcourt, Brace, & Jovanovich, 1977.
11. Cattell, J. P. "Avoiding the Mistakes in Bereavement."

In A. H. Kutscher, et al., eds. *For Those Bereaved.* New York: Arno Press, 1980. pp. 160-163.

12. Decker, D. J. "Grief: In the Valley of the Shadow." *American Journal of Nursing,* 1978. pp. 416-417.

13. DeSpelder, L. A. and A. L. Strickland. *The Last Dance: Encountering Death and Dying.* Palo Alto, Calif.: Mayfield, 1983.

14. DeVaul, R. A. and S. Zisook. "Unresolved Grief: Clinical Considerations." *Postgraduate Medicine,* 1976. 59(5):267-271.

15. Elizur, E. and M. Kaffman. "Children's Bereavement Reactions Following the Death of the Father." *Journal of the American Academy of Child Psychiatry,* 1982. 21(5): 414-480.

16. _____. "Factors Influencing the Severity of Childhood Bereavement Reactions." *American Journal of Orthopsychiatry,* 1983. 53:668-676.

17. Felner, R. D., et al. "Parental Death or Divorce and the School Adjustment of Young Children." *American Journal of Community,* 1981. 9(2): 181-191.

18. Fitchett, G. "Pastoral Care of the Bereaved." *Newsletter of the Forum for Death Education and Counseling,* 1983. 6: 4-5.

19. Fulton, R. and J. Fulton. "A Psychosocial Aspect of Terminal Care: Anticipatory Grief." In R. A. Kalish, ed. *Caring relationships: The Dying and the Bereaved.* Baywood Publishing Company, Inc., 1980. pp. 87-96.

20. Garfield, C. A., ed. *Psychosocial Care of the Dying Patient.* New York: McGraw-Hill, 1978.

21. Gerber, I., et al., eds. *Perspectives on Bereavement.* New York: MSS Information Corporation, 1978.

22. Glick, I. O., et al. *The first Year of Bereavement.* New York: Wiley Interscience, 1974.

23. Graves, J. S. "Differentiating Grief, Mourning and Bereavement." *American Journal of Psychiatry,* 1978. 135:874-875.

24. Hackett, T. P., M.D. "Recognizing and Treating Abnormal Grief." *Hospital Physician,* 1974. 1:49-56.

25. Hammett, E.B., et al. "A Typical Grief—Anniversary Reactions." *Military Medicine,* 1979. 144:320-321.

26. Hecht, M. H. "Dynamics of Bereavement." *Journal of Religion and Health,* 1971. 10:359-372.

27. Hodge, J. R. "They that Mourn." *Journal of Religion and Health,* 1972. 11:229-240.

28. Hodgkinson, P. E. "Abnormal Grief—the Problem of Therapy." *British Journal of Medical Psychology,* 1982. 55: 29-34.

29. Jackson, E. *The Many Faces of Grief.* New York: Abingdon Press, 1977.

30. Jensen, M. "Some Implications of Narrative Theology for Ministry to Cancer Patients." *The Journal of Pastoral Care,* 1984. 38, 3:316-225.

31. Klass, D. "Self-Help Groups for the Bereaved: Theory, Theology, and Practice." *Journal of Religion and Health,* 1982. 21:307-324.

32. Klepser, M. J., "Grief: How Long Does Grief Go On?" *American Journal of Nursing.* 1978. pp. 420-422.

33. Kübler-Ross, E. *On Death and Dying.* London: Tavistock, 1969.

34. _____. *Questions and Answers on Death and Dying.* New York: Macmillan, 1974.

35. _____. *To Live Until We Say Good-Bye.* New York: Prentice-Hall, 1978.

36. LeShan, E. *Learning to Say Goodbye When a Parent Dies.* New York: Macmillan, 1976.

37. Lewis, C. S. *A Grief Observed.* London: Faber and Farber, 1986.

38. Lifton, R. J. and E. Olson. *Living and Dying.* New York Praeger, 1974.

39. Lindeman, E. "Grief and Grief Management: Some Reflections." *Journal of Pastoral Care,* 1976. 30:198-207.

40. Lofland, L. H. *The Craft of Dying: The Modern Face of Death.* Beverly Hills: Sage, 1978.

41. Lopata, H. Z. *Widowhood in an American City.* Cambridge, Mass.: Schenkman, 1973.

42. Meares, R. A. "On Saying Good-bye Before Death." *Journal of the American Medical Association,* 1981. 246(11):1227-1229.

43. Melges, F. T. and D.R. Demaso. "Grief-Resolution Therapy: Reliving, Revising, and Revisiting." *American Journal of Psychotherapy,* 1980. 34(1):51-61.

44. Miller, J. *The Healing Power of Grief.* New York: Seabury, 1978.

45. Mills, L. O. "Issues for Clergy in the Care of the Dying and Bereaved." In D. Barton, ed. *Dying and Death: A Clinical Guide for Caregivers.* Baltimore: Williams & Wilkins, 1977.

46. Mitchell, K. R. "A Death and a Community: Case Conference." *The Journal of Pastoral Care,* 1982, 36, 1, 3-16.

47. Morgan, J. H., ed. *Death and Dying: A Resource Bibliography for Clergy and Chaplains (1960-1976).* Wichita: Institute of Ministry and the Elderly, 1977.

48. Nichols, R. V. "Sudden Death, Acute Grief, and Ultimate Recovery." In O. Margolis, et al., eds. *Acute grief: Counseling the bereaved.* New York: Columbia University Press, 1981. pp. 214-224.

49. Oates, Wayne E., ed. *An Introduction to Pastoral Counseling.* Nashville: Broadman Press, 1959.

50. _____. *Pastoral Care and Counseling in Grief and Separation.* New York: Fortress Press, 1977.

51. _____. *The Psychology of Religion.* Waco, Texas: Word Books, 1973.

52. O'Conner, B., et al. *The Role of the Minister in Caring for the Dying Patient and the Bereaved.* New York: MAA Information, 1978.

53. Orange, D. "Spiritual care of the Terminally Ill." In R. Turnball, ed. *Terminal Care.* New York: Hemisphere Pub-

lishing Corporation, 1986. pp. 76-81.

54. Parkes, C. M. *Bereavement: Studies of Grief in Adult Life.* New York: International Universities Press, 1972.

55. Pattison, E. M., ed. *The Experience of Dying.* Englewood Cliffs, N.J.: Prentice-Hall, 1977.

56. Pincus, L. *Death and the Family: The Importance of Mourning.* New York: Pantheon Books, 1974.

57. Pine, V. R., ed. *Acute Grief and the Funeral.* Springfield, Ill: Charles C. Thomas Publisher, 1975.

58. Platt, L. A. *Death and Dying, Volume I: Grief and Bereavement —A Research Bibliography, 1964-1984.* Georgia Southern College: The Social Gerontology Program, 1985.

59. _____. *Death and Dying, Volume II: The Anthropology of Bereavement—A Research Bibliography.* With Richard Persico. Georgia Southern College: The Social Gerontology Program, 1986.

60. _____. "Grief and Social Support Networks: Anthropological Perspectives." *Georgia Journal of Science,* 1986. 44,1-2:63-64.

61. _____. "Grief Responses to Sudden Death: A Review of the Literature." *Proceedings—8th Annual Meeting of the Forum for Death Education and Counseling,* 1985. 7:66.

62. _____. Patterns of Bereavement: A Cultural Analysis. *Georgia Journal of Science,* 1985. 43, 1-2:50-51.

63. _____. "Social Support Networks and Grief Responses: An Analysis of Current Research." *Proceedings —8th Annual Meeting, Forum of Death Education and Counseling,* 1986. 8:84.

64. _____. "The Impact of Grief on Survivors, A New Dimension to Assessing Damages." *The Journal of the Academy of Florida Trial Lawyers,* 1984. 266:17-18.

65. _____. "Without Warning: The Impact of Sudden Death." *Thanatos,* 1985. 10, 4:18-21.

66. Platt, L. A., R. G. Branch, R. Persico, and D.E. Hill, eds. *Encounters with Death, Dying and Bereavement.* Lexington, Mass.: Ginn Press, 1986.

67. Proulx, J. R. and P.D. Baker. "Grief, Grieving, and Be-

reavement: A Look at the Basics." In O. Margolis, et al., eds. *Acute Grief: Counseling the Bereaved.* New York: Columbia University Press, 1981. pp. 191-200.

68. Rando, T. A. *Grief, Dying, and Death: Clinical Interventions for Caregivers.* Champaign, Ill.: Research Press Company, 1984.

69. Raphael, B. *The Anatomy of Bereavement.* New York: Basic Books, 1983.

70. Rosen, H. *Unspoken Grief: Coping with Childhood Sibling Loss.* Lexington, Mass.: Lexington Books, 1986.

71. Schiff, H. S. *The Bereaved Parent.* New York: Crown Publishers, 1977.

72. Schmidt, D. D. and E. Messner. "The Management of Ordinary Grief." *Journal of Family Practice,* 1975. 2:259-262.

73. Schoenberg, B. M. *Bereavement Counseling: A Multidisciplinary Handbook,* Westport, Conn.: Greenwood Press, 1980.

74. Schulz, R. *The Psychology of Death, Dying, and Bereavement.* Reading, Mass.: Addison-Wesley, 1978.

75. Sheskin, A. and S.E. Wallace. "Differing Bereavements: Suicide, Natural and Accidental death," *OMEGA,* 1976. 76:229-242.

76. Shneidman, E. S., ed. *Death: Current Perspectives.* Palo Alto, Calif.: Mayfield Company, 1976.

77. Simpson, M. A. *The Facts of Death.* New York: Spectrum, 1979.

78. Small, L. *Pathological Grief: The Briefer Psychotherapies.* New York: Brunner/Mazel, 1979.

79. Smith, W. J. *Dying in the Human Life Cycle.* New York: Holt, Rinehart and Winston, 1985.

80. Spiegel, Y. *The Grief Process: Analysis & Counseling.* Nashville: Abingdon Press, 1977.

81. Stephenson, S. J. *Death, Grief, and Mourning: Individual and Social Realities.* New York: The Free Press, 1985.

82. Stern, M. M. "Death and the Child." In J. Schowalter, et al., eds. *The Child and Death.* New York: Columbia University Press, 1983. pp. 19-26.

83. Sullender, R. S. "Three Theoretical Approaches to Grief." *The Journal of Pastoral Care,* 1979. 33, 4, 243-251.

84. Switzer, D. *The Dynamics of Grief.* New York: Abingdon, 1970.

85. Turnball, R., ed. *Terminal Care.* Washington: McGraw-Hill International Book Company, 1986.

86. Uroda, S. F. "Counseling the Bereaved." *Counseling and Values,* 1977. 21: 185-191.

87. Vachon, M. L. S. "Grief and Bereavement Following the Death of a Spouse." *The Canadian Psychiatric Journal,* 1976. 21, 35-44.

88. Volkan, V. D. *Linking Objects and Linking Phenomena: A Study of the Forms, Symptoms, Metapsychology, and Therapy of Complicated Mourning.* New York: International Universities Press, Inc., 1981.

89. Wass, H. *Dying: Facing the Facts.* New York: McGraw-Hill, 1979.

90. Weisman, A. D. *On Dying and Denying: A Psychiatric Study of Terminality.* New York: Behavioral Publications, 1972.

91. Weizman, S. G., and P. Kamm. *About Mourning: Support and Guidance for the Bereaved.* New York: Human Sciences Press, Inc., 1985.

92. Wilcox, S. G. and M. Sutton. eds. *Understanding Death and Dying.* Sherman Oaks, Calif.: Alfred Publishers, 1977.

93. Worden, J. W. *Grief Counseling and Grief Therapy: A Handbook for the Mental Health Practitioner.* New York: Springer Publishing Company, 1982.

94. Young, Richard K. *The Pastor's Hospital Ministry.* Nashville: Broadman Press, 1954.

95. Young, Richard K. and Albert L. Meiburg. *Spiritual Therapy.* New York: Harper and Brothers, Publishers, 1960.